THESAURUS

LINGUÆ LATINÆ;

OR THE ART OF

TRANSLATING ENGLISH INTO LATIN

AT SIGHT;

ON THE PLAN OF LE TRÉSOR:

BY

MONS. LOUIS FENWICK DE PORQUET,

Author of Le Trésor, Parisian Grammar, and other Elementary Works for the study of Modern Languages.

LONDON:

PUBLISHED AND SOLD BY

MESSRS. FENWICK DE PORQUET AND COOPER,

at their Warehouse for Elementary Works,

11, TAVISTOCK STREET, COVENT GARDEN;

And may be had of all other Booksellers.

1832.

The property of the Author, who acknowledges only such copies as bear his signature.

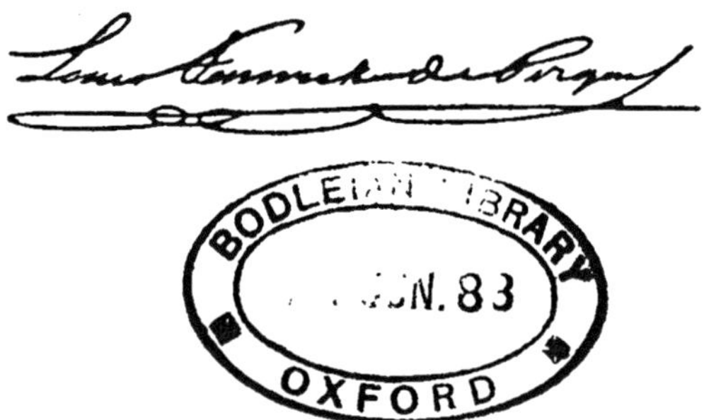

LONDON:
G. SCHULZE, 13, POLAND STREET.

TO THE

ILLUSTRIOUS MEMBERS

COMPOSING THE

COUNCIL OF KING'S COLLEGE,

LONDON;

THIS WORK IS

MOST RESPECTFULLY

INSCRIBED BY

THEIR MOST OBEDIENT

AND HUMBLE SERVANT

The Author.

5, Gloucester Place,
Kentish Town.

PREFACE

TO

THESAURUS.

FOR

THE ATTENTIVE PERUSAL

OF THOSE ENGAGED IN

TEACHING THE CLASSICS.

GENTLEMEN, In promulgating this system of education for the juvenile members of society, I resorted to first principles, at once a difficult mode of invention, and perilous to support in practice: perilous, because it is fairly to run the race of competition with all other *eminent makers* of systems who have advanced their claims to the patronage of the public; thereby exciting, in a few instances, *the professors to turn their acknowledged talent against me* and *this system*, and in other cases encountering the risk of a share in the obloquy which certain *unsuccessful pretenders have merited.*

It is difficult, in this era of fallacious pretension in every profession, to ground the elements of polite learning and useful knowledge upon the simple basis which the unerring rules of nature point to, as their securest foundation. I have, nevertheless, done so, and have rejected the aid of specious ornament, the subsidies of figurative and florid arguments and style, the sophistry of modern masters of the languages, and more particularly the 'vantage ground of surreptitiously enhancing upon the best part and meritorious portion of the recent systems, of thus rising by the labours of men of learning, or through some shadowy, unsubstantial additions, to the favour of the English public.

On the contrary, I have sacrificed fortune, exerted my utmost energy and my best talents, in the service of the youth of this great nation, and shall ever esteem it my pride and consolation *if it be allowed that I have meant well,* and have succeeded so far as to chalk out an *unbeaten* course for the advancement of students in their eager pursuit of learning.

My plan in this extensive set of manuals, for inparting more speedy instruction in the European languages, consists of the judicious application of the *new theory* of tuition, which is *the result of the observation of logicians* upon the imperfection, during many centuries, of the ordinary methods of education. I have not space to point out all these errors; that they exist is acknowledged; they have futilely absorbed some years of the students' lives; they have clouded genius with that night of ignorance which it was the province of instructors of youth to have removed. It has been from a sense of their superior learning alone, *remotâ erroris nebulâ* that poets and philosophers have had the opportunity given them of instructing their fellow-citizens, or that legislators have been first promoted to govern states.

When I deplore, with so many learned men, the frequent loss of several years in the acquisition, by English youth, of the foreign languages, and contemplate the deceptive quality of the mind through which these studies, impressed upon it in *one month*, are *cancelled and obliterated in the next*, a deficiency of memory which has caused fortune to favour Language Masters, as their pupils can seldom emancipate themselves, I resolve to aid, with my best ability, and all my zeal, in subverting this evil *ab ovo*, in its nascent condition; to furnish the youthful memory with all efficacious expedients for the pupil's speedy progress, I shall take every occasion to prompt the student with those resources which experience has taught the guides of mankind to employ in their instruction, I mean the La Fontaines, the La Bruyères, the Fénélons, the Fléchiers, and the Montesquieus, Cicero and Seneca, Milton and Locke, Gay, Dryden, and Pope, Shakspeare and Molière, Burke and Johnson; such great names are a few of our admired guides in languages.

I have lamented the repugnance of young persons in the first study of the elements of knowledge, a disinclination lasting sometimes to eleven years of age, for all learning, an apathy, with regard to beneficial information, which afflicts half the population of each nation. It arises from a cause which I now point out; there is a fame, which reaches the nursery, that learning is not a garden of delightful shrubs and flowers, but a wilderness of briars.

The tender mother alarms her offspring with the expected severity of the schoolmaster.

I shall ask a few important questions in this place: Is it not some disgrace to the French—

is it not a lowering of our national vanity, to find that it is chiefly the speech and pronunciation of a Parisian, of the native of Orleans, Blois, Tours, &c. that the English confide in? Is it not also some disgrace to the universal English people, the colonists of an empire which overspreads the four quarters of the globe, that the court or metropolitan language is alone reputed to be the *best* English, and that the men of Somersetshire or Yorkshire, &c. (excepting the rich class, who have been enabled to breathe the court air) talk in a dialect, and with so uncouth a pronunciation, that they are nearly unintelligible to Englishmen of other provinces? Is it not some disgrace to the Scotch, individually and nationally, that no length of years can efface their provincialism in accent, or the rigidity of their style of English? And to the Irish, that the nation, with the sole exception of the courtiers and barristers, speak English by incantation, having an intonation or song appertaining to each division of their island, and that, according to a favourate word of Milton, they all " exasperate " the language?

These remarks are so just, that no rational mind will take alarm at them, or censure me for considering them a fair argument in proof that there is an improper neglect of language and learning, and that honest exertions are misdirected. I will add, what we are all aware of, that in spite of such accidental or inevitable want of good education, the Frenchman still appropriates to himself his justly merited repute of vivacity of soul, or *esprit*, of elegance and of politeness; the Englishman maintains his old character of sincerity, courage, enterprise, and genius; the Scotch give philosophers to the new generations; and the Irish have committed the malicious blunder of offering a consummate general to controul the destinies of Europe by his success in arms; and many eminent statesmen and lawyers to dictate to their own islanders, to save them from anarchy, rather than enslave them.

Having thus made the *amende honorable*, I shall proceed with my reprehension of the deficient modes of education, which have caused the absurdity of impoverished and ridiculous language, being that of the mass of each people. Estimate the number of teachers in France, in this island, and say should not elegant language have become almost general, either by direct instruction or by the spread of learning, which, if *good*, is expansive? The *old system* is to be *blamed*, not the *enlightened professors* of the two nations.

How shocking is it to our professors to reflect, that the gross blunders of speech are made by a portion of the community endowed with the *usual* education!

I will prove this hypothesis by some example, so absurd that an opponent will scarcely contradict me. I say, then, that there are often boys, who have spent some years at the petty schools, who say habitually, I *don't know no such thing*. If so, why object to the introduction of more efficacious systems of general instruction? Does not that authentic example equal in barbarity the *j'étions* of our uninstructed peasantry of Champagne or Provence?

The teaching must be essentially bad which can *produce* palpable absurdities of speech—a lamentable result! I confess that I purposely employ this verb *produce*, for if the youths who have been misled by exploded and antiquated systems, into ignorance of good language, and have been coerced by perverse tuition, had been left free to use the simplest efforts of their reason, they would have attained to eminence in learning. Is it not perfectly true that some English gentlemen, in a spirit of candour, still say, "*I was at school, and at the university; yet, after all, I had to commence learning on my own plan, for I had learnt little previously at school and college?*"

Those gentlemen probably exaggerated in that statement, yet made so strange a speech, with little hesitation. But how many say, "*I learned Latin and French at school, and have forgotten both?*" I ask, did they effectually learn either?—were they properly taught? Their masters were excellent, but the route was a circle of error, and terminated where it began, in the total ignorance of the pupils.

I flatter myself that *my system* can produce riper fruit: the blossoms are most promising, if I may implicitly trust my kind correspondents, the schoolmasters, who liberally patronize these works; and I think that the students who have acquired a perfect knowledge of French, by the adoption of my rules for pronunciation, the exercises afforded in *Le Trésor*, and my French Reader, Dialogues, Annotations, Grammars, and Collections of Phrases and Idioms, forming the Elements of General Conversation, will not lose, at a period of life when the affairs of the world call them into action, the advantages of this inestimable prize.

By similar modes, indeed by the adaptation of the identical works to other languages, I hope to impart the right pronunciation of the Italian, German, and Latin Languages, with fluency of speech and copiousness of diction, equal to what has been gained by many of the students of these works in French. I have heretofore explained amply my system, and have furnished preceptors and governesses with a catalogue of useful lessons for their scholars. I shall refer to those instructions, rather than repeat them in this place, and now wish to identify the THESAURUS with its predecessors LE TRÉSOR and IL TESORETTO.

I affirm, that he who would, at a future day, speak French, Italian, and Latin with fluency (which latter is by no means an impossibility), must learn by a system which shall tempt onward by its facility, the absence of discouraging difficulties and abstruse classifications and deductions, and which shall charm by the certain hope of ultimate success. If he would speak with elegance, he must have learned with ease.

An infant acquires from its parent a language by the period of its third year: the child speaks its native tongue as early as the tender organs of elocution can be subservient to the important acquisition. Is he at ten years of age taught Latin by as effective a mode ? I ask, is his path made smooth, or are the barricades of pedantry and old custom thrown across his way ? Is he actually taught to speak Latin, or have his instructors rendered that acquisition a fable, a deception, an improbability, nay, an impossibility ? Now I, on the contrary, assert, that if you do not cause your son *to be taught to speak Latin and Greek* with the fluency which you expect from him in French, he will perhaps say, some day, with those I have above alluded to, "*I did learn Latin*, but indeed *I do not know it now*."

Children learn their *own* language, emphatically so named, because they *do* learn it with a charm. Thus is French learned in France —thus might it be taught and learned in England.

The original channels of communication which parents have, from the *cradle*, held with their child's understanding and his active perceptions hitherto unblunted, should certainly not be closed by the pedagogue.

Abstruse grammar *should aid*, and *not supersede*, the instruction of nature and of the paternal house. Yet, at my early schools, how I have taken the *dose* of grammar before breakfast, dinner, and supper, to conjugate the verbs, reckon the declensions, learn the *Propria quæ maribus* of our own instructors, all with little attention, because the language itself was withheld. If grammar is the best vehicle, should this celebrated carriage be always *à vide?*

Here I dare to attack the fortress itself of the old pedants, who have happily given way before the *bonne volonté* of *modern schoolmasters.* For centuries there has resounded the perverse, the interested, the ominous cry against *routine;* yet *routine* is conversation itself. Nevertheless, Theory has been the fashion, Grammar the rage and prescriptive method. Grammar! without *conversation,* without the daily *rendering* lessons from the *vernacular tongue into* the language, *ancient or modern,* which is to be *acquired,* without the truly efficient mode of *translating* and *retranslating.* They might well talk of dead languages, and of having learned French during ten years without any *success at all.* To learn conversation, and daily to practise it; to learn the true pronunciation; to translate rapidly *into the language* which is *the object* of acquisition; to translate from fine specimens of that language and retranslate into the original; to declaim beautiful specimens of the choice poets, with loud and elegant pronunciation; to read the desired language, daily, in the most perfect style of elocution; and almost every week *to read* the grammar through with rapidity, and *accompanied by just remarks, comparisons, analysis and reference,* are some of the favourite modes, with me, of a student's gaining a new language, and which I perpetually recommend in my writings.

"But," say the old literary tyrants, "to learn by *rote* is to learn with the starling and parrot; you must let *us* teach your young gentlemen grammar and theory of language, also to write nonsensical verses, and when to exclaim 'A false quantity! a false quantity!' if another person quotes Tacitus, or caps verses; and the young gentlemen will be fit for the university in *four* or *five* years." These doctors teach *rules* and *exceptions*, but no conversation; THEY IMPART NO GIFT OF SPEECH. But I fortify my student's memory; I make him desirous to investigate the rules of many grammars, because he has *use for them* in their application, when he daily converses in the language studied. I appeal to those who have studied my grammatical works, to say if I can be suspected of a desire to *slight* grammar. In recommending that the scholar shall learn by *rote*, and also learn by *theory*, I simply, but very properly, enable him to *understand* the theory. Indeed what can grammar *effect*, with *a total neglect of conversation?* Conversation and good pronunciation are essential objects acquired by imitation, and imitation is a portion of *routine* or *practice*. To converse in an ancient language is beyond the pretension of the censors, and a good scholar has not even an idea of what was the pronunciation of the ancients. These two objects he has considered beneath his notice, and therefore he knows nothing of them.

The best point of the enlightened schoolmaster's teaching is the *exercises*, which he causes his boys to pay considerable attention to. Here his plan coincides with my system, and he will be the less predisposed to assert the inutility of my mode, of directing the student *to translate at sight*, from the appointed lesson of the *vernacular tongue into Latin, Italian, French, Spanish, Portuguese and German.*

My selection of sentences is calculated to be useful to the student of any of the above languages, in the essential quality of rendering him familiar with the idoms most frequently recurring. My glossaries appended to LE TRÉSOR, IL TESORETTO, and the THESAURUS, have been studiously prepared to elucidate the most difficult words and remarkable phrases, and to convey *succinctly much information on grammar*, and the precision of *genuine idioms*, but not of provincialisms. These glossaries or indices cannot fail, therefore, of being eminently useful, particularly to those who have not my grammars and dictionaries yet placed in their hands.

These volumes, calculated to promote right pronunciation, fluency in conversation, and grammatical accuracy, are in the course of being completed, according to my original plan and proposals.

I subjoin a catalogue of such of them as are in print, and take this opportunity of recommending such of them as have been recently published, to my patrons, the heads of schools in London, Rochester, Dover, Ramsgate, Bristol, Birmingham, Liverpool, Manchester, Edinburgh, Glasgow, Dublin, and Belfast, and the other places in which this system has been introduced.

To conclude, I beg leave to offer this observation, which I consider myself in duty bound to make, viz. that as no one can flatter himself of enjoying peacefully and quietly the fruit or well-earned reward of his labour, without being exposed to the *invidious attacks of jealous* and *less successful candidates* to public favour, who will not scruple to magnify *mole hills into mountains*, and catch at a straw, should there be any typographical errors in the more recent editions of my works (which is most difficult to obviate), I may assure my numerous patrons, that it has been, and always will be, my most anxious desire to revise every edition, till it may be proved faultless; but that even admitting that a few errors might have crept in during the course of printing, it cannot in the remotest degree *deprive* the works of the *high importance* attached to the lineal features of my plan, and that as to the extracts found in the *French Pupil's Own Book*, they have been copied faithfully from the original editions, without *presuming* on my part to correct or chastise my masters in French literature, although repeatedly desired to do so by less celebrated men of the present day.

I remain, gentlemen, respectfully,

Your obedient servant,

(Signed) LOUIS FENWICK DE PORQUET.

11, *Tavistock Street, Covent Garden.*

APPROVALS.

FROM THE EDITOR OF THE CHESTER CHRONICLE ON THE TEACHING OF LANGUAGES.

The great error in the system adopted by most teachers of languages (in schools more especially) is, that they adopt the same plan for teaching the dead and the living languages; whereas the objects in the study of the one and the other are widely different. A person applies himself to the study of the Greek and Roman classics to obtain some acquaintance with grammar as a science; to enrich the stores of his mind with the sublime conceptions of the ancients—unmutilated or undiluted as they are even in the best translations; and to improve his composition, and form his style, by rendering them into his own language. All the other purposes for which the ancient classics were formerly so valuable, are now fulfilled by translations, or the study of them rendered unnecessary by the various works in our own language upon every branch in the whole circle of the arts and sciences.

The great object in the study of a living language is, to obtain not only the ability to read and translate it at sight, and even a critical acquaintance with the genius and grammatical construction of the language, but to acquire *la langue parlée*—a facility of *composing* and *conversing* in the particular language which is the subject of study. To attain this, the mode almost universally adopted in teaching the Greek and Roman classics (and to which teachers of the old school still pertinaciously adhere) is palpably inadequate. In proof of the truth of this assertion, it is only necessary to ask any well-educated Englishman (who has been taught French on the *orthodox* system) to write a letter in French, or to turn a page of any English book into that language, and it will be seen that every phrase will contain an Anglicism, if every third word be not a sin against the grammar of the language. As to conversing in French, that is wholly out of the question. Address him in that language, and after the interchange of a sentence or two (and these for the most part common-place) he declares "*Monsieur, je sais bien traduire, mais je ne puis pas parler français.*"

The object, then, in the study of the dead and of the living languages, being wholly different, the course of study in each should also be different. Without stopping to inquire whether the plan usually pursued in teaching the classics is the very best that might be adopted, it is quite clear as the result of all experience, that the mere turning of French, Italian, or any other language into English, joined with how intimate soever an acquaintance with the grammar, will not give a facility of French or Italian composition or conversation. M. de Porquet, after many years' labour as a teacher, upon the orthodox system, found this to be the result of his experience, and bethought him of devising a remedy. He says, in a letter he has published on the subject,

"At last it occurred to me that, if we were to reverse the order, we might obtain a different result. I tried it, and no sooner had a pupil learned how to read, and become familiar with the nine parts of speech in French, than I caused a small portion of plain and easy English to be translated into French at sight, the pupil having previously prepared his lesson by the help of his dictionary. I thus discovered, for the first time, and perhaps to my shame, that as long as a pupil only translated *Recueil Choisi*, *Numa Pompilius* and *Télémaque*, &c. from

French into English, he was merely *working in English*; and that, on the other hand, in order to meet with no impediment in expressing his ideas in French, he must have been in the habit, not of making English, but of turning his English into French, or, in other words, of working in French."

After what we have already written, it may be almost superfluous to say how entirely we agree with Mons. de Porquet in the efficacy of the plan he recommends; but while we thus bear a willing testimony to its merits, and the admirable arrangement of the works he has compiled to aid in carrying it into practice, we cannot concede to him the merit of perfect originality in his plan, although to him undoubtedly belongs (as far as our experience extends) the merit of being the first to promulgate it. It is more than probable that others engaged in teaching discovered the defect, and applied the remedy, in the same way as Mons. de Porquet; indeed, some friends of our own in the profession have long pursued the same plan in teaching French, although not perhaps to the same extent as he has done. It is, undoubtedly, the very best way of acquiring a facility of French composition, and a great step towards *fluency* in conversation, which latter can be attained by *constant practice only*. A venerable gentleman of our acquaintance assures us that he was taught Latin upon this plan, at a village school in this county, at least half a century ago; and it is owing to a course of discipline somewhat similar that the young men educated at Kerry, and other parts of the south of Ireland, not only write Latin with facility and remarkable purity, but frequently are able to speak it with considerable fluency.

The system of M. Fenwick de Porquet is calculated, we are convinced, to effect a very important revolution in the present mode of teaching French, and this must be our apology for again recommending it to the attention of our readers. We find we were right in our conjecture, that the object of M. Fenwick's visit to this part of the country was to introduce his peculiar system to the notice of the conductors of schools, and we are happy to find that he has been as eminently successful in Lancashire as he had previously been in London and its neighbourhood.—*Liverpool Chronicle.*

EXTRACT FROM M. MORDACQUE'S ESSAY ON THE MERITS OF FRENCH WORKS FOR THE STUDY OF THAT LANGUAGE.

Printed in England, 1831, *and published in the Lancashire Herald, of October,* 1831.

About the same time, however, some French elementary books were silently making their way, and introducing a system of tuition far superior to any thing produced before. We allude to the works of M. Fenwick de Porquet. During his stay in England, as a practical teacher, M. Fenwick remarked a fact which we all have an opportunity of ascertaining, should we not believe it, namely, *that there is no country where French is more generally diffused than in England, and no nation that speaks French worse than the English.* An inquiring mind would naturally look into the cause whence arises such a deficiency, and soon find it in the absurd methods adopted for teaching living languages. "Read the theory of the science," said M. Fenwick to his pupils; "but practice, *and by continually turning your own language into French.*" To enable them so to do, and in order that the conversation be better understood, the indefatigable teacher subdivided his labour, and published it in a series of elementary works, as follow:

Elements of Pronunciation,
Useful Words and Phrases,
An introductory Grammar and Exercises,
Select Pieces for Translation and Reading,
What he called *Trésor*, and Parisian Secretary; or the Art of turning English into French at sight.

This *Trésor* is the *innovation* he introduced, by thus adopting a practical exercise to the former routine which he also simplified. A small pamphlet, by the same author, explains the *Fenwickian System*, which we would not exactly call a system, but a rational division of labour, combining theory and practice, and chiefly intended for the use of beginners. A series of works, on the same plan, and intended to carry on the practical system with persons advanced in the language, will, no doubt, be published in succession. Up to this time, however, M. F.'s publications are certainly *far superior* to any thing known, and best calculated to impart real practical knowledge.

To conclude, and as we have said, without alluding to

our own labours on the subject,—the old routine is bad—the natural plans *will not do*—the without-book plan *cannot* do. An alteration must take place in the modes hitherto adopted for teaching languages. Who is to have the honour of introducing it? Time will tell the public, and the public (that infallible judge) will decide.

DIRECTIONS TO PUPILS AND TEACHERS.

It is intended that the following pages should be read in a loud and distinct manner, in Latin, to a teacher of Latin, as if the pupil were reading a Latin composition out. It may be prepared previously, by the help of the Dictionary, at the end.

THESAURUS LINGUÆ LATINÆ,

OR THE ART OF

READING ENGLISH INTO LATIN

AT SIGHT.

1.

I have a grammar. I have not your dictionary.[1] I had his pen. I shall have a lesson.[2] He has their pencil. He had my box.[3] He will have a better place[4]. He would have a hat. I have spoken to my mother. I had loved. I have not seen his house. I had not spoken.

---

1. Thesaurum.—2. habebo lectionem.—3. arcam.—4. meliorem locum.

Have you given your direction? He has not pardoned his brother.[1] Have I written badly? Had he told my father? I shall not be here before six o'clock. Why? Because I have not a horse. I am very sorry. You have not spoken to my uncle. But why has he not a better house? I do not know.[2] Have you paid your bill? Yes, I have paid[3] my bill, and all my debts.[4] Have you consulted my friend?

2.

I am a native of London.[5] You are now in Italy. I was very sorry. I am not pleased. Where are you? Where were you? Where shall you be? Where am I? I am loved[6] by every one. He had read that book. Have I spoken against you? You shall be punished.[7] For what? My sister is gone to Paris with her governess. When? Yesterday. I have not your book. Who has it? I do not know. You are too good. They are here.[8] His papers are lost. His book is better than mine. Am I angry?[9] You are now in London, and your

1. Ignovit fratri suo.—2. nescio.—3. solvi.—4. æs omne alienum.—5. Londinensis.—6. dilectus sum.—7. vapulabis.—8. adsunt.—9. An ego irascor?

father is in Paris. I am not sorry. Are you not tired?[1] Yes, I am very tired? She is very kind. What is he? They are very ill. Where were they? Where will they be? At your house.[2] We have not learned this lesson. Why not? I have no pen.[3] I had no master. I shall have no horse. Have you a good watch? No, I have none. My garden is very fine. I will have a box.

3.

Your master[4] is come. You are satisfied. I hope so. I did not ask too much.[5] He had read that book I am sure.[6] Are you pleased? Yes. Well; I am not. Is he arrived? Are they come? Is dinner ready? No, not yet. We are very sure. Is the king in London. I am very ill.[7] I shall be very angry. Your drawing is well done. Do you draw? I have learned drawing for five years. I do not draw very well.[8] Do you speak French? Yes, I speak French and Italian also. Where did you learn it?[9] Near London. At Brompton. She has spoken French

1. Imò.—2. domi.—3. stylum.—4. herus.—5. nimis.—6. certo scio.—7. valde ægroto.—8. satis benè.—9. ubi didicisti?

all day.[1] Where is your father now? In the East Indies.[2] I am glad[3] to see you. Speak to that man. Are you determined to follow[4] your brother?

4.

Where are my children?[5] This house is very large. Too large for my family. My son was at school.[6] Has he finished his speech?[7] Sell your land. If you have a novel, lend it to my mother. If you come to-morrow, I will give you something. We shall always have much pleasure in seeing you.[8] I shall have those fields[9] with this farm-house. He has had much trouble. They have arrived. You have played[10] very well. He has taken my hat and my stick.[11] We were rich, now we are very poor. Was I with you? No, you were with Mrs. D. You have done wrong. It is not my fault. Let us have more prudence, and let us be more careful. Have you shewn your writing? Did you shew

---

1. Toto die.—2. Indiâ.—3. gaudeo te.—4. sequi.—5. liberi mei.—6. erat ludo.—7. sermonem.—8. te visendo.—9. agros. —10. lusisti.—11. baculum meum.

your hand? Would you have shewn your letter? I have sung all night.[1]

5.

They have arrived here before me. Divine Providence. I have been there several times.[2] At what time do you go? The door is open. The gate was shut.[3] You have left the window open. Shut it, if you please.[4] Who left it open?[5] She is not here.[6] I have bought this work for one hundred pounds. I have it not. He had purchased that house before his father's death. Is she ill? Yes, she has been very ill. Indeed? Who told you? We have not been angry with you. Where is your master? In the garden or in the yard? Why are you so wicked? Where will your friends be to-morrow? At Dover. Did he send his letters and parcels? believe he has. Speak to him. The passions of men.[7] The keys of the house. The master's desk. Shall we be received in that company?[8] I hope so. If you have still some hope, do not abandon me.[9]

---

1. Totâ nocte, vel per totam noctem.—2. sæpenumerò.—3. clausa fuit.—4. si libet.—5. liquit apertam.—6. adest.—7. hominum motus animi.—8. societate illâ.—9. ne deseras me.

6.

We are ready.[1] The company of that man is dangerous. I have accompanied your son on his travels. Was he prepared? Was he not surprised?[2] Were you not astonished at it? I am glad of it.[3] I have some. I have not any. I will eat some. I give none. I shall have those books next week. They were very polite. His plan was approved by every body. Will he be prepared this evening? I do not know indeed. I knew your cousin Charles. We were in Scotland this summer. Did you speak to her mother? Yes, I did. Speaking and writing are two very different things.[4] I have not bought any pens this week.[5] We shall not have that. Be honest and just. Have pity on your relations. They are not so weak as they were. It is full of faults. Do not be silly. She is in a passion. Life is uncertain. Where are my drawings?[6] In the parlour. I do not see them. Look well. Be more attentive. Look at that. Look for that. I am looking for you.[7] Look at me.[8]

---

1. Parati sumus.—2. nonne miratus est?—3. eâ de re.—4. res sunt valde diversæ.—5. hâc hebdomadâ.—6. adumbrationes meæ.—7. te peto.—8. me inspice.

7.

Have you dined? Have you been invited[1] to breakfast with the Duke of B.? Yes, and also to spend a month at His Grace's seat[2] near Marlow. At what o'clock do you sup generally?[3] About ten. I have dined with him several times. You are an Irishman I believe. Yes, I am. He was a general. I am a surgeon. Are they sorrowful. I have pardoned you more than once.[4] Pray be dutiful. I am not an Englishman. But your name is English, is it not? You are right. Have done. I have done. Are we in danger[5] here? No, you are not in any great danger. My dear, you are always here before me. That is excusable. I am always ill in London. Why? Because I am not used to live in the city. Are you fond of the country?[6] Yes, I like it well enough in the summer. Where will you spend the winter?[7] Perhaps at Bath. Do you know any one in Clifton? She is very pretty.[8] Your sister is handsomer.[9] Sophia is certainly the prettiest of all my cousins. What do you say? I say that you are right.

---

1. Convocatus.—2. in villâ suâ.—3. cænare soles, vel consuescis.—4. semel ataque iterùm.—5. in periculo.—6. rus.—7. quo in loco hibernabis?—8. formosa.—9. formosior.

8.

Do not be silly. You are as tall as I am. But I am older. He is not able to do it. The penknife is lost in the grass.[1] Who is there? The French are very polite. Will you oblige[2] me to punish you? Italy is the garden of Europe.[3] The pens are mended.[4] I write to the King every day. So do I. I received a letter in which they write me news of all our friends. It is a fine country! Do you like Italy? Very much. Were they merry?[5] Who are they?[6] What are they? I did not study this lesson. Why are you so passionate? Silence. There is a post chaise[7] in the yard. He should or would have spoken much better. I am a Frenchman. My father's brother is a German. We often speak French. Your friends from London are come. You have given me a good place. We are, and have been always good friends. I am a merchant, and you are a physician. He is attentive, and they are careless.[8] We are prepared and they are not. Of what country are they? Has he not been a shop-

---

1. In herbâ.—2. coges?—3. hortus Europæ.—4. acuti sunt.—5. hilari, vel jocosi.—6. qui sunt?—7. rheda.—8. negligentes.

keeper? Let us go into the country. I believe he is a merchant.

9.

You have lost my favourite dog. I have found it this morning.[1] I am ashamed[2] of his conduct. She is more useful to her father. Am I not curious? How inquisitive you are![3] What was his intention? We have seen all his prints. That boy is stronger than the other. It would be very strange. My glass was not full. The street was narrow. Their son has been very ill. This lesson is not difficult as the other. I am quite wet. Where were the pupils? You shall be free. Do not be idle. I give you my word of honour. Is she returned from market?[4] Her music master is blind, but not deaf I assure you. You are mistaken. Her gown is very well made. His shoes are worn out. Have they done? The innocent have been oppressed and always will be. He received four wounds in the same battle. She had been educated[5] near London. How kind he is! Be quiet. Be sure that he never will do it. Eliza plays

1. Hodiè manè —2. pudet me illius morum.—3. quam tu es percontator!—4. à foro, vel ex mercatu.—5. nutrita est.

well on the piano-forte. She practices,[1] daily, five hours. It is a great while.

10.

He was delighted.[2] Are you not guilty?[3] Yes, I am. He had learned French and his sister Italian. Have I not shut all the windows, and you all the doors? Have we not danced all the night?[4] Their horse seems tired, does he not? How many children are there? There are eleven children, six boys and five girls. Every body has sent something to that poor family. The clock has struck seven. She is yet too young. She has left school. Indeed! Yet she is not fifteen. I have scolded[5] my servants several times for this very thing. He would have been very useful to his country. Would they have been so ill-natured? Had you not taken the candle? Is he not too weak to take such a journey in this season? Is there another man in the world who could redress these grievances? He is more bold than considerate. It is probable. It is possible. Is it probable?

---

1. Se exercet.—2. valde lætatus est.—3. sons.—4. in choreis per totam noctem versati fuimus.—5. objurgavi.

11.

She is always cross[1] when you are here. What a pretty cross she wears! Is it not of gold?[2] Is it true? Is it not well. It was not true. I am so tired. Enough. She is often cross. How cross they are! Do not be so obstinate. Are you come to quarrel? My gloves are dearer than theirs. This little girl is very naughty.[3] He is very stout.[4] I am at home every day between nine and ten. You would be complaisant.[5] They have been very giddy. I am angry with you. Be as prudent as your dear mother. Do not be proud and vain. A despicable man is not worthy of advice. Has he not been accused of inattention to business? Tea is ready. Napoleon was the first emperor of the French. Have you ever seen him? A thousand times.[6] Is she not pretty? Is she dark? No, she is fair. Your intention[7] is good; that of your uncle is better. Mine is not so good. His is noble and generous. They have been very whimsical. She was as pale[8] as death. You should be rich, if you were more prudent. I am very cold.[9]

---

1. Irata est, vel irascitur.—2. aurea, vel auri.—3. mala.—4. obesus.—5. humanus, vel comis.—6. milliès.—7. propositum tuum.—8. pallida.—9. algeo.

12.

I am very much obliged to you, ladies.[1] She is very genteel.[2] I shall be obliged to send him[3] to Paris. Is dinner ready? Yes, long ago. I shall not dine at home to-day. Very well; I shall not wait for you. These merchants are very wealthy. They have made a considerable fortune[4] in the last war. Has he not consulted all his friends? Yes, he has. The greatest privilege of a king is to pardon. We shall soon have an answer to the letter we sent last night. Have they any acquaintances in Paris? A great many. Have you any thing for me? Nothing. If I had your house I would let it for two years, and would go and live in the west of England, to recover my health. How can I do it? How could I do it? Have I not business in London which I cannot give up? You are, I am sure, rich enough. All that glitters is not gold, according to the proverb.[5] This book was published[6] in France last year, and met with success.

---

1. Dominœ.—2. generosa.—3. cogar illum Lutetiam mittere.—4. rem familiarem satis magnam.—5. sicut aiunt.—6. editus.

13.

You are very tall,[1] and I am very short.[2] You are dull. Leave me alone. I am your very humble servant.[3] Are you married? No, Madam, I am not yet married, but I shall be next year, next month, or next week. The next day he called at my house. Do you call me? Call my daughter. Buonaparte was a great general. Gambling[4] has been the misfortune[5] of many men. Have you been to Russia? Yes, and to America also. You have travelled a great deal. Yes, and if I have gained some information. I shall never regret it. You are right. I have lost a great many friends. In what other countries have you been? I first visited France, where I stayed nine months; I departed thence for Italy. I spent a winter in Rome, visited all the interesting antiquities of that celebrated city, and accompanied by a young and intelligent Greek I went next to Naples and Florence. After a few months spent in studying the

1. Grandis —2. brevis.—3. cupio omnia quæ vis,—vel obsequentissimus tibi sum.—4. alea.—5. exitium, vel infortunium.

beautiful language of Petrarch, Dante, and Ariosto, we resolved to embark on the Mediterranean.[1] Whilst we were cruizing on that sea we were boarded by a South American privateer, which captured us; and when nearly within sight of one of their ports, a Russian squadron retook us, after an action which lasted more than two hours.

14.

Is she a good girl? Pretty well. Who speaks so loud? Is there any paper? Yes, there is some, but not for you. I bought it for my master who wishes to copy my book. As long as you are attentive. I love[2] my children tenderly, but I cannot bring them up as I should like. Bring my cane and hat. Take this coat to the tailor's.[3] Bring your sister to tea this evening. Has he not taken my linen? Where is it? There. Give me my flute. Do not give me my grammar, but my copy book. Are you not sick? Yes, always when I ride in a close carriage. If

---

1. Statuimus navem conscendere.—2. valde diligo.—3. vestem ad sartorem.

you study hard, you will speak French very soon.[1] Do you write well? Look. That is pretty well. Who is your master? I am listening[2] to you. Speak the truth. Speak openly. My parents have been in Germany. You were last week in England and now you are in Paris. Will you be satisfied? Yes, I will. Is he at home? The wine was good, but was it not too dear? If you are tired, rest yourself. My pen is not good. Is it too soft? Rather. You were formerly so diligent, why are you now so idle? Was she at home? My dear son be diligent, and thou shalt be loved.

15.

Had I been[3] in your place, I should have been more prudent.[4] You are sad. If we were glad. Your sister was the prettiest woman in this town. I was a soldier. I am now a general. Interest, glory, and pleasure, are the three motives of men's actions. You are older than I. She is as rich as you. I

1. Brevi tempore.—2. ausculto.—3. fuissem.—4. prudentiorem me præbuissem.

should be the most generous man in the world if I were rich. To be rich and to have been rich, are certainly two very different things. She is lovely. Are you an Italian? She is sulky. Have you much money?[1] Enough for our journey. I have fifty pounds, and my brother one hundred and twenty-five. You had my night cap. Where did you put it? In your closet. I had[2] the headache. My head aches. Have a little charity. We have nothing to give you. The Greeks[3] had no money under Solon. I will have an egg for breakfast. My ill-health remains just the same, and my infirmities are, as they have always been, very troublesome to those who are with me. When will you have a new carriage? When I am rich. When I have done I will speak to you. What a noise![4]

16.

I give a book to my sister. I do not give a pound of tea to the man. I did give a dozen lines to this boy to learn by heart. I will give a fine house to my son. I would give a better

1. Multos nummos.—2. doluit.—3. Græci.—4. o quantus strepitus!

price. She sings as well as I. She sang a very pretty song. She will sing several songs this evening. She should sing if she were not so ill. The fear of death,[1] the love of life, are natural to man.[2] Give her the loaf.[3] Cut the meat. The price of bread is very high. Men ought to shun vice. France is a fine country. England has obtained the praise of travellers from all the other countries of Europe. The creator of heaven and earth[4] is the God of Christians. Bring the mustard.[5] Do you admire Venice? Not so much as Geneva. The kings of France are crowned at Rheims, a town of France. Afterwards I shall return to England. I came from Scotland. I travelled through the county of Cumberland on my return to London. Come to England.

17.

You shall soon be satisfied. Are you not pleased? Pretty well. We shall be better treated. I shall send them back,[6] before two o'clock. If you call upon me to-morrow[7] be-

1. Timor mortis —2. homini.—3. panem.—4. cœli et terræ, —5. affer sinapem.—6. illos remittam.—si me convenias cras,

tween nine and ten you will find me at home.[1] We have begun our defence, and we hope to see the end of this business, perhaps before a fortnight. He will find his handkerchief under the chair. Let us love our neighbour as ourselves. Who lives in the next house? Mr. B——. He is a very good neighbour, I assure you. Is he married? Yes, and he has a very large family. From what county does he come? Sussex. How old is his lady? I believe she is more than forty. Do you forget you owe me some money?[2] When do you mean to pay[3] me? Give her a glass of water. Look yonder. This action does not merit a reward; you surprise me. For shame![4]

18.

Wheat is sold at eight shillings[5] a bushel.[6] Cherries at twopence a pound. Hay sells[7] now for three pounds a load. It is very cheap. It is very dear. Have you ever been in Ireland? Never. It is a fine country. I am speaking of

---

1. Invenies me domi.—2. ut argentum mutuum mihi debeas.—3. solvere.—4. proh pudor.—5. octo solidis.—6. modiu stritici.—7. vehes fœni venditur quatuor libris.

an officer whom you know very well. You are mistaken. I am writing to a gentleman, and my wife to a friend of hers, with whom she was at school for upwards of six years. I come from a very large town in this county, that does not send any member[1] to parliament. London is more populous than Paris; but France is more populous than England. How many inhabitants are there in each country? Thirty-three millions in France, and only twenty-two in England. Have you hunted[2] this week? Yes, I have. Where? In Epping Forest.[3] Bring us something to drink. I will see it with pleasure. You have sent them your horse. You hate them.[4] Very well.

19.

Take my master's hat and my brother's umbrella. The boy's books. The girl's bonnets. Leave the gentleman's coat. He will come on Wednesday.[5] Think on it seriously. Who knocks at the door? Go and see who it is. I want my horse at three o'clock. Do not stay long in Switzerland.[6] I wish to meet

---

1. Senator.—2. an venatus es.—3. saltu.—4. illos odisti.—5. die Mercurii.—6. in Helvetiâ.

you[1] at Geneva. Has he washed the carriage? Wash this handkerchief. Wash your hands. I have washed my hands before them. Now let us go in.[2] Is the company come? Beg of your brother to come to tea. I will buy some cloth in the market. We like certain persons without knowing why: and we hate others in the same manner. When you come, I am always engaged. Take a glass of wine.[3]—What wine do you choose, red or white? Red, if you please. Have they tied the bundle? Have you not many pupils at Miss Taylor's? A great many. I will not fail to ask her where she is going to spend her hòlidays. I spend more than eight hundred a year. He spends most of his time at home. Make haste. Quick.

20.

I often carry letters for my friends,[4] and parcels also. Do you not think I am too good? You are right. I never count them. When I make up my bills. Lace is very cheap in Holland. This letter comes from the king, and

1. Tibi obviam ire.—2. eamus nunc intro.—3. scyphum vel poculum vini.—4. pro familiaribus.

is addressed to the magistrates of this county. I return from town.[1] Go to the post-office; inquire if there are any letters for me. There are four. I have received the order from the General. Did you hear that news? Yes, I heard it at the bank. My father's clerk is very ill, and unable to come to the office.[2] Go to the fisherman's,[3] tell him I shall want some fish on Monday and Tuesday, and also on Saturday, because I expect company to dine at my house. Let us prefer honor to interest.[4] I have bought a sword, a cane, silk stockings, and handkerchiefs. White and black are two opposite colours. The king of England is the patron of the fine arts. Every body admires you. Gaming is the ruin of young men.[5] I do not like winter; that season is too cold for my health. Let us now be merry. Take her to church. Take the arm chair into his bed-room. The enemy have burnt his mansion. Come and see me.

21.

Send me your corn-factor, as soon as possible.

---

1. Ex urbe redeo.—2. ad officinam.—3. pete piscatorem.—4. anteponamus honorem lucro.—5. juvenum.

Never forget,[1] my dear love, all the duties you have to perform. I came to see all the curiosities of London. I come from home. I have sent my cows to your farm.[2] Take care of them. A good wife[3] is a great treasure. Great men are scarce,[4] do you say? His sister is very short, but extremely pretty. Their mother is very handsome; and the father was the finest man in the county. Napoleon, notwithstanding all his faults, was a great man.[5] Napoleon was very short. Napoleon was not a tall man. I know it. The French tongue is spoken in all the courts of Europe.[6] She has brought a considerable fortune. I am content with what I have. God be praised. I believe in God. Show me the Gospel for this day. He has mislaid his prayer-book. Has she a Bible? Who preaches to-day? The curate. Were there many people at church this morning? Who played the organ? The clerk. What does he bring us? The bells of this church are the finest I have ever heard. How many are there? Only eight. They are very excellent bells. Ring the bell,

---

1. Nunquam obliviscere.—2. ad fundum tuum.—3. uxor digna.—4. perpauci.—5. magnus habebatur.—6. in regiis Europæ omnibus.

if you please. I want my newspaper. She is fit for any thing.

22.

Are you a friend to religous people ?[1] She is a friend to the poor.[2] The dog is a friend to man. Many flowers have no smell though they are beautiful. Human life is never free from troubles.[3] I have been forced to go there. Do you see that mill ? Yes, I do. It belongs to a friend of mine. A friend of yours called upon us yesterday. I had a book of yours up stairs. A book of mine do you say ? Go and fetch it. I will ; here it is. It is not mine, I assure you. Whose is it then ? I think it is my uncle's. Clean the candlestick and the extinguisher directly. Has he lighted a fire in my study ? No, not yet, it is very cold ; I want a fire immediately. Seal my letter,[4] or else I shall be too late for the post. He is rich,[5] I suppose ?[6] He has been very rich ; but he has lately lost a great deal of money, by several failures. Where does he live ? In the country. Does he not keep an establishment in town ? Only during

1. Piorum.—2. pauperum.—3. exempta vicissitudinibus.—4. obsigna litteras meas.—5. dives.—6. ut puto.

the winter months, December, January, and February. You have broken[1] four glasses; you shall be scolded. I do not care; I can pay for them. Mind you do then.

23.

What shall I do? I really do not know. Do you know my master?[2] Yes, I know him very well. Does he know that you are here? I do not know; ask him. You do not know your lesson. I know my repetition well; and I know also you are idle. Do they take snuff? No, never. Why? It is a bad habit.[3] So you say. She sings sweetly.[4] Did she learn singing? Yes, for some time. Who taught her? The celebrated master, Signor Della Torre. Is he not a member of the Conservatory at Naples? From what part of Italy is he? He comes from Milan. The Italians understand[5] that delightful art better than we. How long have you been in this country?[6] Seven years. You are almost a native. The husband and wife are ill. Men and women are mortal. Life is precarious.

---

1. Fregisti quatuor calices.—2. novisti dominum meum?—3. mala consuetudo.—4. dulcè.—5. periti sunt.—6. in hâc patriâ, vel in hoc regno.

I keep generally in my study all the morning. Do you keep at home much? We have done it carelessly. What do you look for, pray? I am looking for my pocket-book and my snuff box. Here they are. I thank you for the trouble you have taken.

24.

My sisters are too generous. I shall or will assist[1] your master. We shall publish this book next year. I beg your pardon.[2] I should limit his power. I swear to be faithful to my king and country. We seek the means of doing him good. I will insist upon that condition. I had left the window and the door shut. My mother and my uncle are come. I have six sisters and one brother married. There were thirty-two ladies and nine gentlemen prepared to meet his majesty. Let us imitate our ancestors. Warm your hands. It freezes. So much the worse.[3] I cannot skate. You slide no doubt. Very little. Never mind. I will run the risk[4] of it. She is at school. He sees me; but I cannot see him. I love you because you love me. I

1. Adjuvabo.—2. a te veniam impetro.—3. tantò pejus.—4. periculum faciam.

speak to you because you speak to me. He loves me because I love him. They hate me because I hate them.[1] A bricked house is preferable. He is gone home. Of whom do you speak? From whom did you receive that? Those animals are revengeful. His acts have been crowned with success. All that which you say is false. This wine is dear. Is it not?

25.

What do you say? I do not care. You are angry with me. I am not angry with you. I have abandoned my friends. I am abandoned by every one. He has blamed her conduct. We have buried the dead. She has walked the whole day. Explain yourself. The rule is explained. I should have burnt her drawings. Throw me the ball.[2] Throw it me. I will not leave my father and mother. I have kissed his majesty's hand. Can you swim? Let us swim. Swim over to the other side.[3] Praise me if deserve it. Draw this string. Draw your chair to the fire. Dance with her. Let us play at whist.[4] Do you aim at it? I have

1. Me oderunt quia ipsos odi.—2. pilam jace mihi.—3. nata usque ad alteram ripam.—4. ludamus pictis chartis.

thanked you several times. It is true. He has avoided the danger, has he not? I avoid bad company[1] as much as possible. I will avoid him. Why? Tell me. Is there any fault in your exercise? Are you Mr. B's daughter? Yes, I am. Are you pleased? No, I am not. Are you ill? Yes, I am.

26.

I came from my house. There is a gentleman now in the drawing room, who wants to speak with you.[2] What do you mean? I meant that if——He does not care. What does he mean? He has never learned Latin, although he has been taught several years. Do you not see that high tower?[3] This is a very dangerous game. Comfort your poor mother. These children improve much. He will give the necessary orders. Order, and you shall be obeyed. We began our exercise by four o'clock. Begin your lesson. The beginning is hard. Do not forget the services he has rendered you. Look here. Fly[4] to his assistance. They are speaking

---

1. Malos fugio.—2. qui tecum loqui vult.—3. nonne vides turrem hanc excelsam.—4. advola.

against me, are they not? The admirals will meet this day. This little girl is very pretty. Is she clever? Not so much as her brother. His works[1] are very much admired. Both went to Paris last year, but neither could speak a word of French. What a pity! Have pity[2] on the unfortunate. Those apples seem very good indeed. Bring me some cold beef. What a number of oxen! I am not fond of that. What a noise those boys do make! They love me, at least you say so. I do not believe it. Do you think they do? What a pleasant morning!

27.

No, but it is all the same. I have no pens. What shall I do? Do they sell any at the next shop? I really do not know. Ask Mr. W— I have but one true friend. They are very scarce. I know it as well as you. Is he come? Yes, he is. I shall be punished for that offence. This cloth is very fine; how do you sell it a yard? My sisters are reading in the library. Two gentlemen are come to speak to you. My aunts have arrived. How long have you been

---

1. Ejus opera.—2. miseresce infelicium hominum.

learning[1] French? Upwards of two years,[2] and I cannot yet speak it. Whose fault is it? Do you know? There were but ten[3] at dinner. How long have they been in England? I think they have been two years here. How much a dozen? Four pounds ten shillings. Their shoes were worn out. His poor brother and his children. Her instrument is not in tune. His mother is dead. Who are you? Who makes such a noise? Have they ever travelled?

28.

Give me this or that. Wine is better than brandy[4]. Do not do that, my child. Go out. Keep this. Take that. The same person took that.[5] Nothing pleases her. Both went to the play, but neither of them were satisfied. All that you say is false. I know[6] them well, they are young and handsome. He reads good books. You respect her. The Cardinals have elected a new Pope this year. Our canals are numerous. The Admirals meet this day. A pretty girl is seldom clever. His efforts have

1. Quamdiù didicisti.—2 diutiùs duobus annis.—3. decem tantùm adfuerunt.—4. melius quam aquâ vitæ.—5. idem excepit illud.—6. domus lateritia melior est tugurio.

been blessed. A brick house is preferable to a thatched cottage. That young man is very steady.

29.

I have been waiting for you some time.[1] I promised you to be here by seven, and it is yet but half past six; that does not matter.[2] Have you seen my father? What did he say to you? How dilatory you are! How long you stay. How long you keep the people waiting for you! It pours, or it is pouring. I did not know it. You are very sleepy. She is sleepy. You have been, or were so kind, as to lend[3] me Dr. Granville's Petersburgh, which I read with infinite pleasure[4] or which is very entertaining or interesting.

30.

Who is making a noise! It is I. Who wrote to you? He. My brother and sister are in the garden. You know my father. You do not know[5] my mother. Do you know my brothers? I know them very well.[6] I am sure you

1. Te diù expectabam.—2. paullùm refert.—3. mihi commodare.—4. libentissimè.—5. non novisti.—6. rectè quidem novi illos.

do not know them. Do you know your lesson? He learns French. He does not learn French. Does he learn French? Does he not learn[1] French? Yes, he is learning French and Italian. Do you sell your house?[2] Do you not sell your house? Yes, I do. To whom? Have you received the letter which I wrote to you last Friday? No, I have not. Who has it? I blame you. Do you blame me? Do you not blame me? Do you see me? Do you not see me? I cannot see you, but I can see them very well. I have it. I have not it. Have I not it? Have I it? You have them. How so? Take them. Speak to them. Go with them. Follow them.

31.

Bring me some cold beef.[3] I like good oranges. Let him take good cheese.[4] Never eat meat. Why? It is not wholesome. Do you see that high hill? This is a very dangerous place. Is it indeed? What does he mean? I do not care. He does not care,[5] and in fact[6] we do not care. Are they angry with

---

1. Discit?—2. ædem tuam nonne venundas?—3. pone bubulam.—4. capiat caseum bonum.—5. nihilo curat.—6. equidem.

you? I am pleased with them. He will not care. I shall be very angry with you, if you thus neglect your duties. I do not care. Are you satisfied, Madam? Yes, Sir, I am. We are happy, and they are not. Are you the son of Mr. D.? No, I am not, Madam. There is some one calling me.[1] There are many people who fancy[2] they can learn a language without studying it. He has never learnt French: but he has been taught.

32.

I have given them to your master. I have not given them to your master. I will take the very first opportunity of writing[3] to them. They and my uncle are going to Walton. You and I will stay at home. He and you shall read a pretty story. Do not give me that. I do not like it. This wine is not so good as that cyder. Do not go out all at once. He cannot see me, can he? Will he be angry with me or with them? Give them my books. Examine them. Look at them. Do not read them. You

1. Aliquis me appellat.—2. multi credunt.—3. occasio, vel facultas scribendi.

read them. You do not read often enough. Do you read them sometimes? I am reading them now. What! Those interesting books you bought at the sale. Who sold them?[1] I will sell them cheap. Hold your tongue.[2]

33.

Is there a letter for me? There are three? How much[3] do they come to? Be quiet.[4] Will you talk of it to your acquaintances?[5] Yes, I will. Do not be so quarrelsome. Let us be attentive. Is he come? I have been nearly four years in England. How long have you been learning French? I have only one true friend. We were but ten at dinner. I have but one guinea.[6] I never wrote but five lines. Come here. Is supper ready? This cloth is very fine, how much is it a yard? Seven shillings a yard. My sisters are in the country. Two gentlemen are come to see you. My sister and her cousin are prepared. His shoes were worn out. Their poor brother and his children will be reduced to beggary.[7] I was determined to

---

1. Quis illos vendidit?—2. tace.—3. quantum pecuniæ.—4. quiesce.—5. familiaribus tuis.—6. viginti unum solidos.—7. mendicitati.

follow him. Her piano is not in tune. His mother is ill. Her sons are gone to school. My lesson was very hard. What is he? What were you? Who are you? Your covetousness[1] is despicable. My bounties conferred on the family. This man had always been despised. He is afflicted. The child has been spoiled. Have they ever travelled.

34.

I am thinking of you. He was coming to us. Do that for me. Do not speak against them. Go to them directly. Do not go with her. She is always so cross. They are incessantly speaking ill of one another; I believe they hate one another. Is this your house? Yes, it is. It is well built.[2] It cost me a great deal of money.[3] I dare say it has. Upwards of five hundred pounds. It is very dear. Whose was it? It belonged to my wife's brother. The gardens of these houses were too small. The rays of the sun[4] can pierce through. The toys[5] of the children. Give the pins to the girl and the pens to the boy. Speak to Charles or

---

1. Avaritia.—2. bene ædificata.—3. multum nummorum.—4. radii solis.—5. crepundia.

Frederic. I come from Paris and you from London. When he returns from Dover, I shall then send him to Richmond. Does he write from Vienna? I have some good pears, excellent apples, fine peaches, and beautiful grapes. I shall write to the king, the queen, and the dukes.

35.

This dictionary has been very useful to them.[1] He has lent me some money.[2] You have sent him your address, but you have not seen him. Has she a sister? None. I am sorry for it. This wine is not old enough. Your ink was too thick. His hat is too large for his small head. Did you speak to me? Has the boot-maker made my boots? Did he go to college? Did the servant call me this morning? Did you say I was there? Did we come in time? Did they jump over the ditch?[3] Did he study Greek? Did we read so far? This lane is too narrow. How high is that tower? The ditch is not deep enough. Your stick is not long enough. It is too short. Is it too short? Is

---

1. Hoc dictionarium illis perutile fuit.—2. commodavi mihi pecuniam mutuam.—3. trans fossam.

it not too short? Did I not give eleven shillings for the whole? We were ten at supper. Is it hot? It is very damp. I am not able to finish it. The ink[1] does not run.

36.

September 10, 1825.

My dear Sir,

I received your letter[2] last night, on my return home,[3] and I am very sorry I shall not be able to see your brother to-day, previously to his departure[4] for Bengal. My son who is very ill at college has sent this morning his servant with a note from his physician, who wishes to see me immediately; however, if his indisposition is not very serious, I will endeavour[5] to return to town in the evening, and prepare the letters of introduction[6] which I promised him, the last time he called upon me. Remember me kindly to Mrs. G.

Believe me, yours truly,

James D.

---

1. Atramentum.—2. tuas litteras.—3. cum domum revertissem.—4. ejus discessum.—5. conabor.—6. dare litteras commendatitias.

37.

Did you say that the door and the window were shut, or open?[1] His brother and sisters are happy. I do not think his wife is happy. How[2] do you know? I am told so. You have not been told the truth. Who says he is not brave[3] and generous? The queen was not so generous as her father. This is a long book; I do not like it. He is like his father. My mother and sister are generous, but very prudent. You say, they are prodigal because[4] you are a miser. You are a very good boy and she is a good girl. Yes, they are good children.[5] Have you been to my bed room? No, I came from the dining room. Who has broken the milk jug? The footman.[6] This is the fish-market. No, you are mistaken,[7] it is the hay-market,[8] and on the other side to the right, the corn-market.

38.

He was skilful. How blind we are sometimes to our infirmities! How many lessons do you

1. Apertæ.—2. qui.—3. fortis.—4. quia.—5. liberi optimi. 6. famulus.—7. haud ita est, erras.—8. forum vel mercatus fœnorum.

generally give a day? Sometimes twelve, but more commonly nine. It is probable we shall have a double quantity. It is said that the gentlemen of your country are very changeable.[1] My land is barren;[2] yours, on the contrary, is very fruitful.[3] Their conduct[4] has always been praiseworthy. He will be probably invited. How rough you are, Sir! Her health is weak. It would be painful. Her relations were poor, but honest. Do not be so rash. Were there many people![5] Was there a single man prepared? There will be as many as you want. There is more prudence in his conduct now than formerly. There were four lessons given. There would be many difficulties to encounter. There are two ladies who wish to see you. Last night was very dark. The clock struck twelve when I reached home.

39.

Rise and go out.[6] I cannot[7] walk. My foot is hurt. They are walking in the yard. Give us a yard of ribbon. I walk every morning be-

---

1. Homines mutabiles.—2. ager meus sterilis est.—3. fertilissimus.—4. vita.—5. an plures adfuerunt?—6. surge et exi.—7. nequeo.

fore breakfast. We rise before five in summer, and by seven in winter. That is very early. Ask[1] that gentleman if he has breakfasted. You jest. Indeed, I do not jest. I am speaking very seriously. You have sent your servant away because he has robbed you. We should have played all night. What prevented you? We had no candle. Lend me your purse.[2] No, I cannot. I will lend you twenty pounds. Lend me your horse; I want him. Where do you want to go? To my banker's. He has showed me his watch. Watch his actions, pray. Did you see the watch-maker in his shop? Send for the watchman. I will show you his house. Play well. Where is the play-house? At what game does he play? He plays at cards, and at fives.[3] Gambling is, and has always been, a despicable pastime. You are a very fine player. Mr. Young is the finest player on the English stage. He is considered the first actor in Europe. Does she play on the piano? Yes, she does, but she cannot play on the harp.[4] You know the Gamester; an excellent play in three acts. Will you play a game with me? What

---

1. Interroga.—2. commoda mihi crumenam tuam, vel marsupium tuum.—3. pilis.—4. citharâ.

at? He has married a very handsome lady, who is very poor. How high the wind blows!

40.

Are you pleased with it? He will come to our house. I have spoken[1] to your lady and she does not seem willing[2] to sign[3] the deed. Give me eleven. I have some. You know my intention. He saw all his machinations. We saw their design. Take some.[4] Give me some. Let us send some. My intentions were pure and honorable. Let him eat some for his lunch. Some soldiers were taken up yesterday and locked up.[5] Will you have some? Shall I have some? Will he read some? We have counted nineteen. I will not lose any. To write well, we must have good ink, good pens and good paper. I have brought you some money, will you accept it? That is never refused. He takes snuff every minute. Some cider[6] is preferable to some water. Good cider is better than bad wine. He awoke at six o'clock. At what time do you rise? About four, every

---

1. Locutus sum.—2. nonvult, quemadmodum apparet.—3. obsignare.—4. cape.—5. in carcerem conjecti.—6. succus pomorum.

morning; but on Sunday not before seven, both summer and winter. I shall love you as long as you do your duty.

41.

Do you speak French? Yes, Sir, I do, and also Italian. Where did you learn these two languages? I speak as a father, do not oblige me to speak as a judge.[1] Judge of my embarrassment. I do not deserve[2] your pardon. I do not wish it, and I do not ask for it, therefore I will not accept it, if you offer it me. Your offer was noble.[3] I was offered ten pounds for it. He will discover the whole business. Do not open the window pray,[4] for I have a sad cold. We shall offer him our country-seat for two years. Are you going to leave this county? Yes, we are going to Wales,[5] to spend some time with our mother's sister, or aunt. How old is she? How old are you? How old was he? Are you afraid of thunder?[6]

42.

I shall go to London, to see my brother-in-

1.—Tanquam judex.—2. non mereor.—3. id quod obtulisti munificum erat.—4. obsecro.—5. Walliam.—6. num times tonitruum?

law, who is a clerk to the East India Company. How long has he been in their service? I do not know. How long will you stay? They run as fast as you. You shall lose your time.[1] It is done for ever.[2] We shall dine at six. You do what you please. She goes out too often.[3] We go to church, and they go to chapel. I shall say it, if called upon to do so.[4] Go and see him now. I arrived here before you. You must come back this week, or else you shall be dismissed from his Majesty's service.[5] He died in the arms of an affectionate daughter. I have followed your example. You read better and better. Do you go thither? Shall I go there? Did he go there? Do you see him now? Do not stir.[6] Do you stay there? Do you hear? Do you not understand me? He speaks as well as she. The coach returned empty.[7] Do not all go out at once. He does it on purpose.

43.

I send him my work, to peruse it, and to give me his opinion. He writes to them every

---

1. Tempus perdes.—2. in æternum.—3. sæpiùs.—4. si a me quæritur.—5. ab exercitu regis.—6. ne moveas.—7. rheda vacua rediit.

day.[1] I see him. I owe her a hundred pounds. He obeys them punctually.[2] He loves me more than[3] I love him. I give it to you on condition[4] that you shall not sell it to them. He has bought them too dear. It is, however, cheaper[5] than what you showed me the other day. I consent to it heartily, because I am in hopes it will contribute to the happiness of my children. Have I prepared them for such an undertaking? Has he obeyed him?[6] He opposed it with all his might.[7] You shall not have it before I have given my consent. You will find your snuff box in the drawer. Bring me my work box. I cannot find it. We could not find them yesterday. I could walk much better six years ago. I, indeed, cannot spend so much money. He cannot go without the leave of his parents. That is right enough.[8] They cannot finish to-day. Can you not write to them the day after to-morrow? Can he not come now? We met him[9] at Naples.

---

1. Singulis diebus, vel quotidie.—2. decuratè.—3. plus quam.—4. eâ conditione.—5. est, tamen, minoris pretii.—6. illi paruit.—7. totis viribus.—8. hoc equidem bellè.—9. illum convenimus.

44.

I shall be able to help them now and then. I ought to receive the half of it. We ought to attend to his instructions. I will not see them. I am taller than you. He will go on in spite of all opposition. We will do it. He will not set out before day-light.[1] Have you slept pretty well? Yes, I have slept pretty well; but I cannot sleep after six o'clock, because I am so used to get up very early that I am sure to be ill, or to have the head-ache, if I rise later. We spend about two guineas a week; that makes more than one hundred pounds a year. How do you spend your time? How many[2] horses do you keep now? Two carriage horses and three saddle horses. No hunters? Does he often ride on horseback?[3] No, not very often. It is difficult to find a good, and trusty servant.[4]

45.

What advantages has he? They were ac-

1. Ante diluculum.—2. quot equos.—3. equitat.—4. servum* bonum atque fidelem.

* *Servus* need not be restricted, in translation, to the *slave*, and *domestic*, but may be applied generally.

cused of robbery.[1] By whom? Such an accusation was ill-founded. Address yourself to the magistrates. Who adopted that orphan?[2] Bring me several acts of parliament[3] when you go to town. The fair is abolished.[4] My lesson is not yet finished. How long you are! Relate me your adventures. No, follow my advice, do not. What airs she gives herself! Have you bought an almanack? How amiable they are! Have you ever been to America? Do not take the alarm.[5] Adieu, my dear. You detest me and I abhor you. Why do you hate them? Has he measured the park? Yes, just now. There are one hundred and twenty-five acres.[6] Do not abandon me in my present situation. Which are the four quarters of the world? Europe, Asia, Africa, and America.

46.

How far is it[7] from hence to Paris? Do not push them. How do you go? By water? By land. I will drink after you. Do not take my book instead of hers. Her husband is a very

1. Accusati sunt furti.—2. hunc puerum orbum?—3. decreta senatûs.—4 nundinæ sunt abrogatæ.—5. sis perterritus.—6. jugera centum viginti quinque sunt.—7. quam longè distat.

handsome man. His wife is always scolding.[1] Her father is aged[2] but her mother is much younger. It was under the chair. It is true, and he will not believe you. It was clear. It will be impossible. Is it good? Is it new? Is it in fashion? It would be preferable[3] to deny him such a favor. I will defend you at the peril of my own life. You do nothing but sing. There has been a dispute between them. All the soldiers and sailors. There is now a quarrel about nothing. The silver waiter is in the dining-room.[4] I have bought silk stockings at four francs a pair. When? Two years ago.

47.

I only want a little attention from them. Chelmsford is not so large as Colchester. I give to my servants and their friends[5] on Christmas-day, beef, beer,[6] and plum-pudding. My father's hat is lost.[7] Mr. B's horse has been stolen from the stable. He does nothing but play.[8] They go as far as Edinburgh. They have offered a considerable reward. Go to the

1. Objurgat semper.—2. senex.—3. potiùs fuerit.—4. in cœnaculo, vel tricliniario.—5. famulis atque illorum amicis.—6. cerevisiam.—7. amissus.—8. nil agit, at ludit tantum.

grocer's; I want seventeen pounds[1] of sugar, three ounces of pepper, and nine pounds of his best tea. I prefer Burgundy to Port. She is fit for any thing. We have but two hundred and fifty pounds. Is there any Dutch cheese in the house? I am very sensible of cold. I am very rejoiced to see you. We are very much pleased to receive such good news. Take that, and leave this. Go now, and come again.

48.

She is a good wife. Bring this. Which will you have, this or that? That which, or what I complain of is your incorrigible idleness[2] That which glitters is not gold. What I demand of you[3] is civility. Italian wines are cheaper than French wines. Wine is sold[4] there for two-pence a bottle. It is cheaper than beer.[5] So many books to be bound. So much to say in his behalf. I assure you that I have no time to lose in this manner.

49.

Mrs. W. desires Mr. F. to call upon her in

---

1. Septemdecim libras.—2. ignavia incorrigibilis.—3. quod à te impetro.—4. vinum venit.—5. vilior cerevisiâ.

the course of next week, as her eldest daughter[1] wishes to receive some instructions in Italian.[2]

Chelmsford, March 17, 1821.

Dunmow, Essex.

Mrs. T. presents her compliments[3] to Mr. F. and is sorry to inform him she will decline his further attendance this summer, as her daughters are going to the sea-side.[4]

Saturday Evening, April 9, 1829

Mrs. B. presents her compliments to Mr. F. and is under the necessity of desiring him to postpone his visit to the Castle, till Saturday fortnight, on account of the indisposition[5] of Mr. B.

Tuesday Morning, Danbury, Essex.

50.

I came from Rome, where I resided eight months.[6] What I have given you for that desk[7] is more than it is worth. The brother

---

1. Filia major natu.—2. in linguâ italica.—3. salutem quamplurimam dat.—4. ad littus maris.—5. causâ invaletudinis mariti sui.—6. ubi habitabam octo mensibus, vel per octo menses.—7. pro pluteo isto.

and sister are ill. The father and brother were dead. That which he says is not true. Men and women are mortal. I know that which you are looking for. He knows where it was. I do not like flowers. I shall return to Italy next winter; will you accompany me thither?[1] I am afraid of the banditti or highwaymen. Two yards of French lace at half a guinea. A bushel of coals. A large quantity of ribbons. A crowd of children ran after them.

51.

I go almost every day to the park? With whom? Do they go to dine[2] with him to-morrow? Yes, and we are invited.[3] Shall we go? Do as you please. As for myself, I have more than once offended him; therefore, I will not go. Send me back my music. I did send it back last night. To whom did you give it? To your servant. He will not go unless you command him. Run, run, again. Really I cannot run. Did you gather me a rose? I cannot gather any unless you give me the key of the garden.

---

1. Illùc.—2. num illi ibunt pransum.—3. imò, nos quoque convocati sumus.

—Have you not it? Take it; you will find it in the drawer.

52.

I have seen so many people in the street. They have never bought any thing finer. A troop of men were killed.[1] Do not learn so many lines. There is nothing good in his shop.[2] Have you no more pears?[3] We have enough for the dessert. I have not understood him. Have you yet let or sold your houses? You want too much for them. I sold them this month. I came on foot. Make haste, quick.[4] You may go elsewhere; you will never find a better situation. It will cost you at least twenty shillings. Speak freely now.[5] Never fear to speak the truth. You have acted wisely. You do worse and worse. Let them receive him in private. You do very wrong to go thither.

53.

I will get rid of this horse. He will buy it. How much do you want for him? Put on your hat.[6] They can do that easily. Do you always

---

1. Interempti sunt.—2. in tabernâ ejus.—3. pyra.—4. festina, citò.—5. loquere nunc liberè.—6. indue galerum.

say what you think? Not always. He seldom reads. She always scolds. Does she. He willingly consents to that condition. They did it secretly.[1] So they say. Do not believe such prattlers.[2] I now tell you in earnest that it is good for nothing. He comes regularly. You had too much indulgence for your children. Few things are necessary to make him happy.[3] So you say. Give them much bread, little meat, and a few coals. The number of subscribers amounts to twelve hundred. A number of friends came to his assistance. How much[4] did they give him? This room is I believe ten feet long and seven wide. Did you measure it? I am taller than you by the whole head. Who told you so? Nobody.

54.

He has quite displeased him.[5] They are quite sluggish.[6] There is a house with stables to let and several fields to be sold in our village. I will do it purposely to displease them. Since I saw you I have lost a deal of money.[7] When do you intend going to the Netherlands?[8] Im-

1. Clam.—2. ne credas garrulis similibus.—3. beatum reddere.—4. quantum.—5. displicuit illi.—6. ignavi.—7. multum pecuniæ.—8. ad Belgicas provincias.

mediately after the recess if I have no engagements here. Which way do you go? I have heard a great deal of noise all night. At first we were astonished at his not coming.[1] We almost always give something to the poor on Christmas-day. He is returned from town. I never saw the King of England. I have seen the Prince of Wales. Is she up stairs? I usually take an egg at breakfast. Let him come in the day-time[2] and then I will receive him. Arise, let us be going.

55.

Comb my hair. Your hands are very dirty[3] Has he paired his nails? Cut my nails. Get my shoes mended. Dress yourself quickly. We are going out. He is going to town. Are they gone, tell me? Do not wipe your hands with my towel, if you please, it is dirty. That is no matter. Give me my stockings.[4] Has he mended my coat? Whose[5] hat is that? Your father's. I want[6] a pair of shoes and he a pair of boots. Put on this pair; they are rather too narrrow; take them off. Undress yourself.

---

1. Quòd ille non venit.—2. die.—3. manus sordidæ sunt.—4. da mihi tibialia mea.—5. cujus.—6. volo.

Where are their clothes? In the next room. What! in my bed-room? This coat is out of fashion. I have a mind to put on this blue coat.[1] Try it on me. It does not fit you.

56.

You read a good book. He will come to our house. We have won a hundred guineas. You entered before me. I would not speak to them on your account.[2] I have brought an umbrella for your sister. I am sure we shall have rain[3] before long. This hat is made after the French fashion;[4] It is frightful. I never saw such an ugly thing.[5] I have met him at your house. She shall go with her brother. As to what he says I would advise you to attend to it. He is half mad. I shall begin after you. He is near the fire. Come near. I am travelling now two hundred and seventy miles a week.[6]

57.

That is more than one thousand miles a month.[7] He has travelled by sea.[8] You will

1. Induere vestem hanc cœruleam.—2. tui causâ.—3. imber cadet.—4. gallico modo.—5. rem tàm deformem.—6. hebdomadâ, vel per hebdomadam.—7. per mensem.—8. navigavit.

perceive in the Italian language a great affinity[1] to the French. You will understand French in a short time. Put the candle upon the table,[2] and the snuffers also. You have broken[3] my stool, and you must pay[4] for it. By his assiduity and his diligence he has made a large fortune. You know that gentleman? Yes, I do. He does not know his rules. Yes, he does. He knows neither his articles nor his verbs.[5] I know what you say. I should like very much to know that family. He knows them by sight, not personally. I know all my prepositions by heart.[6] I knew him long before you.

58.

Do not speak so fast. I find it difficult to speak good English. Can you speak German? I have learned it some time ago. Do you pronounce well?[7] As well as you.[8] How long have you learned? Six months. It is a very short time. How long have you been learning? Not long. I shall never learn. Nonsense.[9] Every body speaks French. French and Italian

---

1. Similitudinem.—2. super mensam.—3 fregisti.—4. pretium ponere.—5. verba.—6. memoritèr.—7. rectène pronuntias?—8. rectè æque ac tu.—9. nugæ!

are spoken every where. The sun is rising. What o'clock is it? Look at your watch. It is half-past nine. No, you are mistaken; it is only a quarter to eight. How so? Your watch looses. It gains generally. It is moonlight.[1] How is the weather?[2]

59.

Will you eat any more?[3] He does not want any more. I shall write to your father to send me some money. More prudence[4] is highly necessary in your conduct. I am twice indebted to him for my health. I will write to him as soon as it suits me. We will send it to them. He gives them some. She always takes it with her. I will send them to her. I ask you a favour: do not refuse me.[5] Give it to them directly. Send it to her to-morrow. Take it and eat it. Taste it and eat it, if you like it. Take them and read them. Read to your father this paper. Read that news to them. How many books do you want? Very well. Read them by yourself.[6] Tear them and burn them. Do not grant it them.

---

1. Resplendet luna.—2. cœlum.—3. visne tu plus edere?—4. magis prudentiæ.—5. ne mihi recusas.—6. tecum solùm.

60.

Let us see them. Permit me to open them He answered him very impertinently. France is indebted to him[1] for many useful institutions. Germany never has been so powerful under the last dynasty. You have promised them to them. Will you have any? Will they take some? I shall give it to them. Do not give me four. I am surprised at it. Has he not sent them some? We have some. We have not any. Are you pleased with it? Will you not have any? Do they go from hence?[2] He will treat you with them. He shall not stay there long. I will carry some there. I shall not get any thing by it. Do you not get any thing by it?[3] Do not carry your brother there. Let us send some there. I have received a letter from an officer who was with my brother in France last year. A book well bound. I have given clothes to a man. She speaks of a woman and I of a man. I write to a gentleman and my wife to a lady. The window was open.

---

1. Gallia ab illo accepit.—2. abhinc.—3. nihilne ex eo tibi prodest?

61.

She depends on a friend. Those parcels come from a banker in London. He came in a ship and landed in a boat. We go to a garden belonging to our family. Have you the key. We shall write to him. I have done it myself.[1] We shall do it without them.[2] He has deceived us. It is not him I want, it is her. I am looking for them. He looks for it. I alone have done it. I alone shall be sacrificed. They who are so proud. It is I who saw you. It is they who will undertake the business.[3] I who lost every thing. I who love him so much.

62.

You are always laughing at us. I did not laugh at you. It is very wrong to laugh in people's faces. Do not laugh at me. Be still. I have flattered myself that you will not laugh at her. You mock people so. Go on pray. Look! he is now making faces at us both. You misuse[4] my goodness. What a fog![5] No, it is a mist.[6]. There is very little difference be-

---

1. Ipse.—2. sine illis.—3. qui rem suscipient.—4. abuteris meâ bonitate.—5. nebula.—6. caligo est.

tween them. What a mistake![1] It is a slight error.[2] Try to catch me if you can. Take your aim. Fire. Do not miss me. I am sure you will miss me. Have you not missed me?

63.

It is they who have taken the house. It is I who did it. It is they who robbed the man. He and they have been attentive. I? what have I said? You give it me. You do not give it me. He sends it to them. I think of him. He speaks against them.[3] This young lady reads too many novels.[4] This young man wastes his time. Do not speak to that man. To whom do you speak? I received it from that child. Whose coat is this? What do you mean?[5] This does not please them.

64.

The flowers I have in my garden are very fine. Who has done that? He. Who dines[6] here to-day? I. Who learns French? What do you think of it? The vegetables we have

---

1. Quantus error!—2. error parvula.—3. contra illos.—4. historias fictas.—5. quid tibi vis?—6. quis hic prandebit.

bought at market. It is not what I want. Does this displease you? He who reads his Bible every day. They who pray all day. Those who are poor. They who scold their children.[1] They who sing. I do not know what has happened to them. I want you. I am losing. Are you reading French authors? A few. This is not so handsome as that. Do not take this. Do not do that. Take this. I do not like that. What books do you read? What misfortune is ours? What house do you live in? What lesson have you learned?

65.

What play have you seen? What defence has he made? What are his crimes? What was your remark? What a child! What a pity! What an obstinate child! What a man! What men![2] What fools! This is my father's house. That is my cousin's horse. Such are the king's orders. Take mine not hers.[3] Do not forget ours. What losses!—What kindness! What a misfortune! They have stopped him on the high road. They say the king is much

---

1. Qui objurgant liberos suos.—2. quales homines!—3. meum non suum cape.

better.[1] It is said he is going into the country. I am told you have cut yourselves. She is my own child. I prefer my house to yours. Take my horse and bring me his.

66.

I have taken my books instead[2] of your's. I have met the same gentleman and the same lady. Tell me what you want.[3] That house was ours before it was his. I do not like yours. Give me hers. Somebody wants you. Somebody[4] came to ask for yours. I believe that neither yours nor mine have been sold. I will have neither yours nor mine bound. Look for theirs. My stockings[5] and his are worn out. My master and his are gone into the country for a month. Where is yours? One of my horses and one of yours are lame. Some one stole my mule. I have met nobody.[6] No one speaks to you. I have found another thing against him. The greatest of men commit often the grossest mistakes. I am looking for something. Every country has its customs.

---

1. Convalescere.—2. loco.—3. tu desideras.—4. aliquis.—5. caligæ.—6. neminem conveni.

67.

Every[1] one must do his duty. I see neither of them very often. Each danced all night. I have seen nobody come here. Go directly. I am not fond of high life. I am listening to what you say. Every lesson must be learnt[2] by heart. However kind you may be you shall be reproved. He was then still at school. He takes every thing he sees. Do whatever you like. Have you done already? When I have done my duty I shall leave you. When we go to church we ought to pray for every one. Both are broken.[3] Take both.[4] Do you pay by the week, or by the year? He came lately from France. I expected you the day before yesterday. How is it?

68.

Brompton, September 20, 1829.

My dear Mother,[5]

I thank you a thousand times[6] for the handsome present you sent me by William last

1. Unusquisque.—2. discenda.—3. ambo fracti sunt.—4. ambos accipe.—5. mater dilectissime.—6. millies.

Saturday; I may assure you I will do my utmost to deserve such a kindness.

My master, Mr. H. wishes me to inform you that he is satisfied with my improvement and he hopes to be able to place me next year in the first class and to make me begin Greek. Can you send me to-morrow, or Wednesday, a few good quills[1] and all my Latin and French books, which you will find in my study, as I may want them to complete[2] my studies in those two languages. I wrote the other day a French letter to my uncle Wilson, but have not yet been favoured with an answer.[3] I rather suspect he is puzzled how to write French now, it is so long since he has corresponded in that language; if you see him, tell him I am expecting to hear from him every day.

Believe me, dear Mother,

Your affectionate and dutiful son,

WALTER L.

P.S.—Give my love to Jane and Sophia.

---

1. Pennas bonas.—2. finire.—3. responso, vel responsu.

69.

Afterwards there was a ball. I have extolled his high deeds.[1] I have bathed in the Thames and you in the pond.[2] I go to the play now and then. We have repented our sins. Are you up ?[3] I have risen at five o'clock. I write daily seven pages in Italian and ten in French. What college have you been at ? I came down[4] at nine. We started at about three in the afternoon. He came suddenly. Have you been out[5] to-day ? This work will soon be published. I know his sentiments. They drink red wine[6] I shall drink white[7] wine. It has frozen very hard. It has rained all day. It is very fine weather. I hope you will do better for the future. He came immediately. I shall give it to you bye and bye. Do not speak so loud. I will come and dine with you on Christmas Eve. Do you go to church to-morrow ? I will do it as soon as possible. I always rise early. As for me I often walk before breakfast. I frequently take chocolate. In a short time you will speak French. I am going to France next spring. I

---

1. Res gestæ.—2. lacu.—3. surrexistine ?—4. descendi.—5. exivisit.—6. potant vinum rubrum.—7. album.

have travelled in Italy during several years. Go elsewhere; they will tell you the same thing. My house is situate in the vicinity of Antwerp, in the Netherlands. Robert seldom goes into the country. How do you like London?

70.

I passed through Genoa on my return to England. I shall go this evening as far as the next town. Pray what o'clock is it? It is the custom among the Dutch.[1] Go up stairs; the company is there. Let him go down. Waiter, bring me[2] a candle and a newspaper. He wants the loaf. Do not forget to come and give me a lesson at half past nine. I cannot come before a quarter[3] to ten. My daughter has been well educated. My sister plays on the piano-forte. He is an old bachelor.[4] These boys learn French and Italian. Speak the truth. Let him go and see his friends.

71.

What weather[5] was it? It snowed. The

---

1. Mos est apud Belgas.—2. puer, affer mihi.—3. ante quindecim momenta.—4. cœlebs.—5. qualis tempestas.

moon shines. It is very hot. It was cold. We trust to you. I have grown rich in that country. I nurse myself too much.[1] We go to bed before you. I have taken cold. Let us make haste. They tormented themselves for nothing. He intended to travel.[2] I travel on horseback. You deceived yourself. I do not remember that event. She has fainted away. They have complained of you. He has repented of this faults We walked in your garden. My flowers have faded. I married a year before him. Why do you laugh at him? You had laughed at us. Is it true? It is false. We have exposed ourselves to his anger. He was right. We lost ourselves in the wood. I bathed in the river. We are used to it. I used to read every day a chapter of that book aloud.

72.

She paints badly. You have fancied I was in the wrong, and on the contrary I was in the right. He gives it me. I do not know where he lives.[3] He has sold it to us. He sees her. James, pray tell it to my father-in-law. Do not

1. Me nimis curo.—2. statuit peregrinari.—3. habitat.

give it him. I have invited your sisters; I do not know if they are coming. Where were you? Here, my dear.[1] What have you done with your watch? Here it is, father. Here is your master; mind what you are about.[2] He always minds better his own affairs than those of others. My history is short. My friendship is great. His hope is well grounded. I wish you would read those exercises several times before your master, as if you were reading some French book without the least hesitation.

73.

Then I may assure you, that you cannot fail in being able[3] to speak the language you are studying in a much shorter time than by following[4] the old methods, generally used by most masters[5] in this country. Read them over and over again; never be tired of doing so and you will succeed. Believe a man whose labours have been, for the last ten years, directed to smooth the numerous difficulties[6] which at all

1. Carissime.—2. vide quid facis.—3. aliter fieri non posse quin tu.—4. quam sequendo.—5. à plerisque preceptoribus. —6. quamplurimas difficultates complanare.

times have hindered[1] the progress of those who are studying the most useful and the most fashionable language in Europe. You will not, certainly in this little work, have the exercises upon all the rules, and particular idioms, of the language; but you will find in it the most essential part[2]. When once master of the above practice the reading of some of the best authors will soon enable you to imitate them[3] either in your writing or conversation. Have done.

74.

Which[4] do you chuse, the white one or the black one? Which came first, the youngest or the eldest? Which do you like? Which[5] is the best? Tell me, which have you taken? How pretty she is! How glad I am to see you![6] How dangerous it is to run so fast? How small is that house! How foolish you are! How difficult my lesson is! How pleased she is! How black it is! How strange is his conduct! Many professors of the language, of the highest merit, have seldom found in this country the true way

---

1. Impediverunt.—2. præcipuam partem.—3. eos imitari.—4. utrum.—5. uter, *m.* utrum *n.*—6. quàm gaudeo te videre.

of imparting it to Englishmen. Let them study[1] nature. My brothers are much esteemed. My sisters are very much respected. I have respected my master.[2] I have esteemed your brothers. They are gone to Dover.

75.

I have spoken to[3] my father. My father is loved by his children. My mother is loved by her daughters. I have sold my cow. My cow is sold.[4] My horses are sold. I have finished my narration. I have followed his advice.[5] My counsels were attended to. The ladies have danced.[6] The ladies[7] are come. The daughters of Captain B. are arrived in England. We have admired[8] the works of nature. The works of nature have been admired. They have learned their lessons. Their lessons are learned. We have put out the candle. The candles are put out. I have washed my hands. Will you wash my feet. I should be very much obliged to you. Can you not wash them yourself? No, I cannot stop. What is the matter?[9] I have a pain in

1. Studiunto naturam.—2. honoravi præceptorem.—3. locutus fui cum.—4. vendita.—5. secutus sum consilium ejus.—6. saltaverunt.—7. mulieres.—8. admirati sumus.—9. quid habes, vel quid rei est.

my back. Send for a surgeon. Let us rejoice. Peace is made. Give a chair[1] to the gentleman. Your horse is very lean.[2] You do not feed him well. Yes, I feed him very well, but he is a little indisposed. I did not sleep at all last night. How do you like the books we sent you? I find them very amusing. I am indebted to you for all that I possess.[3] Hush! Silence!

76.

We have received several letters. The letters are sealed, and will be sent to the post. I am come to dine with you. She is come to see you. They were come to play with her, but they were sent away. He entered the room without looking at me. For conversing, I would advise you to be perfect in your adjectives, verbs, and especially[4] in your prepositions. I have sore eyes.[5] She has a sore throat,[6] and a sore tongue. He has hurt his foot. My feet are cold. Her hands are very cold.[7] Be quiet.

77.

We have hurt our feet. She has the

1. Da sellam.—2. equus macer, vel macilentus.—3. à te accepi omnia quæ possideo.—4. præsertim.—5. ego sum lippus.—6. fauces ulceratæ.—7. manus suæ sunt frigidæ.

head-ache.[1] I have often the head-ache.[2] When I go to bed late my head aches. Her head aches. I am hungry, He was very hungry.[3] Are you hungry? I am very thirsty.[4] How do you do? How do the children do?[5] They are very well, thank you. How does she do? She is rather unwell. What is the matter with you? What is the matter here?[6] But what is the matter with him? She has the tooth-ache.[7] The more I see him, the more I esteem him. So do I. So does he.

78.

A fisherman having lost his nets[8] sent to a friend of his to ask him for his. The milliner had no time to sew it. Tell my tailor to make me a suit of clothes, and to send them by coach, in the course of a fortnight. Take my mare to our meadow. Mind to fasten the gate; have you the key and the padlock? I am going to pay a visit to my father, and spend the Christmas week with him. How far is it from

---

1. Caput dolet.—2. dolorem capitis.—3. multùm esurivit. —4. admodum sitio.—5. valent.—6. quid hoc rei est?—7. dolorem dentium.—8. retia.

hence?[1] Indeed! Your horse will never go such a long journey in one day.[2] Attend.

79.

Wait[3] for me till four o'clock. Will you be back in half an hour? Birds fly,[4] fish swim,[5] and quadrupeds walk;[6] and we walk also. Never copy fair[7] your translation of these exercises, until you have read them many times aloud before a master able to instruct you. Fill my glass.[8] I am thirsty. How long will he stay in London? Fifty pounds. This is not an answer.[9] I beg your pardon, such an answer is understood by an Oxonian or Cambrigian. It means that I shall stay in town as long as this sum will last. This is very ingenious. Mend my watch and his. My faults and hers are unpardonable. Your brother and hers are taking a walk on the lawn. What a handsome carriage! It is not so handsome as yours. His horses are very fine; but ours are handsomer; and yours are the handsomest of all.

---

1. Abhinc distat?—2. uno die.—3. expecta.—4. volant.—5. natant.—6. ambulant.—7. transcribere.—8. imple poculum meum.—9. hoc non est responsum.

80.

Teffon, Wilts. Sept. 3, 1829.

My dear Sir,

I begin to fear you have forgotten[1] your old friend. It is now nearly six weeks since I heard last[2] from you; I must attribute, I suppose, such silence to your numerous engagements.[3] I should have written before, but, I expected to go down on the 1st instant to join your shooting party on that day. However, Mrs. H's indisposition could not admit of my leaving her,[4] I am happy to say she is fast recovering and if nothing prevents me, I shall take her to Clifton next month, to spend a few weeks at Major W's, which will enable us to have the pleasure of calling upon you during our stay in that delightful spot.

I remain, dear Sir,
Your's truly,
L. F. H.

81.

Who will bring back the other?[5] What do

---

1. metuo equidem ne sis oblitus.—2. novissimè.—3. hanc silentiam tuis quam plurimis negotiis.—4 non sivit ut eam reliquissem.—5. referet alterum.

you mean[1] the horse? I shall leave it till I return next week. What an expense![2] Let him take this bill to my banker's, he lives close to the Mansion-house. Ask for three pounds of silver[3] and the remainder in gold and bank-notes. They shake this table so much that I really cannot write. When I play[4] at cards, I do not like to lose the game. At what game does he play? How did you spend your time last Midsummer? I advise you to avoid idleness;[5] which is the mother of all vices. He admired the beauty of the gardens. The cares of a tender mother. What does my brother do? What does my uncle think? When you return from town,[6] bring me some ribbons, an umbrella, a lamp, and a few French books, well bound in calf with gilt-edges.

81.

What does he ask[7] for? What will you say? What were they looking[8] for? The lady of whom I was speaking, is my wife's father's

1. Vis dicere.—2. magnus sumptus!—3. tres libras argenti. —4. cum ludam.—5. ignaviam vitare,—6. ex urbe.—7. petit. —8. quæsiverunt.

sister. The young lady[1] who sings so sweetly, is my friend's niece, to whom you applied last year[2] to fill the situation of governess in her family. Is it possible?[3] The reasons upon which I rely[4] are good. It is an argument to which there is no reply.[5] It is a malady to which there is no remedy and the cause of which is not known. Read this book often into Latin, without the practice of which, you will not gain a perfect knowledge of that ancient language. Hand me the book which is on the table. Avoid the faults into which I have fallen. The world is a stage upon which[6] men appear always masked. Idleness is a vice for which you[7] cannot have too much abhorrence. How do you translate the English word which? I ought to know now. Against which.[8] For which. After which. Into which. I thank you for having given me so good an exercise, without a rule at the top of the page and an example, which I should have copied no doubt. How are my brothers and sisters?

---

1. Puella.—2. anno præterito.—3. num id fieri potest?—4. rationes quibus ego confido.—5. argumentum hoc haud negandum.—6. theatrum est in quo.—7. vitium est pro quo.—8. contra quod.

82.

The happiness of the people makes that of the prince. The front of the houses.[1] I am going away, will you accompany me?[2] We have built a very handsome country house. Give my little brother his night-cap. I passed through the butter-market, where I met the rabbit-man. I have given him good books. The king's guards. I always carry fire-arms at night when I travel.[3] We often see the king's troops[4] pass under our window. I want the mustard pot. Hand me the cream jug[5] and sugar bason[6].

Paris is a delightful city, which I intend visiting again soon. You were there last winter. Yes; I returned from hence on Monday last. Will he go with me? I should very much like to go there, if I had no business here. I shall take you there next year. I will not go.

83.

Did you not hear what I said? You gave

1. Frons ædium.—2. tune vis me comitari?—3. noctu cùm forem in itinere.—4. copias regis.—5. cantharum floris lactis.—6. poculum sacchari.

me the milk. Go to the hay-market and buy me a load of hay; but do not give more than two pounds[1] for it. I shall send the boys to school with a plum-cake. I do not like to go on foot.[2] Come and dine with us. We have rice soup, apple tart, roast beef, and vegetables.[3] The money which my father sent me last year. Onions, celery, cabbages, with a little meat,[4] make very good soup. I have no apple-trees in my orchard. We have two little boys, seven little girls, and eleven tall servants. My brother and sister are gone out. I give her a lesson three times a week. She lives in Paris.[5] My friend is open and frank, but yours is cunning This book is very small; that much smaller.[6] A sweet apple is better than a bitter orange.[7] That young lady has an harmonious voice. I have called a hundred times at your house. Although I am not rich, yet I am humane towards the poor. He bid them good bye with tears in his eyes.[8]

---

1. Plus duobus libris.—2. nolo pedester transire.—3. atque olera.—4. caules cum cibo paullulo.—5. Lutetiæ vei in Lutetiâ.—6. multò minor est.—7. aurantio amaro.—8. lachrymans.

84.

I have seen him, and have spoken to him. I expect him to-day. I am obliged to him. I am going to show it to you. Behold that fine house, it is well built. Go with him. We have lost much time. You should have been more diligent in your studies. I have completely learned all the lessons of grammar appointed for the week. I do not like cards at all. Because you often lose,[1] is it not? You are a very bad player. Whose deal is it? I dealt last time; it is your turn. I beg your pardon;[2] it is my wife's. It is growing late.[3] Your fire is very low, stir it up a little. I must get rid of this animal. You should get rid of your bad habits.[4] You must know the whole business[5] as soon as possible. We must content ourselves. He is called.

85.

In the year one thousand eight hundred and eleven. It was in the year one thousand seven hundred and seventy-seven the battle was

1. Sæpè perdis.—2 veniam impetro.—3. jam advesperascit. —4. malas consuetudines.—5. rem totam.

fought.[1] She praises herself a great deal too much. Speak as long as you like. I will have either of them. I can neither eat nor drink.[2] This carriage cost me two hundred guineas. Do not cry, my child. She cries for nothing. This is the road to Paris. We dress ourselves after the French fashion.[3] His hat is after the English fashion. He died like a Frenchman,[4] on the field of battle. The guards fell into the ditch ; many were drowned ;[5] others swam to the ramparts.[6] If France were as rich as England, it would be the best country in the world.[7] I know who speaks to me.

86.

Whose house is that ? My uncle's. I have seen the letter you sent me on Saturday. This is the very word I spoke to you of. She held a purse which she gave me, and in which I found a great quantity of gold and silver. I have good eyes. I know whom you love. Do you like him better than her ? Return me the pen-knife.

---

1. Pugnatum est.—2. nequeo aut edere aut potare.—3. nos vestimus gallico more.—4. ut Gallus.—5. plures submergebantur.—6. nonnulli vallis natabant.—7. regnum totius mundi amœnissimum.

Who has my flute?[1] I have lent you my slate. Come and fetch your hat, which is on the shelf. I see him coming. Such is always the fate[2] of the idle. At the beginning of the battle[3] I was very much afraid. When you return hither I will pay you that bill.[4] He is stronger than you[5] by much. When you have done your work come[6] and see us. When I have written all my accompts I shall read the books you have had the goodness to lend me. Till we meet again.

87.

I do not deserve your pardon.[7] I did not ask for it, I do not wish it, I do not demand it; and therefore I will not ask for it, and I would not request it, if I were sure to obtain it. She did not take them, she does not take them, and will not take them, because she does not wish for them, and would not demand them even if she thought you would give them to her. His sister would have learned them if you wished it. His mother has been very ill. Her son is not

1. Tibias, vel fistulam.—2. talis semper est sors.—3. in principio pugnæ.—4. solvam hoc debitum.—5. fortior ille est te.—6. opus perfeceris.—7. non mereor indulgentiam.

yet returned. What is agreeable is often hurtful. What I like, is exactly what she dislikes.[1] What! are you playing at marbles? Fie, for shame! a boy at your age to play at marbles! Any body knows that.[2]

88.

When we are in company,[3] we generally make a point of being as agreeable as we can. When she scolds I get out of the house. When I am at church I behave as you do. When you have played that piece of music,[4] Madam, I shall take the liberty of asking you to play, God save the King. When I write in Latin[5] I seldom use the Dictionary.[6] When I have finished these exercises. We sup at nine, in summer;[7] and at ten in winter.[8] I am very fond of them. I forgive my pupils their faults, when they promise not to do the like again. We never thought of it.

89.

Whoever you meet. Apply to any body who thinks like you. Whatever riches he may

---

1. Illi præcipuè displicet.—2. cuivis hoc notum est.—3. cùm in societate versemur.—4. hanc compositionem musicam.—5. Latinè.—6. rarò dictionario utor.—7. æstate.—8. hieme.

possess, he is never satisfied; and whoever he frequents[1] will tell you so.[2] I know him so well. I am told he is worth twenty thousand a year. However amiable she is, yet she is not so amiable as her mother.[3] Whatever may be your motives, I advise you to mind what you are about. Let them be ever so attentive. Are they stupid? I assure you these words, Whatever, Whoever, and Whosoever are very hard. I can hardly remember them. Repeat the exercise five times. And then write it down in your copy book. A certain gentleman[4] who taught me for several years, never would allow me to read off my themes. Whereby he had the advantage of attending you as many years as he ought to have taught you months. That is very probable.[5]

90.

They may excuse you to-morrow. She is heming a handkerchief. You learn the task now, which you ought to have done last month. They were approaching the city.

---

1. Quemquam ille frequentat.—2. idem tibi dicet.—3. tam amabilis quàm mater.—4. quidam præceptor.—5. probabile quidem hoc est.

Smell this flower. They jumped over the wall. Here are some mulberries, which are not ripe.[1] I throw it to her. I feel the strength of your argument. I promise him. It did appear very bad. I shall esteem[2] you for it. His cows and mine are in the meadow. My watch and theirs are out of order. Our country is more extensive[3] than yours.

91.

I am *in the* right and you are wrong. Who is right? Who is wrong? Throw some crumbs to the birds[4] and to the chickens. I was in the kitchen. I saw some flower and some dough on the dresser. Do you give any bran to your horses with their corn? Yes; also some beans. There are fine prints in the parlour. The upholsterer[5] is in the hall; he has brought you a new screen, a Turkey carpet, a new sofa, a feather-bed, and bedstead. Bid him to walk in. Ask if she has had the measles[6] or scarlet fever. She had then the small-

---

1. Mora quæ non sunt matura.—2. diligam.—3. patria nostra latior.—4. micas avibus.—5. lectorum fabricator.—6. rubiolas.

pox. Will you come with me? No: why? I have chilblains. Is my whip mended?[1] Is your father in the country?[2] Is his horse in the stable? Is your carriage in the coach-house? I am very fond of birds; buy me a lark.

92.

I have now a dozen of canary birds, seven chaffinches, six dozen of sparrows,[3] four tom-tits, one blackbird,[4] several larks,[5] and nine or ten thrushes. The butcher always calls[6] when I am at breakfast. Tell him to call again; also ask him if he has a leg of mutton,[7] a calf's head, and some veal cutlets. What can you be afraid of? What do you fear? Gardener, I want some rose-trees, currant bushes, and strawberry beds this year. My vine wants cutting.

93.

Have you swept[8] all the walks? Did you water the French beans? There are a great

---

1. Flagellum reparatum.—2. Rure.—3. passer.—4. merulam.—5. nonnullas alaudas.—6. lanius semper venit.—7. coxam ovinam.—8. verristine?

many leaves. Cut a few grapes for dinner. Mend my pen, if you please. He has been dangerously wounded.[1] Have you mended your stockings? Do not blame anybody. She is rocking her infant. Has she not warmed the bed? My child will be baptized to-day. I would borrow that sum at the rate of four per cent. Calm[2] her anger. Guess who he was. I cannot guess[3] whom you mean. Do you learn to draw or dance? Do not rub out[4] my writing. The India rubber.

94.

The wheels of my carriage want greasing. You are married, and we congratulate you. I have won the bet. I am in mourning for my grandfather. Cut me some slices of ham. He was lucky at play. The shepherd leads his flock;[5] see him yonder in the pastures.[6] The dress-maker has sent home a new gown, and the shoe-maker a pair of shoes, and a pair of pumps for dancing.[7] You attend our balls, I suppose? Where was it? Here.

---

1. Gravitèr sauciatus est.—2. placa.—3. nequeo divinare. —4. ne deleas.—5. agit pecus.—6. illic in pascuis.—7. calceos ad saltandum.

95.

I took care of her during her stay in Paris. Shortly we are going to see a review.[1] Riches are a burden to the wealthy. If you are again a naughty girl, surely your papa will never give you a kiss.[2] You are a good-for-nothing fellow.[3] He beats me for nothing. I live in the front part of his house. The king was overjoyed at his arrival. Dutch cheese sells for sixpence a pound. Their journies are rather tedious. The French eggs[4] that are sold in this country are most of them very good. What do you look for? I am looking for my purse. This wall is fourteen feet high; our ditch is seven feet deep. The paths of our garden are three feet wide, and the roads of our park about ten. The air of this town[5] is very wholesome. He is digging a well in the orchard, to get water for the plants. You have a nice ring on your middle finger. The grossest insult was to invite us without asking him[6] to come. I look upon this work

---

1. Recensionem copiarum.—2. osculabitur.—3. nebulo.—4. ova e Galliâ asportata.—5. aër urbis hujus.—6. atque illum non rogare.

as one of the most useful performances of our age. They went to St. Helena last week.

96.

My niece[1] is the loveliest girl I ever met. I had rather[2] sing than play. Had you rather go than wait for him? Who is there? I. Who speaks? He. Who plays? I do. Who will come? She. I must lay a snare[3] for those thieves. Have you set a trap in your orchard? Let us go into the poultry yard. We certainly were in the wrong.[4] Were we not? They will do it afterwards. Brush my hat. Let us give it to him. I never mentioned it to them. He has sent it to them. Let him read it aloud. He feels it. Take it and burn it. We are going.[5]

97.

Study it. He has promised them to him. He has sealed it with black wax. Bad omen!

---

1. Fratris, vel sororis filia.—2. mallem.—3. insidias.—4. erravimus.—5. ibimus.

This knife is not cleaned. His shoes are too dirty, he must not come into the drawing room. I am willing to help you. Let her alone. Do not tease her. You will suffer for it. He has deceived him.[1] I have deceived myself. Undeceive him.[2] Do not undeceive him. See it. Do not see it. Write it. Do not write. I am happier than if I had married her. Her temper is so peevish, that there is no living with her in peace.[3] You behave with all the prudence becoming your age.[4] We had rather walk than ride. Ladies babble too much. Girls prattle, and will always prattle. Hearken to the warbling of the birds. Tell the maid to put on the table pepper and salt, vinegar[5] and mustard.

98.

Send her away. She is a great deal too careless. If we could tame our passions, how much happier we should be. The silver forks which I bought in Paris are not so strong. He has been dragged into the most fatal errors,

---

1. Illum fefellit.—2. illum errore libera.—3. potestas secum in pace vivere deest.—4. idonea ætati suæ.—5. acetum.

which have ruined his constitution. They now receive me in the most civil manner. I had rather beg my bread than submit to such hard conditions. Have you seen them? I do not scold them. He has finished my picture; is it like me? The likeness is excellent, indeed. How many sittings did you give? Half a dozen.[1] He draws well.

99.

I was overturned last summer,[2] and my horse very much injured, but I escaped unhurt.[3] Was it not near to our bridge? Yes, close to it. I never was dazzled by his immense wealth. Do you swim? No, I do not, I am no swimmer;[4] but I regret very much my natural aversion to this useful exercise. I am trying to induce them to do it. The whole is not worth five pounds. How much does the whole weigh? He is wholly taken up[5] in composing some new works for the use of his pupils. Drawing is a pleasant amusement.

---

1. Sex.—2. vehiculo eversus fui ultimâ æstate.—3. sine injuriâ.—4. ego non sum natator.—5. prorsus est occupatus.

100.

There are in this stuff several colours well intermixed, viz. yellow, red, green, blue, brown.[1] I was standing by the door when I saw his Majesty the King of France pass. The horses of this farmer[2] are very lean; you do not give them enough oats.[3] They are blood horses, Sir, and you are aware they never look much better were I to give them three times as much. I have reckoned[4] your bill twice, but I think you have made a mistake.[5] I will call the landlord, Sir, for I am only waiter at this house. Who preached this morning? The curate, Sir. How is that? Is the rector ill?[6] No, Sir, he is gone to London for a short time.

101.

Take my boys to school, James,[7] and mind to drive carefully. Is the mare[8] put to? The minister will never give your memorial to the

1. Flavus, ruber, viridis, cæruleus, fuscus.—2. equi hujus agricolæ.—3. satis avenæ.—4. supputavi.—5. te autem in errore esse existimo.—6. an rector ægrotat?—7. filios meos ad ludum, Jacobe.—8. equa.

king, because its contents are contrary to his plans. The lands in that country are unfruitful[1] but might be improved if properly cultivated by the husbandmen. Leave it or take it. Copy my manuscript fair, and bring it me on Saturday morning, as I intend sending it to the printer, on Friday[2] next. Undress these children, they are quite sleepy. Put them to bed. Sell them to us. Buy them some sugar plums. Kill him.[3] When I have given you a lesson, I must go to the vicarage.[4] Children are fond of them. When you have forgiven him his faults, I expect you will forgive me mine also. You say perfectly right.[5]

102.

When I have heard him, I may be able to judge of his abilities. When I have learned French I intend to study German.[6] When they have answered my letter, I will then go and see them. When I have friends staying with me, I seldom study. When I am in France I do as

---

1. Agri steriles.—2. die Veneris proximo.—3. illum interfice.—4. ad domum vicarii.—5. recte equidem loqueris.—6. linguam Germanicam.

they do in France. When she is at Brighton she goes to the royal chapel. When I have finished this little book. I have seen him but I have not spoken to him.[1] Do you send any more of it? Pray do not send any more of it. I believe him. I do not believe him. You are a Frenchman?[2] Yes, I am, Sir. Are they rich? Yes, they are. Are they come? No, they are not. Were you there?

103.

I have been ill,[3] and I am so still. I am very sorry to hear it; do not be frightened. She is joking.[4] I thank you, Madam, for all your kind attentions to my children. I hope they have not been troublesome. He launches into company[5] to forget his grief. You have softened his heart. Besides all my household expenses,[6] I have taxes to pay.

304.

Little by little,[7] he will make a fortune. I

1. Sed cum illo non sum locutus.—2. Gallus.—3. ægrotavi —4. illa jocatur.—5. in societate versatur.—6. sumptus domesticos.—7. paullatim.

play fairly, but you always cheat. I have at most learned six lines.[1] She sets every thing wrong. Hereafter I will give you my custom. I usually rise at five, both summer and winter; breakfast at eight, dine at two, and go to bed at nine. I ran to his assistance. She fell suddenly. How far do we say?[2] How far did you read last time? I hardly ever see them, except on a Sunday, at church.[3] Go that way, you will meet her. I had rather go this way. This field[4] has been sown with turnips.[5]

105.

Can you play at chess? Do not stir, my dear child. My land is sown with wheat.[6] This field is planted with potatoes. I have lived this year in four different places.[7] Is he still alive? He was then alive. Was she living when your uncle died? Louis XVIII died in the year one thousand eight hundred and twenty-four. I have counted ninety-seven

---

1. Didici sex versus.—2. quousque dicere debemus?—3. die Dominicâ, ecclesiæ.—4. hic ager.—5. rapis.—6. seritur tritico.—7. in quatuor locis diversis.

pages in this book. George IV was crowned in the year one thousand eight hundred and twenty-one.

106.

The same year his consort died.[1] Does he owe, really, so much money?[2] You come too soon; it is only a quarter to ten. We agreed last time that I should receive my lesson at eleven. He travelled by land.[3] Between you and him, there is something I cannot find out yet. A servant walks[4] behind his master.[5] For want of assiduity, he will never succeed. He is gone to meet his master, instead of minding his business. You receive company, and neglect that which would support your family. I lent him,[6] last month, seven hundred pounds, at the rate of four per cent. This old miser never spends[7] a shilling. They have blemished her reputation. Pour some oil into the bottle. Go to my father.

---

1. Uxor ejus mortua est.—2. tantos nummos.—3. terrâ iter fecit.—4. ambulat.—5. herum.—6. dedi illi mutuò.—7. avarus nunqnam expendit.

107.

Have you seen the new weights and measures? Do it quickly. All the goods which were in his warehouse were burnt. At what time did that fire happen? The General was attended by the chief officers of the staff. I am in hopes now to overcome all the difficulties of that beautiful language.[1] Do they attend church? I attend lectures on chemistry every Friday. He never attends to his French. My master attends me once a week. Who attended your daughter[2] during her last illness?

108.

He generally attends the family. Whom do you mean? Dr. B. Now, my dear children, attend to what I say. He attends the market every Wednesday. Does he condescend to do that? A man of such abilities. We shall go over to France[3] next summer. Will you go over the water? There is a boat and two watermen ready to take us[4] over to the other

---

1. Superare omnes difficultates illius elegantis linguæ.—2. quis medicinam fecit tuæ filiæ.—3. transibimus in Galliam.—4. scapha atque duo remiges præsto nobis sunt.

side. What a story! The Bishop is expected here next Tuesday. If he believes such stories, he must be a great simpleton. A bull defends himself with his horns. A mad dog has been killed.[1] He is sunk into misfortune; who will take him out of it? I have a large family to provide for. I am tired of writing. It rains hard. I delight in reading such books. Peruse[2] my newspaper.

109.

He takes pleasure in hunting.[3] We cannot hear each other speak. What stuff is your gown[4] made of? Look at that fop, or dandy; he seems quite pleased with himself. They have declined having any thing to do with it. They bear his insulting conduct with patience.[5] I could not, I am sure.[6]

110.

I cannot bear him.[7] The bee is the emblem

1. Canis rabiosus occisus est.—2. lege.—3. in venatu.—4. stola tua.—5. ejus contumeliam ferunt patientiâ.—6. hanc rem me non posse ferre, planè scio.—7. hunc ferre nequeo,

of industry, and was taken by the late Emperor of France as his arms. The slave-trade has been abolished in this country for several years. We cut the ears of our dogs. It is very cruel. They are talking together. If we were to listen to them. We cannot bear the sight of them. They are likely to talk till to-morrow. A cat is sly. That man is deceitful.[1] Cats are fond of mice.[2] Children are fond of pleasure. What county[3] do you come from? Sussex. Leave off crying. Have you left off doing it?[4] Has he left off going to bed at nine? Drunkenness has been at all times looked upon as a vice,[5] which destroys the happiness of families. Let us sit down under the shade of this oak tree. I have forbidden the maid to use this set of china.

111.

A man of wit and education is not always the richest. Do not hinder him from studying. After having declared my sentiments. They were quite intoxicated; so much so, as not to

---

1. Falsus est.—2. mures edunt.—3. ex quâ provinciâ.—4. id facere.—5. ebrietas semper habita est tanquam vitium.

be able to return home that night. He ill-treats his children. What a fine poplar tree. You must cut down that walnut-tree. Wolves destroy in France yearly a great deal of cattle.[1] My last servant was a great rogue. The storm began at three in the morning, and lasted nearly four hours. It thundered,[2] it lightened,[3] and it rained as fast as it could pour. Let us spend merrily this Christmas. So we will.[4]

112.

My library contains[5] above ten thousand volumes; viz. Travels, Histories,[6] French, Italian, Greek, German and Latin authors; some excellent books on Geometry, Astronomy and Mathematics. You will not find in it one single novel; I have banished them. The carpenter has forgotten his hammer. Give it me, I want to nail this picture. I am told you have learned music,[7] will you have the goodness to tell me, what difference there is, between a flat and a sharp?

---

1. Pecoris.—2. tonuit.—3. fulguravit.—4. ita faciemus.—5. bibliotheca mea habet.—6. itinera, historias.—7. musicam vel artem musices.

113.

How many quavers are there in that bar? Count the time. You do not keep time. I am sorry to say your fingering is very bad indeed. How many do you count in a bar? That note is too flat, the other is too sharp. You have no ear.[1] My ear is excellent.[2] Who tunes your instrument? Mr. W. of Chelmsford. It is a good instrument. Now mind your time. He seldom brews any good beer. Yield to his entreaties. Subdue your own passions. My child is quite spoiled. She never spoils her children.

114.

I have broken my whip,[3] take it to the collar-maker's. You have dropt your thimble, pick it up. Take the yard, and let us measure this Gros-de-Naples. It is as sweet as honey.[4] Buy me some lemons and oranges. A pick-pocket[5] has stolen from me a few sovereigns.

---

1. Aurem.—2. auris meâ excellens est, ad musicen distinguendam.—3. fregi meum flagellum.—4. æque dulce est ac mel.—5. fur.

His child died before he was of age. Hold your tongue, I cannot read. Sailors[1] seldom become rich. In my opinion, a hogshead of beer is not worth a dozen of wine.

115.

The doctor entertains very little hopes[2] of her recovery; the physician also attends her once a week. I wear silk stockings, they are nearly worn out; I must buy another pair. They are tight, they do not fit you. It snows and has snowed all night.[3] In case you should want any thing. I have placed the bell on the table. I am going to the tea dealer's and the tailor's. She is a pretty girl, but very idle.[4] Whatever his intention may be. They will be condemned. The ape resembles man.[5]

116.

On Twelfth night we have generally a few friends to supper with us; it is an old custom

---

1. Nautæ.—2. medicus minimè sperat.—3. ningit, atque ninxit per totam noctem.—4. illa est formosa puella, at desidiosa.—5. similis est homini.

and I like to keep it. My grand-daughter is gone to school. Whatever be your faults they will forgive you. Whatever you may ask they will accede to your desires. As tall as she is, she has no strength. They cannot surely be endured. Thou art a madman. How canst thou speak thus to a man of his rank? It is a very genteel family.[1] It is all over with him.[2] Did you succeed in catching him? Has he been able to tame him? This ink is too thick,[3] it does not run. I have finished my task.

117.

Though he may be ever so attentive, yet something is wanted.[4] Rub out all these lines.[5] The washerwoman has not brought back your linen; there are many things wanting; viz. one collar, three pocket handkerchiefs, black silk stockings, a white under waistcoat, two pair of wristbands, three frills, and one nightcap. Every one who is accused is not always guilty.[6] His friends were at a very great expense to

---

1. Familia generosa.—2. factum est de illo.—3. atramentum hoc nimis spissum est.—4. aliquid deest.—5. dele omnes has lineas.— 6. non semper sons est.

educate him. Has he any money left? Put in some cinnamon. When my uncle was in India he had several camels, and brought one over to England. London is far more populous than Paris.

118.

I have not followed his steps[1] in every thing. The rules of the grammar are not always intelligible to young people.[2] This turkey[3] is fat. I have a pain in my back. Pare your nails nicely. The church bells[4] have been ringing all day. On what occasion? The mark has been passed. The loss of time is to be lamented. The mob did a great deal of damage in King-street. Were there many mistakes in your exercise? There is not a rose without a thorn. Who sent me that? To play well, on any instrument, is a gift of nature.[5] The king's death happened about three years after the coronation of his cousin. His faculties were very much impaired long before his late illness,[6] which

1. Vestigia sua non sum secutus.—2. juvenibus.—3. gallina Numidica.—4. campanæ.—5. ludere egregie quovis instrumento musices.—6. Multò ante morbum ejus ultimum.

ended his frail existence. Lend me your horse.

119.

The Duke's carriage has just passed. I am just arrived from Scotland, where I passed the summer. The cat has scratched my hand. If you play with the dog, he will bite your finger. Will you wash her head? Give your hand to her as a sign of reconciliation. Snuff the candles. Blow your nose.[1] I have hurt my foot.[2] You tread upon my feet. We do not always see those who see us. We often love those who do not love us. He loves us. We love him. We love them and fear him.[3] We speak of him.

120.

We know them.[4] We understand them. It is evident he has improved in his studies. It is necessary to attend to one's own affairs to

1. Emunge te.—2. pedem meum læsi.—3. illum timemus.—4. illos novimus.

thrive in this world. I like those whom we have met, but those who called on us do not seem to like us.[1] The boy cut his tongue in playing with the scissors. He loves play. My hands are cold. Warm yours. Church begins at eleven in the morning, and at three in the afternoon. They all went out.[2]

121.

Who preaches to-day? Do you mean in the morning? Yes. Doctor W. Had you a good sermon last sunday? What time[3] did you get there? Very late.[4] It was not our fault:[5] the clocks differ so much. Put every book in its place. He commits faults every minute. He has the tooth-ache.[6] What a service he has rendered to his country! He will be rewarded. I am in want of a good servant, who can wait at table. Nothing can prevent you going there. I have been watching this hour.[7]

---

1. At illi qui nos viserunt, non nos diligere videntur.—2. omnes exiverunt.—3. quo tempore.—4. serissimè.—5. nostra culpa.—6. dens illi dolet, vel dolor dentium illum tenet.—7. vigilavi per totam horam.

122.

Every one is afraid of them. Did you take your prayer-bŏok to church? What do you think of my work? If it may in some measure improve my pupils, I shall think myself fully rewarded. Do not look at that tree. Do not forget that. Take this. Carry it to your poor father, and tell him I wish I could do more for him. He is a dangerous man.' The English fleet sets sail this day at three. What? on a Sunday? Yes, sailors prefer[1] that day to any other.

123.

I may say, for certain, that among ten ships sailing[2] from our ports, seven sail on a Sunday. I have made this remark[3] during my stay at Gravesend; where most of our East Indiamen stay a short time previous to their sailing for Madras and Bombay. Do not plague[4] her, I say.

---

1. Imo, nautæ præferunt.—2. ex decem navibus navigantibus.—3. hanc rem observavi.—4. vexare.

124.

I am ordered to follow you[1] wherever you go. Spare your health[2] more than your money. The king's palace[3] will be illuminated. A quire of paper. Half a hundred pens. A bottle of red ink. Your copy-book is not ruled;[4] give me your ruler and your pencil that I may rule it. Have you any blotting paper? I want to rub out this line; give me your India-rubber. Our glass is cracked.[5] The coach starts at five on Monday.

125.

He stares[6] in her face. Do not stare at us. He smokes in the presence of the ladies.[7] It is a French fashion. It does not matter; it is not genteel. The chimney smokes uncommonly.[8] Send for the bricklayer.[9] This poker is red hot. Do not leave it in the fire.[10] It is dangerous. Is your tea sweet enough? Ann, I have no

---

1. Te sequi.—2. serva valetudinem.—3. basilica.—4. charta plumbo non directa.—5. poculum pertusum.—6. obtutu hæret.—7. coram mulieribus.—8. valde.—9. accerse laterum structorem.—10. ne linquas in igne.

spoon. Put my bunch of keys in the cupboard. It is very vulgar. Here are rolls[1] quite hot. I prefer toast. May you be blessed! How thick the fog is! At what o'clock is the tide to-day? What a dust you make!

126.

You must have new gravel on the walks of our garden. A spark flew and set fire to the whole building. There are seven days in the week. Say them in French.[2] Yes, Sir. I think I have learned them; I will try to remember them; Monday, Tuesday, Wednesday, Thursday, Friday, Saturday, and Sunday.[3] Very well![4] there are twelve months in the year;[5] be so good to say them, also, in French:—January, February, March, April, May, June, July, August, September, October, November, and December. The four seasons, if you please: the Spring, the Summer, the Autumn, and the Winter. In what month is your birth-day?[6] I passed the Easter week with them at Morton

---

1. Crustula.—2. Gallicè.—3. dies Dominica.—4. benè.—5. anni duodecim menses.—6. dies natalis.

Hall, the country seat of my uncle. Christmas[1] will soon come.

127.

The beard of this old man nearly reached down to the ground. He fell on his knees, and prayed to God to save him from such a perilous situation.[2] Give me your left hand, I want to try this ring on your finger. I have cut my thumb. Your nails are too long, you should cut them. Lend me a nail, I want to drive it in the wall. She has learned dancing, and yet she does not possess a genteel carriage. Have you slept well?[3] I always sleep well. Your sleep has not been interrupted. My horse had a fall.

128.

The noise of the carriages[4] in London often prevents my sleeping, but never in the country, where, of course, the bustle is not so great.[5]

---

1. Christi festum.—2. ex tanto periculo.—3. bene dormivisti vel dormisti.—4. strepitus vehiculorum.—5. tumultus non ita magnus.

There are five senses, viz. sight, hearing, smell, taste, and feeling. The small-pox[1] is in the village. I would advise you to take care of yourself. I do not fear it; I have been inoculated several years ago. Did you not cough[2] in the night? Yes, nearly the whole night.

129.

I was bled last winter for a very obstinate cough. I have a pain in my arm.—Your finger bleeds. I see, it is nothing but a scratch. No one can be free from envy. His firmness was admired even by his enemies. His eagerness in fulfilling his duty. He grumbles for nothing. He is never pleased. The plough is one of the most useful instruments[3] in husbandry; how could we till our lands without it? My ploughmen[4] earn eighteen shillings a week. The cart is loaded.[5] I am sorry.

130.

What is his complaint? What is she crying

---

1. Variolæ.—2. an non tussivisti?—3. aratrum est instrumentum utilissimum ad.—4. aratores.—5. carrus est onustus.

for? The shovel is bent. The tongs are so rusty that they cannot be placed in the drawing room. A pack of cards costs more in England than five packs in Paris. The pillow is too hard.[1] The hands of my watch are broken; I must send it to the watch-maker's to have them mended. The jeweller is waiting to show you some earrings. They are right down gamblers.[2]

131.

The ashes were thrown away. I am going to have some to-night. Has he enquired after me? What is the meaning of that? I thought it was later. I have hurt my hand. Let us go and skip with the rope. Have you a ball? I have missed the ball.[3] I will make room.[4] May[5] we go out now? I thought that it was later. Is there a lump?[6] Bear it patiently.[7] The sun shines.[8]

---

1. Pulvinar nimis durum.—2. aleatores.—3. non excepi pilam.—4. locum præbebo.—5. licetne?—6. tuber.—7. æquo animo.—8. resplendet.

132.

The wind blows hard. It is sultry.[1] The weather is cloudy this morning; is the wind changed? I beg you will excuse them. I have made a good breakfast. Let us take a walk. Let us put off the walk to another day. I prefer your small beer. I must go this morning to an auction. I hate the fashions of that country. Is he out of doors? This is the lowest price. Is it right? I wish you a pleasant walk. It stops sometimes. The moon rises early.

133.

There will be enough for that. We shall be delighted to see them. He takes much pains[2] to do it. He heard it. They are lazy.[3] The sea is rough.[4] Do not make a noise. Do not be so stiff. I cannot bend.[5] Bend slowly.[6] Your head is upright. It is as smooth as velvet. Feel my pulse. Show me your doll, sister.

---

1. Magna vis æstûs est.—2. magnoperè laborat.—3. ignavi sunt.—4. æstuat mare.—5. nequeo flectere, vel curvare.—6. inclina lentè.

Let us cut for deal. You have taken my fishes. We will not go.

134.

Feel my hand.[1] You did not look at the rules.[2] You do not improve. I have made a new apron. What a sloven he is! Is it right? I do not play high. How much has he paid?[3] Whence came you?

135.

Bring in the card table. She looks well. She is quite recovered from her last illness. There is too much of it already. I shall discharge my clerk within a month. What ails your hand? What is the matter with you? I will have them do so. Give me ten. They say he is dead. I am told you have acted very much to the displeasure of your friend.[4] They pity him very much. They accuse them wrongfully.[5]

---

1. Palpa manum meam.—2. regulas.—3. quantum solvit, vel dedit.—4. valdè te displicuisse amico tuo.—5. accusant injustè.

136.

It is said we shall be rewarded[1] soon. We have been told that it will not be necessary. They follow fashions.[2] My eyes have at last been opened. They have amused the children. I am assured that he has left the country. They have sung a very fine song. They have not attended to the orders.[3] They have been falsely accused.—It is very much lamented. It is expected every day. That has been well played.

137.

I am eight years old. Lay the cloth.[4] Pull off your shoes. To whom do these belong? I sell cherries for twopence a pound. Is the fire out?[5] Are my boots mended? Let us come. Let us dance. Let us read.[6] I do not like cards. How many tricks have you made? Seven. What are they?

---

1 Munerati erimus.—2. modos observant.—3. præceptis non obediverunt.—4. mappam instrue, vel pone.—5. ignis, vel focus, estne extinctus?—6. legamus.

138.

I see a windmill, silk-worms, and a flower-pot.[1] He wants a watch, gunpowder, and a colour-box.[2] I have bought a tea-chest, fire-arms, and a coffee-mill. Bring us a wine glass, letter or post paper, and the ink bottle. I was in the corn market, where I met the pie woman. I bought an apple tart, and a cream cheese, also a silver milk-pot. I never eat rice pudding. Has he called the oyster-girl? Where is the flower-basket?[3] Tell the butter-man to bring me next week three pounds of fresh butter. Tell the wine merchant[4] I do not like his wines. I will settle his bill, when I am in town next month.

139.

I was born, said he to me,[5] in this happy island. They were walking on the sea-shore.[6] This is not accordant with your feelings. Will you not speak to her on my account? Give me

1. Molam, bombyces et vas florum.—2. cistam colorum.—3. cophinus, vel corbis florum.—4. nuncia œnopolæ, vel vinario.—5. natus sum, mihi dixit.—6. ambulabant in littore maris.

your account. Agreeable to your orders, I have hired a good house with a large garden and a fish-pond. There is a pump, a well, stables[1] for twelve horses, a coach-house, two water mills, a small windmill on the top of a hill, twenty-five acres of meadow land,[2] three fields of arable land, with a brook, and a small nursery for trees. What is the rent of the whole estate? The house, with all the out-buildings, one hundred and sixty pounds per annum, upon a lease of twenty-one years: the land about one pound an acre. Do you think it a high rent? No, it is rather cheap. The house must be very large, I suppose? Why, there is a great deal of room. Did you go all over it? Yes, I did, sir. There are fourteen bed rooms, two small parlours, two drawing rooms, a hall, servant's hall, two kitchens, five sleeping rooms for servants, an excellent cellar, a pantry, a nursery, and several other rooms. Is there a library? Yes, and a study; a hot-house and green-house, an orchard, a shrubbery, a beautiful lawn in front of the mansion, with a piece of water.

---

1. Sunt antlia, puteus, stabula.—2. viginti quinque jugera pratorum.

140.

The meat was not done.[1] How tiresome you are! I have done. By whom is England governed? Who destroyed that city? He did. What does your uncle think?[2] What are the children doing? Who did that? I did. How large is that country? A great number of children came to meet us. What may be the number[3] of our pupils? He has pulled down the wall[4] which was standing before his house. Will you put that on the table? Who has broken that bottle? Now put an end to that. Have you taken your measures and your baskets.[5]

141.

Do not put me off. I must postpone my journey to another day, because it is such very bad weather. There is one wanting,[6] I will lay you what you like. Done. Let us go fishing.

---

1. Caro non est satis cocta, vel tosta.—2. quid hâc de re tuus patruus arbitratur.—3. qui potest esse numerus.—4. evertit murum.—5. mensuras et cophinos tuos.—6. unus deest.

I never sin, but you are a sinner. Give me that peach. Call the fisherman.[1] Plant a peach tree in your garden. Waiter ?[2] Here, sir.[3] Bring me a glass of brandy. Put this cup upon a waiter. Where does he sleep ? At his uncle's. I cannot sleep in London owing to the noise.[4] Does he sleep in London or in the country? Is my cheek red? What is the matter with it? My master has just given me a good box on the ear. The case of this watch is not strong enough. Where did you sit in the theatre[5] last night. In the duke's box. Bring your box, let us pack up, for the coach gets here by six; so make haste. What wood is that ?[6] I think it is rose-wood. Do you not see that it is box ? He is shooting.

142.

I did not give it. I do not give it, or I will not give it to any one, even if you ask for it. Go on faster. He did not like them, he does not like them, and he never will like them. Go

---

1. Voca piscatorem.—2. puer.—3. adsum, domine.—4. strepitus causâ.—5. quam in partem theatri sedisti.—6. quale est hoc lignum.

on now.[1] Get on.[2] Do not get on.[3] Do you get on ? Do you not get on ? Has the clock struck ten ?[4] Has not the clock struck ten ? Did the clock strike ten ?[5] Will the clock strike seven ? Will not the clock strike ? Does it strike ten ? Does it not strike ten ? Is it striking ten ? Is it not striking ten ? You have lost your pocket-book. You have not lost your pocket-book. Did you loose your pocket-book, or have you lost it ? Have you, or did you not lose your pocket-book.[6] Had you lost your pocket-book ? Had you not lost your pocket-book ? Should you have lost your pocket-book ? Should you not have lost your pocket-book ? It was just as you say.

143.

Where are the relations ?[7] Where were the relations ? Where were the friends of that gentleman ? Where will be the children ? Where would be the servants ? He was useful. He was not useful. Will he be useful ? Would

---

1. Perge nunc.—2. I longiùs.—3. ne longiùs eas.—4. sonuit? 5. horam decimam.—6. nonne perdidisti tabulas tuas, vel libellum tuum ?—7. ubi sunt parentes, vel consanguinei.

he be useful? Would he not be useful? Would he not have been useful? I give you my word. I did, or have given you my word. I gave you my word. I will give you my word.[1] I would give you my word. I should not have given you my word. Now, I give you my library.[2] Had I given you a receipt? Should I have given you my address?[3] Have you written?

144.

They have said so. They have not said so, or they did not say so. They had said so to every body. They would have said so to me. Have they said so? Have they not said so?[4] They would, or should have said so to your mother. Would they have said so to my father? He speaks to me, or is speaking to me.[5] He was speaking to you.

145.

We have done so far. They say the plague is

---

1. Dabo promissum.—2. bibliothecam.—3. nunciaverim locum ubi habito.—4. non ita dixerint.—5. mihi, vel mecum loquitur.

at Adrianople.[1] Do not plague me. What a plague! Is it not the end of the book yet? Have patience. I want a little nutmeg, and a drop of brandy for this pudding, and you shall take it to the baker's.[2] Give him a glass of beer.[3]

What a fine goose! Is there any stuffing in it? You have made no gravy. I dislike pickled pork, but I am fond of minced meat. He takes no food but a little soup very weak. Cut me some stale bread. I have none.—Will you have some new bread? Whither did you send the servant? In the dining room.[4] There is some cold veal. What a fine calf I see yonder. Take a dose of salts. I will if you will give me a lozenge. I do not like crumb, I prefer crust.[5] Did you seal your letter? Yes, with a wafer. Have you no wax? Send us some slates and tiles. Has she any lodgings to let? Yes, near the brewery.[6] Tap the cask of wine. Take that hoop off first. Knock at the door. There is no knocker. Lift up the latch.

---

1. Nunciatum est pestem esse in Hadrianopole.—2. ad pistorem.—3. poculum cerevisiæ.—4. in tricliniario.—5. medullam panis, sed crustum magis cupio.—6. juxta zythepsarium.

146.

You are a fop, and a dandy.[1] This is a pretty compliment; to whom is it addressed? He is a story-teller, an outlaw,[2] and an adventurer. Why do you call me a traitor?[3] Because I can prove my words. He is a dunce[4] and you a mocker.[5] They say you are very rich. I should like to know what it is to you? Excuse me. I mean no offence.[6] Now are you satisfied? Yes, I am. Our studies are delightful.[7] Your father is pleased with your rapid progress. Did he write a letter[8] to me? He did, and anxiously expects your return home.

---

1. Nugator.—2. mendosus, exul.—3. vocas proditorem?—4. hebes.—5. tu es derisor.—6. lædere nolo.—7. studia nostra valde amœna.—8. litteras is scripsit?

THESAURUS

LINGUÆ LATINÆ.

A, art. The indef. art. is understood, not expressed, in Latin.
Abbot, s. *abbas*, 3 d. masc.
Ability, s. *facultas*, 3 d. f.
Able (to be), v. *posse*, irr.
—— I am, *possum*
—— he is not, *ille non potest*
—— adj. *hăbĭlis, e. potens*
Abominable, adj. *ăbōminandus*, part.
Abolish (to), v. *ăbŏlēre*, pret. *ăbŏlui* or *ăbŏlēvi*
About, prep. *circum, circa*
—— four o'clock, *circĭter horam diei quartam*
—— it, (I was speaking), *hac de re locutus eram*
—— the garden, *in horto*
—— it (I know nothing), *de hoc quidem nihil prorsus scio*
About the damage, *de injuriâ*
—— it (set), *age, incipe*
Above, prep. *sŭper*
Above sixpence, *supra sex asses*
—— mentioned, *jam citatus, suprà*
—— all, *super omnia, supra modum*
—— ten pounds, *plus decem minarum*
Abroad (from home), *fŏris*, adv.
—— (in foreign climes), *pĕrĕgrè*, adv.
Ace (at cards), s. *monas, ădis*, 3d. f.
Accede (to) v. *accēdĕre, assentīri dep.*
Acceded, p. p. *assensus*
Accept (to), v. *accĭpĕre*

Accept of my offers, *accipe quæ tibi propono*
Acceptable, adj. *acceptabilis e.*
Accident, s. *căsus, ûs,* 4 d. m.
Accompany (to), v. *comĭtāri,* 1 c. dep.
Accompt, s. *compŭtatio,* 3 d.f.
Accuse, v. *accŭsāre,* 1 c. act.
Accustom, v. *assuēfăcĕre,* 3 c. act.
Accustom one's self, v. *solēre,* 2 c. neut. irr. *sŏlĭtus sum,* pret.
Ache (to), v. *dŏlēre,* 2 c. n.
Acknowledge, v. *fătēri,* dep. *fassus sum,* pret.
Acknowledgment, s. *assentātio,* 3 d f. *confessio,* 3 d. f.
Acquaint, v. *certiorem aliquem facere, nuntiāre,* 1 c. *indicāre,* 1 c.
Acquaintances, s. *fămĭliāres, sive nĕcessārii*
Acquainted with him (I am not), *haud novi hominem*
Act, v. n. *ăgĕre,* 3 c. irr.
Action, s. *actio,* 3 d.
Address, s. *concio,* 3 d. f.
——— v. *allŏqui,* 3 c. dep.
——— to harangue, *concionem habere*
Adjective (an), *adjectivus,* adj. used substantively
Admiral, s. *classis præfectus*
Admiration, s. *admīrātio,* 3 f.
Admire, v. *admīrāri,* 1 c. dep.
——— or wonder at nothing, *nil admirari*
Admit, v. a. *admittĕre,* 3 c.
Advance, v. forward, *progrĕdi,* 3 c. n. dep.
——— to promote, *augēre,* 2 c. act. *prōmŏvēre,* 2 c. act.

Advice, s. *nuncium,* 2 d. n. *consĭlium,* 2 d. n.
Advise, v. *commendāre,* 1 c. *suadēre,* 2 c.
Affairs, s. *res,* nom. plur. f. *negotia,* nom. plur. neut.
Affection, s. *amor,* 3 d. m. *dilectio,* 3 d. f.
Affectionate, adj. *dīlĭgens, amans*
Affinity, s. *affīnĭtas,* 3 d. f.
Affirm (to), v. n. *affirmāre,* 1 c.
—— (to), v. a. *confirmāre,* 1 c. *firmāre,* 1 c.
Afflict (to), v. a. *affligĕre,* 3 c.
Afflicted, adj. *afflictus,* p. p.
Afford (to), v. a. *præbēre,* 2 c. act.
Afraid, adj. *păvĭdus,* adj. *trĕpĭdus,* adj.
——— (to be), *păvēre,* 2 n. *tĭmēre,* 2 c.
——— (I am), *tĭmeo, perterrĭtus sum*
Africa, *Afrĭca, æ* f.
After, prep. *à, post, ex, secundum,* &c.
—— (the day), *post illum diem, postridiè*
—— the French fashion, *modo Gallico*
—— all, *nĭhĭlōmĭnus, neque eo sĕciùs*
—— noon, *post mĕrīdiem*
—— the example of, *isto exemplo,* abl. abs. *sĕcundum*
—— the example of your father, *exemplo tui patris*
—— my taste, *sĕcundum me, modo meo*
—— (to look), *curare, quærere*

Afterwards, adv. *posteà*
Again, adj. *ĭtĕrum*
—— (afresh), *dēnuo, de integro*
—— (to come), *rĕvĕnīre*, 4 c. neut.
—— (to give), *rursus dăre*
—— (to begin), *de novo incipere*
—— (to see), *rĕvīsere*
Against, prep. *adversus, contra*
——— me, *adversus me*
——— them, *adversum illos*
——— his will, *illo invito*
Age, s. *ætas*, 3 d. f.
What age are you? *quot annos natus es?*
Twenty two, *viginti duo*
Aged, adj. *ætate provectus, senex*
Age (I am of), *mājor sum ætate*
—— (she is not of), *illa minor est ætate*
Ago, adv. (long), *jamdudum*
—— (five years), *his quinque annis*
— (half an hour), *abhinc dimĭdium horæ*
— (is it long), *eratne dūdum?*
Agree (to), v. a *assentīre*, act. *assentīri*, dep. 4 c.
—— upon (with), v. n. *consentīre de re aliquā*, 4 c. n.
—— to it (I), *consentire de eo*
Agreed, p. p. *assensus*
Agreeable, adj. *gratus, jūcundus*
Agreeably to, *secundum*, prep.
Agreement, s. *concordantia*, 1 d.
Ague, s. *febris, quartāna*

Ail (to), v. n. *ægrotare*, 1 c. *dolēre*, 2 c.
Ailing, adj. (she is always), *semper ægrotat*
Aim at (to), v *collinēre*, 2 c.
——, purpose, s. *propŏsĭtum*, 2 d.
Airs she gives herself (what), *quōmŏdo illa jactat vide*
Alarm. s. *terror*, 3 d.
Alderman, s. *dĕcūrio*, 3 d. m.
Alight (to), v. n. *dēsĭlire ex ĕquo*
Alive, ad. *vīvus*
—— (when), *adhuc vivens*
—— (is he still), *vivitne nunc etiam?*
All, adj. *omnis, tōtus*
— after, *demum, posthæc*
— the morning, *toto tempore mātūtīno*
— day, *toto die*
— the evening, *toto vespere*
— night, *totā nocte*
— the year, *toto anno*
— that (for), *neque eo sēcius*
— over (it is), *actum est*
— things (in), *omnibus in rebus*
— (not at), *prorsus omnino*
Allow (to), v. a. *permittĕre*, 3 c.
Almanack, s. *călendārium*, 2 d.
Almighty, adj. *omnipotens*
Almost, adv. *pēne*
——— twelve o'clock, *ferme meridiem*
——— done, *prŏpĕmŏdum factus, fere fīnītus*
Alms, s. *ĕleēmŏsyna*, 1 d.
Alone, adj. *sōlus*
Aloud, adv. *clarā voce*

Aloud (speak), *lŏquere clarè*
—— (he said), *clarâ voce locūtus est, clamavit ille*
Already, adv *jam*
Also, adv. *ĕtiam*
Altar, s. *ara*, 1 f. *altare* 3 d. neut.
Alter (to), v. a. *variare*, 1 c. *mutare*, 1 c.
Alteration, s. *mutātio*, 3 d. f.
Although, adv. *quanquam, lĭcet*
—— I am, *etsi sim*
—— you have dined, *quanquam prandisti*
—— you spoke, *etsi lŏcūtus fueris*
—— you have learned, *tu licet didicisti*
Always, adv. *semper*
—— comes (he), *semper venit*
Am (I), from *esse*, to be, *sum, ego sum*
— (I), cold, *frīgeo*
— (I), hot, *căleo*
— (I), ten years old, *decem annos natus sum*
— come (I), *vēni*
— told (I), *nuntiatum est mihi*
— just arrived (I), *modò ex itinere advĕnio*
— ill (I), *ægroto*
— informed (I), *audīvi*
— forty (I), *quadrāginta annos natus sum*
— very sorry (I), *valde me pœnitet*
America, s. pr. *America, æ* f.
American, *Americanus, a, um.*
Amiable, adj. *amabilis*
Amidst, prep. *in medio*

Among, prep. *inter*
Amount (to), *cresco*, 3 c. *făcio*, 3 c.
—— to (how much do they), *quantum faciunt?*
—— s. *summa*, 1 f. *totum*, 2 n.
Amuse (to), v. *oblectāre*, 1 c.
Amusement, s. *dēlectāmentum* 2 n. *oblectatio*, 3 f.
Ancestors, s. *majores, ăvi, ătăvi*
Ancle, s. *tālus*, 2 d. masc.
—— (to put out one's), *talum vertere*
And, conj. *et, ac, atque*
Anger, s. *ira*, 1 f. *iracundia*, 1 f.
Angle (to), v. n. *piscāri*, 1 c. dep.
Angling, s. *piscātus, ûs, vel i*, masc. *piscatio*, 3 f.
—— rod, *arundo piscatoria*
—— hook, *hāmus*, 2 m.
Angry, adj. *iratus*
—— at it (I am), *irascor, iratus sum hâc de re*
—— (to be), *irasci*
Animal, s. *ănimal*, 3 d. neut.
Another, adj. *ălius*
Annum (per)
Answer, s. *responsum*, 2 d.
—— (to), *respondere*
—— for it (I), *spondeo pro hoc*
Answered, *responsus*
Ant, s. *formica*, 1 f.
Antiquities, s. pl. *antiquitates*, 3 f.
Any more (do they sell), *vendunt ne plūra?*
— thing (fit for), *aptus cuilibet rei*

Ape, s. *simia*, 1 d. f.
Appear (to), *appārēre*, 2 c.
——— (they), *apparent*
——— bashful (to), *verecundiam præbēre, esse modestos*
Appearance, s. *aspectus*, 4 d. m. *persōna*, 1 d. f.
Appellation, s. *nomen*, 3 d. n. *appellatio*, 3 d. f.
Appetite, s. *appĕtītus*, 4 d. m.
Apple, s. *pōmum*, 2 d. n. *mālum*, 2 d. n.
—— pie, tart, *poma crustâ farreâ incocta*
—— tree, *mālus*, 1 d. f.
Applied, *applicans*, p. act. *applicatus*, p. p.
Apply (to), *applicāre*, 1 c.
—— oneself to study (to), *ad studium animum applicare*, 1 c.
—— to any one (to), *adire aliquem*
Appoint (to), *nomināre*, 1 c. *designare*, 1 c. *præstituere*, 3 c.
Appointed to meet Trebatius at Capua (I have), *constitui Trebatio obviam ire Capuam*
Appointment, s. *loci constitutio*
Appraise, v. *pretium æstimare*
Apprehend, v. *suspicāri*, 1 c. dep. *intelligere*, 3 c. *capere*, 3 c.
Apprize (to), v. *certiorem aliquem facere*
Approach (to), v. n. *accedere*, 3 c. *ădīre*, 4 c.
Approve (to), v. n. *plaudĕre*, 3 c. *approbāre*, 1 c.
Approved, p. p. *approbatus*

April, s. *Aprilis*, 3 d. m.
Apron, s. *præcinctōrium*, 2 n.
Arabia, s. pr. *Arābia*, æ f.
Arable, adj. *arabilis*
Are to be found (they), *possunt invĕnīri*
— to have soon (we), *debemus citò habere*
— we to do it? *an debemus id facere?*
— never accustomed to (we), *haud sōlēmus unquam*
— you cold? *frīgesne?*
— you pleased? *esne contentus?*
— the children warm? *num liberi călent?*
— there many, *sunt ne plures*
Argument, s. *argumentum*, 2 d. n.
Arise (to), v. n. *surgĕre*, 3 c. *nasci*, 3 c. dep.
Aristotle, s. p. *Aristŏtĕles, is*
Arm, (limb), s. *brăchium*, 2 d. n.
Arms, (weapons), s. *arma*, 2 d. n. plur.
Arm (to), v. *armāre, arma sūmere*
Army, s. *exercĭtus*, 4 d. m.
Arrival, s. *adventus, ûs*, m.
Arrive (to), *advenīre, accēdĕre*
Arrived (I have), *adveni*
——— (I am just), *modò adveni*
Arrows, s. *sagittæ*, 1 d. f.
Art, s. *ars*, 3 d. f.
As, conj. *ut*
— he speaks I speak, *ut ille lŏquitur ego lŏquor*
— well as I, *et ego quŏque*
— good as that, *tam bonus ut istud*

As you like, *ut lŭbet*
— long as you are attentive, *tam diù quam studiosum te ostendis*
— long as my cane, *æque longus ac baculus meus*
— a friend, *ut amicus*
— tall as she is, *grandis sĭcut illa*
— tall as I am, *celsus æque ut ego sum*
— far as London, *Londĭnum usque*
— far as here, *hùc usque*
— soon as possible, *quamprīmum*, adv.
— many as, *tot, quotquot*
— much as, *quantùm*, adv.
— to him, *quòd ad illum attinet*
— her father is gone to, *quia pater ejus profectus est ad*
— her daughter wants, *quia ejus filia eget*
— civil as he is, *ut sit cōmis*
— soon as it suits me, *quum prīmum perplăcet mihi*
— far as the next town, *quoădusque vīcīnam urbem*
— long as you like, *quamdiu vis*
— near as I can guess, *quam accūratè possim dīvīnāre*
— to what he says, *de eo quod ille dicit*
Ashamed, adj. *pudore suffusus vel suffusa*
Ash-tree, s. *fraxinus*, 2 d. f.
Ashes, s. *cĭnis, cineris*, m. *et* f. 3 c. in plur. *cineres*
Asia, s. pr. *Asia, æ* f.
Ask (to), v. a. *rogāre, quærĕre*
— (to), for him, *illum pĕtĕre*
Ask (to), of him, *ab illo quærere*
—— your brother, *a fratre tuo quære*
Asked (being), *rogatus*
Asparagus, s. *aspărăgus*, 2 d. m.
Ass, s. *ăsinus vel ăsĭna*
Assiduity, *sedulitas*, 3 d. f.
Assist (to), v. *juvāre*, 1 c. *opem ferre*
Assistance, s. *opis*, 3 d. f. *auxĭlium*, 2 d. n.
Assure (to), v. *firmāre*, 1 c. *pollicēri*, 2 c. dep.
Astonish (to), v. a. *stupefacere*, 1 c. irr.
Astonished at it (I am), *hâc de re multùm mīror*
Astronomy, s. *astrŏnŏmia, æ* f.
At, prep. *ad*
— Paris, at Rome, *Lŭtētiæ, Rōmæ*
— what time do you go? *quando properas?*
— my father's, *dŏmi patris*
— what o'clock do you sup? *quotâ horâ cœnabis*
— it, *id faciens*
— the grocers, *ad aromatopolium*
— the rate, *hâc ratione*
— our warehouse, *ad repositorium nostrum*
— your house, *dŏmi tuæ*
Attachment, s. *dīlectio, onis*, 3 d. f.
Attack (to), v. a. *aggrĕdi* 3 c. dep. *provocāre*, 1 c.
Attend (to), v. a. (i. e. to mind), *studēre*, 2 c. *auscultāre*, 1 c.

Attend as a master (to), *docēre*
——— (to be present), v. *adesse*
——— (to accompany), *comitāri*, 1 c. dep.
——— (to), as a medical man, *cūrāre*, 1 c. *medicinam alicui facere*
——— to church, *comitāri ad templum*
——— to market, *simul ad mercātum ire*
——— balls, *saltāre in chŏrēis*
——— lectures, *audire philosophum vel lectorem*
——— to one's desire (to), *facere quod præceptum est*
——— diligently to your wishes (I shall), *faciam sedulò quæ cupis*
——— to your orders, *præcepta tua observare*
Attendance (surgeon's), *cūrātio, ōnis*, 3 d. f.
Attended to (my counsels, were not), *consilium meum non secutum erat*
Attention, s. *attentio*, 3 d. f. *stŭdium*, 2 d. n.
Attentive, adj. *attentus, stŭdiōsus*
Attorney, s. *prōcūrātor causarum*
Attribute (to), v. a. *attribuĕre* 3 c.
Auction, s. *auctio, ōnis*, 3 d. f.
August, s. (the month), *Augustus*, i. m.
Aunt, s. *ămita, æ.*
Author, s. *scriptor*, 3 d.
Autumn, s. *autumnus*, i. m.
Avail (to), v. *valēre, prodesse*
Aversion, s. *fastidium*, 2 d. n.
Avoid (to), v. a. *ēvītare*, 1 c.
Awake (to), v. a. and n. *excitāre*, 1 c. act. *expergisci*, 3. c. n. dep.
Aware (to be), v. *cavēre*, 2 c. *præscium esse*
Away (to take), v. a. *tollere, auferre*
Awoke (he), v. n. *experrectus est*
Away (to go), *abire*
—— (I am going), *abeo*
—— (to drive), *expello*
Axle-tree, s. *axis, is*, m.
Axe, s. *securis*, 3 d. f. *dolabella*, 1 d. f.

B

Babble (to), v. n. *garrīre* 4 c.
Babbler, s. *garrulus, i* 2 d.
Bachelor, s. *cælebs*, 3 d. m. *baccalaureus*, 2 d. m.
Back, s. *tergum*, 2 d. n.
—— (to go), v. *rĕdīre*, 4 c.
—— (to come), *rĕvĕnire*, 4 c.
—— (to give), *reddĕre*, 3 c.
—— of a house, *posticum domi*
Backwards, adv. *retrò, retrorsùm*
Backward, adj. *remissus, alienus*
Back (to send), *remittere*, 3 c.
Bad, adj. *malus, pravus*
—— (this is), *hoc malum est*
Badly, adv. *malè, pravè*
Bag, s. *sarcina, æ* f. *succus, i* m.

Bailiff, s. *apparitor*, 3 d. *villicus*, 2 d.
Bait (to horses), *dīversāri*, 1 c. dep. *ĕquos ad diversōrii stabulum ducere*
Bake (to), v. a. *pinsĕre*, 3 c. *cŏquĕre*, 3 c.
Bakehouse, s. *pistrīnum*, 2 d. n.
Baker, s. *pistor*, 3 d. m.
Ball, s. *pila*, *æ* f.
—— (a dance), s. *chŏrea*, 1 d. f.
—— (a foot), s. *pila pedalis*
Banditti, s. pl. *latrōnes*, 3 d. pl.
Baneful, adj. *noxius*, *fātālis*
Banish (to), v. a. *mittere in exĭlium*
Bank, s. of England, *thēsaurus Britanniæ*
—— or mound, *tŭmŭlus*, 2 d. *collis*, 3 d. f.
—— or shore, *rīpa*, 1 d. f.
—— notes, s. *syngraphæ thesauri publici*, *tesseræ argentariæ*
Banker, s. *nummŭlārius*, 2 d.
Baptize, v. a. *baptizāre*, 1 c.
Baptism, s. *baptisma*, *ătis*, 3 d. neut.
Bar or bolt, s. *vectis*, *is*, m.
Barricade, s. *impĕdīmentum*, 2 d. n.
Barriers, s. *līmĭtes*, *fīnes*
Barber, s. *tonsor*, 3 d. m.
Bargain, s. *pactum*, 2 d. n.
Barge, s. *nāvĭgium*, 2 d. n.
Bark, v. n. *latrāre*, 1 c.
—— of a tree, s. *cortex*, 3 d.
Barn, s. *horreum*, 2 d. n.
Barrel, s. *cadus*, 2 d. m. *dolium*, neut.

Barren, adj. *sterilis*
Bashfulness, s. *pudor*, 3 d. m.
Basket, s. *cophinus*, 2 d. m. *corbis*, 3 d.
Bason, s. *crāter*, *crātēris*, m. *pelvis*, 3 d. f.
—— (sugar), s. *sacchări*
Bath, s. *balneum*, 2 d. n.
Bathe, v. a. *ire lăvātum*, *lăvāre*
Bathed, adj. *lōtum*, *lăvātum*
Battle, s. *pugna*, æ
Bay (a colour), adj. *fulvus*, *bădius*, *a*, *um*
— (a horse), s. *ĕquus bădius*
Be (to), v. n. *esse*
— so good as, *quæso ut facias*
— (I shall), *ero*
— (I shall not), *non ero*
— quiet, *esto tranquillus*, *quiesce*, *sile*
— (let them), *taceant*, *requiescant*
— imper. *sis*, *es*, *esto*
— (do not), *ne sis*
— so rash (do not), *ne sis tam tĕmĕrārius*
'Beadle, s. *præco*, *onis*, 3 d.
Beans, french beans, *făbæ*, 1 d. f. *phaseoli*, 2 d. m.
Bear (to), v. a. *ferre*, *portāre*
—— with (to), *indulgēre*, 2 c. *ferre*
—— him (I cannot), *non possum ferre hunc*
—— the sight of (to), *ferre conspectum*
—— an animal, s. *ursus*, m. *ursa*, f.
Beard, s. *barba*, *æ* f.
Bearer, s. *portitor*, 3 d.
Beast, s. *bestia*, f. *fera*, f. *bellua*, f.

Beasts, s. pl. *bestiæ, arum*
Beat (to), v. a. *verberāre*, 1 c. *cædĕre*, 3 c.
Beautiful, adj. *pulcher, pulchra, pulchrum, formosus*
Beauty, s. *pulchritudo*, f.
Beaver, s. *castor*, 3 d. m.
Because, conj. *quia, quòd*
Become (to), v. n. *fieri*
Becoming, adj. *gracilis, aptus*
——— your age, *ætati tuæ congruens*
Bed, s. *lectus*, 2 d. m. *cubile*, 3 d. n. *torus*, 2 d. m.
— clothes, *stragula*, s. pl. n.
— room, *cŭbĭcŭlum*, 2 d. n.
— side, *prope lectum*
— stead, *sponda*, 1 d. f.
Bee, s. *apis*, 3 d. f.
Beech, s. *fagus*, 2 d. f.
Beef, s. *caro bŭbŭla*
—— (roast), s. *bŭbŭla assata vel tosta*
Being, part. of to be, use at times in Lat. *an ablative absolute*
Been (he has), *fuit, ille fuit*
Beer, s. *cĕrĕvisia*, 1 d. f.
Befal, v. n. *evenire*, 4 c.
Before, *ante, prius*
——— long, *multo ante*
——— *or* in the presence of the king, *coram rege*
——— seven o'clock, *ante horam septimam*
Beg, v. *rogāre, pĕtĕre, mendicāre, orāre, supplicāre, obsecrāre*
—— leave (I), *permittas velim*
—— pardon (to), *veniam petere*
Beg your pardon (I), *oro ut mihi ignoscas*
—— bread, v. *panem rogāre*
Beggary, s. *mendĭcĭtas*, 3 d. f.
Begin (to), v. a. *incĭpere*, 3 c.
Beginning, s. *principium, initium*
Begun, p. p. *inchoātus*
Behalf (in my), *mei gratiâ*
Behave, v. n. *se præbĕre*
Behaviour, s. *mores, consuetudo*
Behind, prep. adv. *post, pone*
Behold! *en! ecce!*
Being, s. *ănimal*, 3 d. n. *res creata vel existens*
—— part, *pars*, s. 3 d. f.
—— asked, *rŏgātus*
—— told, *certior factus*
Belief, s. *fides*, 5 d. f.
Believe (to), v. a. *credere, fidem dare*
Believed, p. p. *crēdĭtus*
Bell of a church, s. *campāna*, 1 d. f.
— of a room, s. *tintinnābŭlum*, 2 d. n.
— (ring the), *sona tintinnabulum, tinnito*
Bellowing, s. *mūgītus*, 4 d. m.
Belong, v. n. *pertinēre*, 2 c.
Belonging to, *attinens*
Beloved, p. p. *ămātus*
Below, adv. *sub*
Belt, s. *cingŭlum*, 2 d. n.
Bench, s. *sĕdīle*, 3 d. n.
Bend, v. *curvāre, flectĕre*
Benefited, *profectus, se meliùs habere*
Bengal, *India*, æ f.
Bent, (inclination), s. *dispŏsĭtio, inclīnātio*

Bent part. *flexus, a, um*
Berry, s. *bacca*, 1 d. f.
Beseech, v. *obsecrāre*, 1 c.
Besides, prep. *præter*
Beside, adv. *prætĕreà*
Best, super. of good, *optimus, a, um*
Bestow, v. a. *largiri, dōnare*
Bet, s. *pignus*, 3 d. n.
— v. *pignus deponere*
Betimes, adv. *tempori, manè*
Better, comp. of good, *mĕlior, mĕlius*
——— place, s. *melior locus*
——— and better, *melius atque melius*
——— day the better deed, *optima quæque dies rem optimè gestam debet præbere*
Between, prep. *inter, in medio positus*
Beverage, s. *pōtus*, 4 d. m. *pōtio*, 3 d. f.
Beyond, prep. *ultra, trans*
Bible, s. *biblia, ōrum*, pl. s. n.
Bid, invite (to), *rogatus, vocatus*
Bier, s. *fĕretrum*, 2 d. n.
Big, adj. *magnus*
Bill, s. *syngrapha*, æ f.
Bills of exchange, *tesseræ nummariæ*
Bind, v. *ligāre*, 1 c.
Bird, *avis*, 3 d. f.
—— cage, s. *căvea*, æ f.
Bird's nest, s. *nīdus*, i m. *nīdŭlus, i*, m.
Birth, s. *ortus*, 4 d. m. *partus*, 4 d. m.
—— day, s. *dies natalis*
Biscuit, s. *panis nauticus*
Bishop, s. *episcopus*, 2 d. m.
Bit, s. (a piece), *frustum, pars*
— (of a bridle), *lupatum, i*, n.
Bite, v. a. *mordēre*, 2 c.
—— (a), s. *morsus*, 4 d. m.
Bitten, p. p. *morsus, part.*
Bitter, adj. *amarus, a, um*
Bitterness, s. *amaritudo*, 3 d. f. *asperitas*, 3 d. f.
Black, adj. *nĭger, nigra, nigrum*
—— berries, s. *mōra*, 2 d. n.
—— bird, s. *merula*, æ f.
—— lead, s. *stibium*, 2 d. n.
—— smith, s. *faber ferrarius*
—— silk, s. *sērĭcum nigrum*
Bladder, s. *vesica*, 1 d. f.
Blade, s. *cultri vel ensis lamina*
—— of corn, *caulis frumenti*
Blame, v. a. *culpāre*, 1 c.
Blanket, s. *stragulum*, 2 d. n.
Bleed, v. *sanguinem amittere*
—— any one (to), v. a. *vēnam alicui incidere*
Bled, p. p. *venâ incisus*
Blemish, v. *maculare*, 1 c.
Bless, v. a. *bĕnĕdīcĕre*, 3 c.
Blessing, s. *bĕnĕdictio*, 3 d. f.
Blessed, p. p. *beatus, benedictus*
Blind, v. *cæcāre*, 1 c. *fallĕre*,
—— adj. *cæcus, captus aculis*
—— of an eye, *luscus*
Blindness, s. *cæcĭtas*, 3 d. f.
Blister, s. *vesicatorium*, 2 d.
Blockhead, s. *stipes*, 3 d. m.
Blood, s. *sanguis*, 3 d. m.
—— horse, *ĕquus gĕnĕrōsus*
Blossom, s. *flos*, 3 d. m.
———— v. n. *florēre*, 2 c.
Blot, s. *litura, macula*
Blotting-paper, *charta bibula*

Blow (a thump), s. *cŏlăphus*, 2 d. m. *ictus*, 4 d m.
—— (to), as flowers, v. n. *florere, efflorescere*
The wind blows hard, *vehementer ventus perflat*
—— out the candles (to), *efflāre lucernam*
—— your nose, *te emunge*
Blue, adj. *cærŭleus*
—— bottle, s. *musca*, 1 d. f.
Blunder, s. *error, hallūcĭnātio*
Blunt, adj. *obtusus, hebes*
Blush, v. n. *erubescere*, 3 c.
—— s. *rubor*, 3 d. m.
Boar, s. *aper*, 2 d. m. *porcus*, 2 d. m.
Board with planks (to), v. *contăbŭlāre*
—— and lodge a person, *accipere quemquam mensâ et domo*
—— (to go on), *in navem conscendere*
Boarding-school, *convictio literaria*
Boast (to), v. n. *jactāre*, 1 c. *gloriāri*, 1 c. dep.
—— s. *jactatio*, 3 d. f. *gloriatio*
Boaster, s. *jactĭtātor*, 3 d. m.
Boat, s. *navicula, cymba*, 1 d. f.
—— man, s. *remex*, 3 d. m.
Body (dead), *cădāver*, 3 d. n.
Bodily, adj. *corporeus*
Body, s. *corpus*, 3 d. n.
—— (a busy), s. *ardelio, ōnis*, c. g.
—— (every), *unusquisque, singuli*
—— (no), *nēmo*
—— (some), *quidam, ălĭquis*

Boil, v. *bullīre*, 4 c.
Bold, adj. *audax*
Boldly, adv. *audacter*
Boldness, s. *audacia*, æ f.
Bolster, s. *pulvīnar*, 3 d. n.
Bolt, s. *pessulus*, 2 d. m.
Bone, s. *os*, 3 d. n.
—— of fish, *os piscis*
Book, s. *līber, libri*, m.
—— (day), s. *diarium*, 2 d. n.
—— (pocket), s. *libellus in loculis portandus*
—— binder, s. *bibliŏpēgus*, 2 d. m.
—— (prayer), *liber precum*
—— seller, *bibliŏpōla*, 1 d. m.
Booth, s. *velabrum*, 2 d. n.
Boot-maker, s. *sūtor ocrearum*
Boots, s. *ocreæ*
Border, s. *margo*, 3 d. *finis*, 3 d.
—— v. a. *accolĕre*, irr. *finire*, 4 c.
Born, adj. *natus*
—— (to be), v. *nasci*, dep. irr.
Borough, s. *municipium*, 2 d. n.
Borrow, v. a. *mutuo sumere, mutuāri*
Bosom, s. *sinus*. 4 d. m. *gremium*, 2 d. n.
Both, pron. *ambo, uterque*
—— my brother and I were there, *et frater meus et ego adfuimus*
Bottle, s. *uter*, 3 d. m. *ampulla*, 1 d. f.
Bottom, s. *fundus*, i m.
—— of a hill, *radix montis*
Bough, s. *ramus*, 2 d. m. *frons*, 3 d. f.
Bought, p. p. *emptus*

Bound for (to be), *vadāri* dep. *confirmatorem esse pecuniæ, obligari*, 1 c.
——— (as a book), *compactus*
Bountiful, adj. *bĕnĕficus*
Bounty, s. *largitas, benignitas*
Bow, s. *salutatio*, 3 d. f.
—— the soldier's, *arcus*, 4 d. m.
—— rain, *iris, irĭdis*, f. *arcus cœlestis*
—— (to), v. *salutāre*, 1 c.
—— or bend, *flectĕre*, 3 c.
Bower, s. *pergula*, 1 d. f.
Box, s. *arca*, 1 d. *cista*, 1 d.
—— (money), *arca nummorum*
—— (christmas), *strena*, æ f.
—— of a play-house, *casa theatralis*
—— on the ear, *alapa*, æ f.
—— tree, *buxus*, i 2 d. f.
Boy, s. *puer*, 2 d.
Bracelet, s. *armilla*, æ f.
Brain (the), *cĕrĕbrum*, 2 d. n.
Bran, s. *furfur, ŭris*, m.
Branch, s. *rāmus*, i
Brandy, s. *vini spiritus ardens*
Brass, s. *æs, æris*, n.
Brave, adj. *fortis*
Braying of an ass, *rŭditus*, 4 d.
Bread, s. *pānis*, 3 d. m.
——— (new), *recens panis*
——— stale, *durus panis*
Breadth, s. *lătitūdo*, 3 d. f.
Break of day, *diluculum*, 2 d. n.
Breakfast, s. *jentaculum*, 2 d. n.
Breakfast (to). v. *jentāre*, 1 c.
Breast, s. *pectus*, 3 d. n. *uber*, 3 d. n.
Breath, s. *spiritus*, 4 d. m. *halitus, flatus*
Brew, v. *cŏquere cerevisiam*
—— house, s. *zythepsarium*, 2 d. n.
Brewer, s. *cerevisiæ coctor*
Brick, s. *later*, 3 d. m.
—— house, s. *domus lateribus ædificata*
—— layer, s. *laterum structor*
Bricked, p. p. *laterum constructus*
Brier (sweet), *cynosbătos*, i f.
Bride, s. *nupta*, æ 1 c.
Bridge, s. *pons*, 3 d. m.
Bridle, s. *habena*, 1 d. f. *frænum*, 2 d. n.
Brief, adj. *brevis*
Bright, adj. *splendens, lucidus*
Brim of a hat, *limbus galeri*
Bring, v. a. *afferre*
—— back, v. *referre*
—— up, v. *educāre*, 1 c. *alĕre*, 3 c.
British, adj. *Britannicus*
——— Museum, *Museum Britannicum*, n.
Broad, adj. *latus*
Broken, adj. *fractus, a, um*
Brook, s. *rivulus*, 2 d. m.
Broom, s. utensil, *scopa*, f. sing. *et scopæ*, f. pl.
——— s. plant, *genista*, 1 d. f. *spartum*, 2 d. n.
Broth, s. *jus*, 3 d. n. *jusculum*, 2 d. n.
Brother, s. *frater*, 3 d.
——— in law, s. *frater mariti*
Brought, p. p. *latus, adductus*

Brown, adj. *fuscus*
Brush, s. *scopula*, æ f. *verriculum*, *i* n.
—— v. a. *scopulâ purgare*, *verrĕre*
Brute, s. *bestia*, 1 d. f.
Brutish, adj. *ferinus*, *brutus*
Bucket, s. *sitŭla*, 1 d. f.
Buckle, s. *fibula*, 1 d. f.
Bud, s. *germen*, 3 d. n.
— v. n. *germināre*, 1 c.
Bug, s. *cimex*, 3 d. m.
Build, *ædificāre*, 1 c.
Building, s. *ædificium*, *ædes*
Built, p. p. *extructus*
Bull, s. *taurus*, 2 d.
— finch, *rubicilla*, 1 d. f.
Bunch of grapes, *răcēmus*, 2 d. m.
—— of keys, *fasciculus clavium*
Bundle, s. *sarcinula*, æ f.
Burden, s. *onus*, *eris*, n.
Burgundy, s. *Burgundia*, æ f.
Burial, s. *exequiæ*, s. pl. *funus*, 3 d. n.
Burn, v. a. *urĕre*, *cremāre*
Burst, v. a. *disrumpere*, 3 c.
—— out crying, *in lachrymas effundi*
—— out laughing (he), *in risum prorupit*
Bury, v. a. *sĕpĕlīre*, 4 c.
Burying, s. *sĕpultūra*, 1 d.
Bush, s. *rŭbus*, 2 d. m.
Business, s. *negotium*, 2 d. n.
Busy, adj. *occupatus*, *diligens*
But, conj. *sed*
— why has he not? *cur autem ille non fecit*
— the most surprising, *sed res mirabilior*
But how are we to do, *at nos quomodo agemus?*
— (in the sense of only), *tantum*
— we have but ten thousand, *habemus decem millia tantum*
— I have but a guinea, *habeo tantum viginti unum solidos*
Butcher, s. *lanius*, 2 d. m.
Butler, s. *promus*, 2 d. m.
Butter, s. *butyrum*, 2 d. n.
—— market, s. *mercatus butyri*
—— man, s. *vendĭtor butyri*
Butterfly, s. *papilio*
Button, s. *fibula*, æ f.
Button hole, *fissura fibulæ*
Buy, v. a. *emĕre*, 3 c. *mercāri* 1 c. dep.
By, prep. *à*, *per*, *juxta*, *secundum*
— (to put), v. a. *seponĕre*, 3 c.
— (praised), *laudatus à*
— (loved), *dilectus ab*
— oneself, *solus*
— all means, *certè*
— no means, *nullo mŏdo*
— the bye, *obiter*
— three o'clock, *ad horam tertiam*
— yourself, *tu solus*
— and bye, *continuò*, *mox*
— giving, *dante*, part. *dando* ger.
— speaking, *loquendo*, ger.
— two feet, *duobus pedibus*
— it, *ab eo*
— much, *multò*
— Mr. F. *à F.*

By one o'clock, *ad horam primam**
— stander, *astans*
— whom, *à quo*
By water, *aquâ*
— sight, *visu*
Bye-way, *semita devia*

C

Cabbage, s. *caulis*, 3 d. m.
Cabin, s. *stega*, æ f.
—— boy, s. *puer nauclero serviens*
Cage, s. *aviarium, cavea*
Cake, s. *placenta*, æ f.
Calamity, s. *calamitas, atis*
Calf, s. *vitulus*, 2 d. m. *vitula* 1 d. f.
Calf's-head, s. *caput vitŭlinum*
Calico, s. *tela xyli*
Call, v. a. *vocāre*
—— upon, v. *visĕre*
—— again, v. *rursùm visĕre*
—— out, v. *evocare*
—— (a), s. *visitatio*, 3 d. f.
—— at (to), *compellāre*, 1 c.
—— up in the morning, *expergefacere*
—— my servants at five, *expergeface servos meos ad quintam horam*
Called upon to do it (if I am), *ego si vocatus sim ad id faciendum*
Calling me (there is some one), *aliquis me appellat*
Calm, s. *serenitas, atis*
—— (to), v. a. *placāre*, 1 c.
Cambric, s. *tela lini, sindon* 3 d. f.
Came (he), *vēnit*
Camel, s. *camelus*
Camp, s. *castra, orum*, s. pl. n.
Canal, s. *canalis*, 3 d.
Can, v. defect, *posse*
— (I), you can, they can, *possum, potes, possunt*
— you swim ?, *potesne natāre ?*
I cannot, *nĕqueo*
It cannot be, *non potest esse*
Canary bird, s. *avis Canaria*
Candle, s. *candela, lucerna*, 1 d. f
——— stick, *candelabrum*, i.
Cane, s. *canna*, 1 d. f. *calamus*, 2 d. m.
Cannon, s. *tormentum novum bellicum*
——— ball, shot, s. *glandes ferreæ*
Cap, s. *calyptra, pileus*
Capable, adj. *idoneus, habilis*
Capital, s. *metrŏpŏlis, eos*, f.
——— adj. *capitalis*
Capon, s. *căpo, ōnis*, 3 d. m.

* The Romans, like the Turks, reckoned from sunrise; but in elementary books it is not customary, in speaking of the hour, to observe that distinction.

Captain, s. *centurio*, 3 d. *dux, ducis*
Card, s. *charta*, æ f.
Cards (a pack of), *chartæ lusoriæ vel pictæ*
—— (to play at), *illudere chartis*
Cardinal, s. *cardĭnālis, is*, 3 d.
Care, s. *cura, anxietas*
—— v. *curare*
—— to beware, *prōvĭdēre*
—— (I do not), *non equidem curo*
Careful, adj. *sedulus, solicitus*
Careless, adj. *negligens*
Carelessly, adv. *inconsideratè*
Carnation, s. *caryophyllon*, 2 d. n.
———— color, s. *color caryophylli, minium*
Carp, s. *carpio*, 3 d. m.
Carpenter, s. *faber lignarius*
Carpet, s. *tapes, ētis*, 3 d. m. *storea*, 1 d. f.
Carriage, s. *vehiculum*, 2 d. n. *rhēda*, 1 d. f.
———— (air, demeanour), *gestus*, 4 d. m.
Carry, v. a. *gerĕre, portāre*
—— to prison, *conjicere in carcerem*
—— away, *auferre*
Cart, s. *carrus*, m. *plaustrum*, n.
Case, s. *res, conditio*
—— (in), *si hoc eveniat*
Cash, s. *nummus*, 2 d. m.
Cashier, s. *nummularius*, 2 d. m.
Cask, s. *cadus*, m. *testa*, f.
Castle, s. *castellum*, 2 d. n.
Cat, s. *felis*, 3 d. f.
Catch, v. a. *prehendere, arripere*
—— a cold (to), *gravedine laborare*
Catching, adj. *pestiferus*
Caterpillar, s. *volvox, ōcis*, m.
Catholic, s. *catholicus*, m. *catholica*, f.
Cato, s. prop. *Cato, onis*, 3 d.
Cattle, s. *pecus*, 3 d. n.
Cauliflower, s. *brassica florida*
Cause, s. *causa*, æ f.
Cease, v. n. *intermittĕre*, 3 c.
Ceiling, s. *lacunar, laquear*
Celebrated, adj. *celebris*
Cellar, s. *cellārium*, 2 d. n.
Cent (per.) *per centum*
Centage (per), *per centum*, (*qu. agere*)
Century, s. *seculum, ævum*
Ceremony, s. *cærĕmōnia*, æ f.
Certain, adj. *certus, a, um*
Certainly, adv. *certè*
Certainty, s. *vērum*, 2 d. n. *vērĭtas*, 3 d. f.
Chaff, s. *pālea*, 1 d. f.
Chaffinch, s. *frīgilla*, 1 d. f.
Chain, s. *catena*, æ
Chair, s. *sella, cathedra*
—— (arm), s. *sŏlium*, 2 d. n.
Chaise (post), s. *rhēda*, 1 d. f.
Challenge, s. *provocatio*, 3 d.
Chamber, *cămĕra, cubiculum*
Chandler (tallow), s. *candelarum venditor*
——— (wax), s. *cērārius*, 2 d. m.
Change, s. *vicissitudo*, 3 d. f.
——— of air, *varietas loci*
——— (money), *commutatio auri et argenti, pecunia*

Changeable. adj. *inconstans*
Channel (the), s. *fretum*, 2 d. n.
Chapel. s. *sacellum*, 2 d. n.
Character, s. *fama, existimatio*
Charcoal, s. *carbo lignarius*
Charge, s. *accusatio*, 3 d. f. *munus*, 3 d. n.
——— v. a. *imperare, accusare*
Charitable, adj. *benignus*
Charity (begins at home), *benignitas domi primùm*
Charles, s. *Carolus*, 2 d.
Charm, s. *incantamentum, illecebra*
——— v. a. *delectare, incantare*
Chatter, v. n. *garrīre*, 4 c.
Chattering, s. *loquacitas*, 3 d. f.
——— fellow, s. *garrulus*, 2 d.
——— of parrots, s. *garrŭlitas, ātis*, f.
Cheap, adj. *vilis pretii*
Cheaper, comparat. of cheap, *vilior, us*
Cheap (very), *pervilis pretii*
Cheat, v. a. *fraudāre*, 1 c.
——— at play, v. *fraudāre ludendo*
Cheat, s. *impostor*, 3 d.
Cheerful, adj. *hilaris, lætus*
Cheerfulness, s. *hilaritas, ātis*, f.
Cheese, s. *cāseus*, 2 d. m.
Chemistry, s. *chymia*, æ f.
Cherry, s. *cĕrăsum*, 2 d. n.
——— stone, s. *ăcĭnus*, *i* m.
——— tree, s. *cĕrăsus*, 2 d. f.
Chess, s. *ludus latrunculorum*
Chest, s. *cista*, æ f.
——— of drawers, *cistulæ tractiles*
Chestnut, s. *nux castanea*
——— tree, *castanea*, æ f.
Chicken, s. *pullus gallinaceus*
Chief, s. *dux, princeps*
——— officers, *duces, centuriones*
Chilblains, s. *perniōnes*, m.
Child, s. *infans*, 3 d.
Childhood, s. *pueritia*, 1 d. f.
Children, s. pl. *liberi*, pl. m.
Chimney, s. *cămīnus*, 2 d. m.
Chin, s. *mentum*, 2 d. n.
China, s. *Sīna*, æ f.
——— ware, *vasa Sinensia*
Chinese, s. *Sinæ, arum*, pl. *Sinenses, ium*, pl.
——— adj, *Sinensis*
Chòcolate, s. *cacao, potus*
Choice, s. *electio, delectus*
Choose, v. a. *eligĕre, seligĕre, malle*
——— (which do you), *utrum mavis?*
Christ, s. pr. *Christus*
Christmas, *Christi festum*
——— eve, *pridie diei Christi natalis*
Christen (to), v. a. *baptizāre*
Christening, s. *baptisma*, n. *baptismus*, m.
Church, s. *ecclesia, templum*
——— yard, *cemeterium*, 2 d. n.
Cider, s. *succus è pomis*
Cinders, s. *cinis*, 3 d.
Cinnamon, *cinnămōmum*, 2 d. n.

Circumstance, s. *res*, 5 d. f.
Citizen, s. *civis*, 3 d.
City, s. *civitas*, 3 d.
Civil, adj. *civilis*, *urbanus*
Civility, s. *cōmĭtas*, *urbanitas*
Clasp, s. *fibula*, 1 d. f.
Clean, v. a. *mundāre*, 1 c.
—— adj. *nitidus*, *mundus*
Cleaned, adj. *abstersus*
Cleanliness, s. *mundities*, 5 d. f.
Clear, adj. *lucidus*
Clemency, s. *clementia*, 1 d. f.
Clerk, or clergyman, *clĕrĭcus*, 2 d.
—— (church), s. *sacrista*, 1 d. m.
—— for writing and accounts, *scriba*, 1 d. m.
Clever, adj. *hăbĭlis*, *solers*
Client, s. *cliens*, 3 d. c. g.
Climate, s. *regio*, *clima*
Clock, s. *horologium*, 2 d. n.
—— (church), s. *horologium*, 2 d. n.
—— (parlour), s. *horologium*, 2 d. n.
—— (what is it o'), *quotâ est horâ*
Closet, s. *conclāve*, *is*, m.
Cloth, s. (linen), *linum*, 2 d. n. *linteum*, 2 d. n.
—— (woolen), *pannus*, 2 d. m.
—— (table), *mappa*, 1 d. f.
—— (horse), *pannus equi*
—— (lay the), *instrue mensam*
Clothe, v. a. *vestīre*, 4 c.
Clothes, s. pl. *vestes*, *vestimenta*
—— (suit of), s. *vestimentum*, 2 d. n.
Clothes (bed), s. *stragula*, s. pl. n.
Clothing, s. *vestitus*, 4 d. m.
Cloud, s. *nubes*, 3 d. f.
Cloudy, adj. *nubilus*
Clover, s. *trĭfŏlium*, 2 d. n.
Club, s. *fustis*, 3 d. m.
Clump, s. *massa*, *gleba*
Coach, s. *vehiculum*, 2 d. n.
—— (by), adv. *vehiculo*
—— (hackney), s. *currus meritorius*
—— house, s. *stabulum rhedarium*
—— maker, s. *faber vehiculorum*
—— man, s. *conductor*, *auriga*
Coal, s. *carbo*, 3 d. m.
—— house, s. *rĕceptācŭlum carbonarium*
—— (load of), *carrus carbonum*
—— pits, *carbonariæ fodinæ*
—— (pit), *carbo ex fŏdinis*
Coarse, adj. *crassus*, *a*, *um*
Coast, s. *ora*, f. *littus*, 3 d. n.
Coat, s. *tunica*, f. *vestis*, f.
Cobweb, s. *aranea*, f. *araneus*, m.
Cock, s. *gallus*, 2 d.
Coffee, s. *kupha*, 1 d. f.
—— mill, s. *mola kuphæ*
Coffin, s. *sandăpĭla*, *loculus*, *sarcophagus*
Coin, s. *moneta*, *nummus*
Cold, adj *frigidus*, *gelidus*
—— (to have a), *gravedine laborare*
—— (I have a very bad), *valde ægroto ex gravedine*
—— (it is), *friget*
—— (I am), *frigeo*

Cold (it was), *frigescebat*
—— (to be), *frigescĕre, rigēre*
—— (he is), *frigescit*
—— (I was), *frixi*
—— (my feet are), *pedes meæ frigent*
—— (my hands are), *manus meæ algore dolent*
Collar, s. *căpistrum, i* n.
College, s. *collēgium*, 2 d. n.
Colonel, s. *chĭliarchus*, 2 d.
Color, s. *cŏlor*
—— box, *cista colorum*
Colt, s. *pullus equinus*
Comb, s. *pecten*, 3 d. m.
—— (to), v. a. *pectĕre*
Come, v. n. *venīre*, 4 c.
—— (are they), v. *venerunt ne?*
—— back (to), v. *redīre*
—— to (how much do they), v. *quantum faciunt?*
—— again (to), v. *rursùs venire*
—— forward (to), v. *procedĕre*, 3 c.
—— out (to), v. *exīre*, 4 c.
—— down (to), v. *descendere*, 3 c.
—— here, *hùc veni*
—— near, *appropinqua, veni propius*
Comedy, s. *cōmœdia, æ* f.
Comfort, s. *solatium*, 2 d. n.
Comfortable, adj. *consolans, dulcis*
Coming (they are), *vĕniunt*
—— (he is), *vĕnit*
Command, v. a. *imperāre*, 1 c.
Commit, v. a. *committĕre*, 3 c.
Common, s. *communis vel compascuus ager*
Common, adj. *commūnis*
Commonly, adv. *communitèr, vulgò*
Commons (House of), *senatus inferior*
Companion, s. *cŏmes, socius, commilito, consors*
Company, s. *societas*, 3 d. f.
—— (East-India), *societas mercaturæ Indiæ Orientalis*
Compare, v. a. *comparāre*, 1 c.
Complain, v. n. *quĕri*, 3 c. dep.
Complained of, *accusatus*
Complaint, s. *querela, morbus*
Complaisant, adj. *comis*
Complete, adj. *perfectus*
Completely, adv. *perfectè*
Compliments, s. *salutatio*
Compose, v. a. *componĕre*, 3 c.
Conceal, v. a. *celare, occultare*
Condescend, v. n. *concedĕre, obsequi*
Condemn, v. a. *damnare, culpare*
Condition, s. *status, conditio*
—— (on). *eâ conditione*
Conduct, s. *vitæ ratio*
Confess, v. a. *confitēri*, dep.
Confusion, s. *confūsio*, 3 d. f.
Congratulate, v. a. *gratulāri*, dep.
Connection, s. *connexio, parens, affinis*
Conscience, s. *conscientia, æ*
Consent, v. n. *assentīre*, 4 c.
—— s. *assensus*
Consequences, s. *effectus*, 4 d. *exitus*, 4 d.
Conservatory, s. *conservatorium*, 2 d. n.

Consider, v. *meditari, considerare*
Considerable, adj. *magnus, clarus*
Consist, v. *consistĕre*, 3 c.
Consort, s. *conjux*, 3 d. f.
Conspiracy, s, *conjūrātio*, 3 d. f.
Constancy, s. *constantia*, 1 d.
Constant, adj. *constans, fidelis*
Constantly, adv. *constanter*
Constitution (the), *magna charta, constitutio regni*
————, bodily, *habitus corporis*
Consult, v. a. *consultāre*, 1 c.
Contain, v. a. *continēre*, 2 c.
Contempt, s. *despectus, contemptus*
Contemptible, adj. *vilis*
Content, v. a. *placēre*, 2 c. *satisfacĕre*, 3 c.
Contented, *contentus*
Contents, s. *res inclusæ, argumentum*
Contentment, s. *oblectatio*, 3 d. f.
Continent, s. *continens*, 3 d.
Continental, adj. *ad continentem pertinens, continentalis*
Continue, v. n. *continuĕre*, 3 c.
Contradict, v. a. *contrădīcĕre*, 3 c.
Contrary, adj. *contrarius, oppositus*
Contribute, v. a. *contrĭbuĕre*, 3 c.
Conversant, adj. *versatus*
Conversation, s. *collŏquium*, n. *diălŏgus*, m.
Converse, v. n. *collŏqui*, 3 c.
Convince, v. a. *convincerè, persuadere*
Cook, s. *cŏquus*, m. *ancilla culinæ*
—— v. a. *cŏquere*, 3 c.
—— shop, s. *pŏpīna*, 1 d. f.
Cool, adj. *frigidus, opacus*
—— v. a. *refrigerāre*, 1 c.
Copper (a), s. *caldārium*, 2 d. n.
——— (the metal), s. *orichalcum, cŭprum*, n.
Copy, v. a. *imitāri*, dep. *transcrībĕre*
—— s. *exemplar, apographum*
—— book, s. *chartæ*
Cork, s. *sūber*
—— screw, s. *cochlĕa*, æ f.
Corn, *far, seges*, &c.
—— (or oats), s. *avena*, æ
—— (on the toe), s. *callus*, 2 d. m.
—— market, s. *mercatus frumenti*
—— factors, s. *venditores farris*
Corner, s. *angulus*, 2 d. m.
Coronation, s. *inauguratio*, 3 d. f.
Correct, v. a. *castigāre, corrĭgĕre*
——— adj. *accuratus*
Correspond, v. n. *literas scribere*
Cost, v. *constāre*, 1 c.
—— costs, s. *sumptus, ūs*, m.
Cottage, s. *căsa*, æ f.
Covetous, adj. *avarus, avidus*
Covetously, adv. *cupidè, avarè*
Cough, v. n. *tussīre*, 4 c.
——— s. *tussis*, 3 d. f.
Could, v. *possem*

Could yesterday (I), *potui heri*
——— do it (if I), *id si possem facere*
——— I but see them, *si modo illos videre possem*
Coulter, s. *culter*, 2 d. m.
Council, s. *concĭlium*, 2 d. n.
——— ecclesiastical, s. *synodus*, 2 d. f.
Counsel, s. *consilium*, 2 d. n.
——— s. *jurisconsultus*, 2 d. m.
——— v. a. *monēre*, 2 c.
Count, v. a. *computāre, numerāre*
——— time in music, *reddere ictus musicæ*
——— (a title), s. *comes*, 3 d.
Counter, s. *loculus vel abacus*
——— at cards, s. *calcŭlus*, 2 d. m.
Country, s. *rus*. 3 d. n.
——— house, s. *villa*, æ f.
——— man, s. *rusticus*
——— seat, s. *villa*, 1 d. f.
——— (in the), s. *rure*
——— (native), s. *patria*, 1 d. f.
County, s. *provincia, comitatus*
Courage, s. *virtus*, 3 d. f. *constantia*, f.
Courageous, adj *fortis, strenuus*
Course, s. *via*, f. *cursus*, 4 d. m.
——— (of), *sicut mos est*
——— of a fortnight (in the), *intra dies quatuordecim*
Court, s. *regia*, 1 f.
——— yard, s. *area*, 1 f.
Cousin, s. *consanguĭneus*, 2 d. m.

Cow, s. *bos, vacca, juvenca*
——— house, s. *bŏvīle, is*, n.
Coward, s. and adj. *timidus, ignavus*
Cowardice, s. *timiditas*, 3 d. f.
Coxcomb, s. *fătuus*, 2 d. m.
Crack, s. *rima*, 1 d. f.
Cracked, p. p. *pertusus, rimas habens*
Cradle, s. *cūnābŭla*, pl. *cūnæ*, pl.
Cravat, s. *collārium*, 2 d. n.
Cream, s. *flos lactis*
——— cheese, s. *caseus ex flore lactis*
——— jug, s. *canthărus*, 2 d. m.
Creator, s. *creator*, 3 d. m.
Creature, s. *creātūra, animal*
Credit s. *fides*, 5 d. f.
Credulous, adj. *crēdŭlus*
Creed, s. *symbolum fidei*
Cricket, s. *ludus baculi et pilæ*
Cries, s. *clamores, lamentationes*
Crime, s. *facinus, delictus, crīmen*
Criminal, s. *sons, reus*
——— adj. *crīmĭnālis*
Crimson, adj. *coccĭneus*
Cross, s. *crux, ŭcis*, f.
——— (to be), *irasci*, 3 c. dep.
——— (she is always so), *illa semper irascitur*
——— over (to), v. *transīre*, irr.
Crotchet, s. *semiminima*, 1 d. f.
Crow, s. *cornix*, 3 d. f.
Crowd, s. *turba*, 1 d. f.
——— of children, s. *turba puerorum*

Crown, s. *cŏrōna, diadema*
——— (money), s. *cŏrōnātus* 2 d. m.
——— of a hat, s. *superior pars pilei*
——— v. a. *coronāre*, 1 c.
Crowned, p. p. *cŏrōnātus*
Cruel, adj. *crudelis*
Cruelty, s. *crudelitas*, 3 d. f.
Cruet, s. *ampulla*, æ f.
—— stand, s. *admĭnĭcŭlum ampullarum*
Cruising (we were), *circumnavigabamus*
Crumb, s. *medulla panis*
Crust, s. *crustum*, 2 d. n.
Crutches, s. *grallæ*, s. pl. f.
Cry, s. *clamor*, 3 d. m.
—— v. n. *clamāre*, 1 c.
—— for help, v. *implorāre*, 1 c.
—— to lament, v. *lamentari*, 1 c. dep.
—— out, v. *exclamāre*, 1 c.
Cucumber, s. *cucumis*, 3 d. m.
Cultivate, v. a. *colĕre*, 3 c.
Cunning, adj. *astutus, versutus*
——— man (a), s. *homo versutus*

Cup, s. *poculum*, 2 d. n.
— board, s. *abacus*, 2 d. m.
Cupola, s. *fastigium rotundum*
Curate, s. *clericus, vicarius*
Curb, s. *lupatum*, 2 d. n.
Cure, v. a. *sanāre*, 1 c.
Curiosity, s. *curiositas*, 3 d. f.
Curious, adj. *curiosus*
Currants, s. currant bushes, *uvæ Corinthiacæ*
Curry-comb, s. *strigilis*, 3 d. f.
Cushion, s. *pulvinar*, 3 d. n.
Custom, s. *mos, consetudo*
Customer, s. *emptor*, 3 d. m.
Custom-house, *telonium*, 2 d. n.
——— officer, s. *publicanus*, 2 d. m.
Customs (the), *vectīgal, ālis*, n.
Cut, s. *plaga, scissura*, f.
— v. a. *secāre*, 1 c.
— down, v. a. *cædĕre*, 3 c.
— oneself, v. a. *se secare*
— out, v. a. *exscindĕre*, 3 c.
Cutler, s. *faber cultarius*
Cutlets, s. pl. *segmina*, pl. n.
Cutter, s. *lembus*, 2 d. m.

D

Daily, adv. *quŏtīdiānò*
Daintiness, s. *dapes*, pl. f.
Dainty, adj. *delicatus*
Dairy, s. *lactarium*, 2 d. n.
Daisy, s. *bellis*, 3 d. f.
Damage, s. *injuria*, æ f.
Dame, s. *hera, domina*
Dampness, s. *humor*, 3 d. m.
Damp, adj. *humidus*
——— (it was), *erat humidus*

Dance, s. *chorea*, 1 d. f.
——— v. n. *saltāre*, 1 c.
Dancing master, s. *saltandi magister*
——— room, s. *locus choreis aptus, orchestra*
Dandy, s. *nugator*, 3 d. m.
Danger, s. *periculum*, 2 d. n.
Dangerous, adj. *periculosus*
Dangerously, adv. *periculosè*

Dare, v. *audēre*, 2 c.
Dark, adj. *tenebrosus*
—— (it is), *tenebræ jam supervenisunt*
Darling, s. *corcŭlum*, 2 d. n.
Darkness, s. *cālīgo*, *ĭnis*, f.
Dated, p. p. *dătus*
Daughter, s. *filia*, 1 d.
—— (God), *filia lustrica*
—— (grand), *neptis*, 3 d.
—— in law, *nŭrus*, 4 d. f.
Dawn, s. *aurora*, *diluculum*
Day, s. *dies*, *ēi*, m. *vel*, f. in sing. *dies*, in pl. masc.
—— after to-morrow, *perendie*
—— (all), *toto die*
—— (so much a), *tot per diem*
—— before (the), s. *pridie*
—— (this), s. *hodie*
—— (on this), s. *hodie*
—— (every), s. *quotidianus*
Days (dog), s. *cănĭcŭla*, 1 d. f.
—— light, s. *lux*, *lumen*
—— time, s. *de die*
Dazzle, v. a. *præstringĕre*, *præstinguĕre*
Dazzled, p. p. *præstrictus*
Dawn, s. *aurōra*, æ f.
Dead, adj. *mortuus*
Deaf, adj. *surdus*
Deal (a great), *magnus numerus*, *multùm*
—— wood, s. *ăbies*, *ĕtis*, f.
—— at cards, s. *distrĭbutio*, 3 d. f.
—— (it is my), s. *mea distributio est*
—— in goods (to), *mercāri*, 1 c. dep.
Deal is it (whose), *cujus est distributio?*
Dealer, s. *factor*, *nĕgōtiātor*
Dealt last time (I), *dedi chartas novissimè*
Dear, adj. *carus*
—— (it is very), *pretiosus fuit*
Dearer, comp. of dear, *carior*, *pretiosior*
Dearly, adv. *carè*
Dearth, s. *fămes*, 3 d. f.
Death, s. *mors*, *tis*, f.
Debt, s. *dēbĭtum*, 2 d. n.
Decanter, s. *lagena transfusioni apta*
Deceit, s. *dŏlus*, 2 d. m.
Deceitful, adj. *subdolus*
Deceive, v. a. *fallĕre*, 3 c.
December, s. *Dĕcember*, *bris*, m.
Decide, v. *decernĕre*, 3 c.
Deck of a ship, *transtra* pl. s. n.
Declare, v. a. *dēclārāre*, 1 c.
Decline, v. a. *declināre*, 1 c.
Decorum, s. *dĕcōrum*, 2 d. n.
Deed, s. *factum*, 2 d. n.
—— (title), s. *tĭtŭlus*
Deep, adj. *profundus*
——, cunning, *astūtus*, *văfer*
—— (two feet), *altus duobus pedibus*
—— (it is one foot), *altum unius pedis est*
Deeply, adv. *altè*
—— afflicted, *valdè afflictus*
Deer, s. *cerva*, æ f.
Defence, s. *dēfensio*, 3 d. f.
Defend, v. a. *defendĕre*, 3 c.
Degrees, s. *gradus*, 4 d. m.
—— (by), adv. *gradatĭm*

Degrees at University, *gradus*
Deign, v. a. *dignāri*, 1 c. dep.
Delay, s. *mora*, 1 c. f.
—— v. *differre, procrastinare*
Delicate, adj. *dēlĭcātus, tener, exquisitus*
Delicacy, s. *elegantia, mollities*
Delicacies, s. pl. *cupediæ*, pl. f. *dapes*, pl. f.
Delight, s. *oblectatio, voluptas*
—— v. *delectāre*, 1 c.
Delighted, p. p. *delectātus, lætus*
Delightful, adj. *gratus, jucundus*
Demand, s. *postulatum*, 2 d. n. *rogatum*
—— v. a. *requirĕre, postulāre*
Den, s. *antrum, lătĭbŭlum*
Denial, s. *repulsa*, 1 d. f. *nĕgātio*, 3 d. f.
Deny, v. a. *negāre*, 1 c.
Departure, s. *profectio, discessus*
Depend, v. *dependĕre*, 3 c.
—— upon it (you may), *potes fidem adhibere*
Deranged (to be), *insānīre*, 4 c. n.
Deserve, v. a. *merēri*, 2 c. dep.
Desert, s. *deserta*, s. pl. n.
Desiring him, *rogans illum*
Desired him (he), *eum rogavit*
Desire, s. *desidĕrium*, 2 d. n.
—— v. a. *cŭpĕre, orare*
Desires, s. *vota*, pl. n. *optata*, pl. n.
Desires her compliments to your sister (Maria), *Maria quamplurimùm salutat sororem tuam*
Desirous, adj. *cŭpĭdus*
—— (I am), *cŭpĭo*
Design, s. *propositum*, 2 d. n.
—— a drawing, s. *dēlĭneātio*, 3 d. f. *pictura*, f.
Desk, s. *abacus*, 2 d. m.
Despicable, adj. *aspernandus*
Despise, v. a. *spernĕre*, 3 c.
Dessert, s. *bellāria*, pl. n. *fructus* m.
Destroy, v. a. *consumĕre, delēre*
Determine, v. *statuĕre*, 3 c.
Dew, s. *ros*, 3 d. m.
Dexterity, s. *dextĕrĭtas, agilitas*
Dexterous, adj. *expĕditus*
Dial (sun), *solarium*, 2 d. n.
Diamond, s. *adamas*, 3 d. m.
—— ring, s. *annulus adamantibus perfectus*
—— at cards, s. *angulatus*
Diaper, s. *sindon*
Dice, s. *tesseræ*, s. pl. f.
Dictionary, s. *dictiōnārium*, 2 d. n.
Did (I), *feci, egi*
Did you laugh? *risisti? tune riseras?*
— he jump, *saltavitne?*
— that (who), *quis id fecit?*
— (I), *ego quidem feci*
— I come? *num vēni?*
— they jump? *illi num saltavērunt?*
— you? *fecisti tu?*
— you set off? *fuistine profectus?*

Did (yes I), *profectus sum*
— we read? *legebamusne?*
———— so far? *legimusne ad hunc usque locum*
— he study? *studuit ille?*
— you receive? *recepistine?*
— I not? *an non recepi?*
— he answer? *respondit ne?*
— (yes he), *imo respondit*
— he go there? *illùc ivit ne?*
— not see you (for I), *nam ego te non vidi*
— you say? *num dixisti?*
— you not see? *an tu non vidisti?*
— you have? *audistine?*
— not look at the rule (you), *regulam non studuisti*
Die, v. n. *mŏri*, dep.
Diet, s. *regimen, diæta, cibus*
Differ, v. *variāre*, 1 c.
Different, adj. *dīversus, alter*
Difference, s. *discrĕpantia, diffĕrentia*
Difficult, adj. *diffĭcĭlis*
Difficulties, s. *diffĭcultātes, res angustæ*
Dig, v. a. *fodĕre*, 3 c.
Dignity, s. *dignĭtas*, 3 d. f.
Diligent, *dĭlĭgens, solers*
Diligence, *assiduitas, diligentia*
Dine, v. n. *prandēre*, 2 c.
Dining-room, *cænaculum*, 2 d. n.
Dinner, *prandium*, 2 d. n.
Dint of (by), *consuetudine vel usu*
Direct, v. *dirigĕre*, 3 c.
——— letters (to), *inscribere epistolas*
Directed, p. p. *instructus*
Directed (whose labors have been) *cujus labores jampridem directi fuēre*
Direction of a letter, *superscriptio epistolæ*
Directly, *statim*
Dirt, *lutum, cœnum*, 2 d. n.
Dirtiness, *sordes, iniquitas*
Dirty, *cœnosus, immundus*
Disappoint, v. a. *fallĕre*, 3 c.
Disappointed, *frustratus, deceptus*
———— (to be), *suâ spe falli*
Disappointment, *frustratio*, 3 d. f.
Discharge a servant (to), *dimittĕre servum*
———— bills, *solvĕre syngraphas vel debita*
———— one's duties, *fungi munere*
Discover, *aspicĕre, detegĕre*, 3 c.
Discovery, *inventio, indicium*
Discourse, v. n. *disserĕre, confabulāri*
Discreet, *prudens, consultus*
Disease, *morbus*, 2 d. m.
Dish, *pătĭna*, 1 d. f.
Dislike, s. *fastidium, odium*, 2 d. n.
——— v. a. *aversāri*, 1 c. dep.
——— (this I), *hoc ōdi*
Dismiss, v. a. *dimittĕre*
Dismissed, *dimissus*
Display, v. a. *expandere, monstrare*
Displayed, part. *expositus*
Displease, v. a. *displicēre*, 2 c.
Displeasure, s. *offensa, simultas*

Dispute, s. *contentio*, 3 d. f.
—— v. *disputare, contendere*
Dissatisfy, v. a. *offendĕre, displicēre*
Dissemble, v. a. *dissimulāre, simulāre*
Dissimulation, s. *simulatio*, 3 d. f.
Distance, s. *distantia, intervallum*
Distant, adj. *longinquus*
Distinguish, v. a. *discernere*, 3 c.
Distress, s. *afflictio*, 3 f. *paupertas*, 3 f.
Ditch, s. *fossa, vallum*
Divide, v. a. *dīvidĕre*, 3 c.
Divine, adj. *dīvīnus*
Divinity, s. *theologia*, f.
Do (to), v. a. *agĕre, facĕre*
— over again, *denuo facĕre*
— the like again, *idem iterùm facere*
— you speak? *loquerisne?*
— not speak to him, *cum illo ne loquaris*
— you like that? *an hoc tibi placet?*
— ? (how do they), *quŏmodo valent?*
— ? (how does your father), *pater tuus quomodo valet?*
— with them (to), *cum illis agere*
— it? (does she), *hoc illa num facit?*
Dock, a weed, *lăpăthus*, 2 d.
—— (West India), *navale*, 3 d. n. *Ind. Occ.*
—— for building ships, *navale*
Doctor, s. *mĕdĭcus, doctor*
Dog, s. *canis*, 3 d. m.
Dog days, *canicula*, f.
Doing it (I have left off), *cessavi jam id facere*
—— justice (it is but), *id est tantummŏdo justitiam reddere*
Doll, s. *pūpa*, 1 d. f.
Dolphin, *delphinus*, 2 d. m.
Done, p. p. *factus*
—— (have), *cessa*
—— (it is), *factum est*
—— (I have), *fēci*
—— his dinner (he has not), *non finivit prandere*
—— (the meat was not), *caro non erat satis cocta*
Doom, s. *fatum, judicium*
Door, s. *ostium, fores*, pl. f.
Dose, s. *dosis*, f.
Double, adj. and s. *duplex, duplum*
Doubt, v. *dubitāre*, 1 c.
—— s. *dubium*, 2 d. n.
Dough, s. *farina subacta*
Dove, s. *columbus*, 2 d. m. *columba*, 1 f. *palumbus*, 2 m.
—— house, *columbarium*, 2 d. n.
—— (turtle), *turtur*, 3 m.
Dover, s. pr. *Dorobernium*
Down, adv. *deorsùm*
——— (to come), *descendere*
——— (to pull), *evertere*
Downfall, *casus, ruina*
Downs, s. (plain), *planities*, 5 d. f.
——— (hill), *grumus*, 2 d. m.
Dowry, s. *dos*, 3 d. f.
Dozen, *duodecim*
Drag, *trahĕre*, 3 c.
Drank, (he) *bibit*
Draw, v. *trahĕre, ducĕre*

Draw with a pencil, *delineāre*, 1 c.
Drawing, s. *adumbratio, lineatio*
——— room, s. *penetrāle, is*, n.
Dreadful, *horrendus*
Dream, s. *somnium*, 2 d. n.
——— v. *somniāre, delirāre*
Dress, v. *induĕre, comāre*
—— s. *vestitus, cultus, vestimenta*
Dresser, s. *mensa coquinaria*
——— (hair), *tonsor*
Dress-maker, *sutrix stolarum*
Drink, v. *bibĕre, potāre*
Drinking-glass, s. *poculum, scyphus*
Drive, v. *agĕre, agitāre, aurigāri*
—— (to take a), *paululùm in essedo excurrere*
—— a horse, *equum agere*
—— away, *abigĕre*, 3 c. *arcēre*, 2 c.
—— a nail, *clavum suffigĕre*.
Drone, s. *fucus*, 2 d. m.
Drop, v. *dimittere, stillare*
—— s. *gutta, stilla*, 1 d. f.
Drove to London, (I) *aurigavi Londinum usque*
Drown, v. *mergĕre*, 3 c. act. *demergi*, pass.

Drowsiness, s. *stupor*, 3 d. m.
Drum, s. *tympanum*, 2 d. n.
Drunk, adj. *ebrius*
Drunkard, s. *ebriosus*
Drunkenness, s. *crapula*, 1 d. f.
Dry, adj. *siccus, siticulosus*
Duck, s. *ănas, ătis*, f.
—— v. (to plunge) *submergĕre*, 3 c.
Due, s. *debitum*, 2 d. n.
—— adj. *debitus*
Dug, part. p. *fossus*
Duke, s. *dux*, 3 d. m.
Dull, adj. *insulsus, hebes*
—— of apprehension, *stŭpĭdus*
Dulness, s. *segnities*, 5 d. f.
Dumb, adj. *mutus*
Dunce, s. *stīpes*, 3 d. m.
During, *per, inter*
Dusk of evening, *crĕpuscŭlum*, 2 *d. n.*
Dust, s. *pulvis*, 3 d.
Dutch, *Batavus*
——— cheese, *caseus Batavus*
Dutiful, *obediens*
Duty, s. *officium*, 2 d. n.
Duty, (the king's) *vectigal regis*
Dwarf, s. *nanus*, 2 d.
Dye, v. *tinctura*, 1 d. f.
Dyer, s. *tinctor*, 3 d. m.
Dynasty, s. *dynastia*, *æ* f.

E

Each, adj. *quisque, singuli*, pl.
—— book, *singuli libri*
—— of them, *uter illorum*
—— other, *mutuò*
—— other, (they speak against) *invĭcem contra se loquuntur*

Eager, adj. *vehemens*
Eagerness, s. *aviditas*
Eagle, s. *aquila*, 1 d. f.
Ear, s. *auris*, 3 d. f.
—— for music, *auris apta musicæ*
—— of corn, *spīcum*, 2 d. n.

Ear, (a box on the) s. *alapa*, 1 d. f.
—— ring, s. *inauris*, 3 d. f.
Earl, s. *comes*, 3 d.
Early, adj. *matutinus*, *mātūrus*
Early, adv. *matutinè*, *citò*
Earn money, (to) *lucrari*, *merēri dep.*
Earnest, (in) *seriò*, adv.
Earth, s. *terra*, *tellus*
Earthen, adj. *fictilis*, *terreus*
Easier, adj. comp. *facilior*, *us*
Easily, adv. *facilè*
East, s. *oriens*, *ortus*
Easter, s. *pascha*, 3 d. n.
—— week, *hebdomada paschalis*
East Indies, *India*, *æ* f.
—— Indiaman, *navis Indiam versus navigans*
Easy, adj. *facilis*
Eat, v. *edĕre*, 3 c.
Eating-house, s. *caupona*, 1
Economical, adj. *frugālis*
Economy, s. *frugalitas*, 3 d. f.
Edge, s. *margo*, *ĭnis*, m. *vel* f.
—— of a knife, *acies*, 5 d. f.
Educate, v. a. *educāre*, *instituĕre*
Eel, s. *anguilla*, 1 d. f.
Effort, s. *cōnātus*, *ûs*, m.
Egg, s. *ovum*, 2 d. n.
Eight, adj. *octo*
Eighteen, adj. *octodecim*
Eighteenth, adj. *decimus octavus*
Eighth, adj. *octavus*
Eighty, adj. *octoginta*
Either, conj. *vel. aut*
—— you or George, *vel tu vel Georgius*
Elbow, s. *ulna*, *cubitus*
Elder, adj. *senior*
Eldest, adj. *maximus natu*
Elect, v. a. *eligĕre*, 3 c.
Elephant, s. *elephas*, 3 d. m.
Eleven, adj. *undecim*
Eleventh, adj. *undecimus*
Eliza, *Eliza*, *æ*
Ell, (a measure), s. *ulna*, 1 d. f.
Elm-tree, *ulmus*, 2 d. f.
Else, adj. *alter*, *alius*
—— conj. *prætereà*, *sive*, *utrum*, *porrò*
—— (something), *aliquid amplius*
—— where, *alibi*
—— (somewhere), *alicubi*
Embark, v. *navem conscendere*
Embarrassment, s. *difficultas*, *impedimentum*
Emblem, s. *emblema*, 3 d. n.
Embrace, v. a. *amplecti*, 3 c.
Embroider, v. a. *acu pingere*
Embroidery, s. *ars pingendi acu*
Eminence, s. *eminentia*, 1 d. f.
Eminent, adj. *eximius*
Emotion, s. *agitatio*, 3 d. f.
Emperor, s. *imperator*, 3 d. m.
Empiric, s. *empiricus*, 2 d. m.
Employ, v. *occupāre*, 1 c. *præponĕre*, 3 c.
Empty, adj. *vacuus*, *inanis*
—— v. a. *transfundĕre*, 3 c.
Enable, v. *vires suppeditare*
Enclose, v. *præcingĕre*, 3 c. *includĕre*, 3 c.
Encounter, v. *congrĕdi*, 3 c. dep.
Encourage, v. *hortāri*, dep. *instigāre*, 1 c.
Encouragement, *hortatus*, 4 d. m.

End, s. *finis*, 3 d.
—— v. *finire*, 4 c. *termināre*, 1 c. *desinĕre*, 3 c.
—— crowns the work, (the) *finis coronat opus*
Endeavour, v. *conāri*, dep.
—— s. *cōnātus*, *ūs*, m.
Endive, s. *intybum*, 2 d. n.
Endure, v. *pati*, 3 c. dep. *perdurāre*, 1 c.
Enemy, s. *hostis*, 3 d.
Engage, v. *spondēre*, 2 c. *confligĕre*, 3 c.
Engagement, s. *vadimonium*, *pugna*, *prælium*
England, *Britannia*, æ f.
English, adj. *Britanni*
Englishman, s. *Britannus*
Enjoy, v. *frui*, 3 c. dep.
Enormous, adj. *enormis*, *vastus*
Enough, adv. *satis*
—— (it is), *sat est*
Enquire, v. *inquirĕre*, 3 c.
Enquiries, s. pl. *inquisitiones*
Ensign, or standard, *vexillum*, 2 d. n.
—— or standard-bearer, *ăquĭlĭfer*, *signifer*
Ensure, v. *præstāre*, 1 c.
Enter, v. *ingredi*, 3 c. dep.
Entertain, v. a. *delectāre*, 1 c.
Entreat, v. a. *orāre*, 1 c.
Envy, v. a. *invidēre*, 2 c.
—— s. *invidia*, 1 d.
Equal, adj. *æqualis*
Erase, v. a. *delēre*, 2 d.
Erect, v. a. *erigĕre*, 3 c.
Errors, s. pl. *errores*, *errata*
Escape, s. *fuga*, æ f.
Escape, v. *effŭgĕre*, *evadĕre*, 3 c.
Especially, adv. *præsertim*
Essential, adj. *essentiālis*
Establish, v. a. *stabilire*, 4 c. *confirmāre*, 1 c.
Establishment, s. *stabilimentum*, 2 d. n.
—— (school) *lūdus*, *i* m.
—— (household) *dŏmus*, *ūs*, f. *domus*, *i* f.
Estate, s. *ordo*, 3 d. m. *status*, 4 d. m. *res*, f.
Esteem, v. a. *æstimo*, *duco*, *pendo*
—— s. *æstimātio*, 3 d. f.
Esteemed, p. p. *habitus*, *æstimatus*
Eternity, *æternĭtas*, 3 d. f.
Eve, s. *vigiliæ*, pl. f.
Even, adv. *etiam*, *vel*
—— adj. *æquus*, *par*
Evening, s. *vespera*, 1 d. f. *vesper*, 3 d. m.
Event, s. *ēventus*, 4 d. m.
Ever, adv. *perpetuò*, *æternùm*
—— (for), adv. *in æternùm*.
Evergreen, *semper virens*
Every, *omnis*, *quisque quilibet*
—— article, *quæque res*
—— body, *quisque*
—— thing, *quæque res*
—— day, *quotidiè*, *quotidianò*
—— minute, *momentaneus*, *singulis momentis*
—— morning, *singulis matutinis*
—— one, *quisque*, *unusquisque*
—— who is accused, *quisquis accusatur*
—— time, *quotiès*
—— where, *ubiquè*
—— year, *quotannis*
—— body, (I gave) *unicuique dedi*

Evidence, s. *testimonium*, i n.
Evident, adj. *perspicuus*, *evidens*
Evil, adj. *mălus*, *a*, *um*
—— s. *mălum*, *i*, 2 d. n.
Europe, *Europa*, *æ* f.
European, adj. *Europæus*, *a*, *um*
Exact, adj. *accuratus*
Exactly, adv. *accuratè*
Examination, s. *examen*, *ĭnis* n.
Examine, v. a. *examinare*, 1 c.
Example, s. *exemplum*, 2 d. n.
Exceedingly, adv. *valdè*
Exceed, v. a. *transcendĕre*, *præstāre*
Excellent, adj. *excellens*, *eximius*
Except, conj. *nisi*
—— v. s. *excipĕre*, 3 c. *excludĕre*, 3 c.
Excess, s. *excessus*, 4 d. m. *intemperantia*, 1 d. f.
Exchange, v. a. *commutāre*
—— s. *commutatio*, 3 d. f.
—— merchants', *excambium*, 2 d. n. *bursa*, 1 d. f.
Excise, s. *census*
Excite, v. a. *excitāre*, 1 c.
Excusable, adj. *excusabilis*
Excuse, s. *excusatio*, 3 d. f.
—— v. *ignoscĕre*, 3 c.
Execution, s. *supplicii inflictio*
Executioner, *carnifex*, 3 d. m.
Exercise, s. *exercĭtatio*, 3 d. f. *pensum*, 2 d. n.
—— v. *exercēre*, 2 c.
Exhaust, v. a. *exhaurīre*, 4 c m.
Exhort, v. a. *hortāri*, 1 c.
Exile, s. *exilium*, 2 d. n.
Existence, s. *vita*, *existentia*
Expect, v. a *expectāre*, 1 c.
Expectation, s. *expectatio*,
Expend, v. a. *expendĕre*, 3 c.
Expense, *sumptus*, *ûs*, 4 d. m.
—— (at his own) *proprio suo sumptu*
Expensive, adj. *carus*
Experience, s. *experientia*, 1 d. f.
Explain, v. a. *explicāre*, 1 c.
Expose, *exponĕre*, 3 c.
Extensive, adj. *lātus*, *a*, *um*
Extinguish, v. a. *extinguĕre*, 3 c.
Extinguisher, s. *suffocatorium*, 2 d. n.
Extol, v. a. *laudāre*, 1 c.
Extreme, adj. *extremus*
Extremely, adv. *summè*, *valdè*
Extraordinary, adj. *insolitus*
Eye, s. *oculus*, 2 d. m.
—— ball, s. *pūpilla*, *æ* f.
—— brow, s. *supercilium*, 2 d. n.
—— glass, s. *vitrum oculis aptum*
—— lids, s. pl. *palpebræ*, 1 d. pl.

F

Face, *vultus*, *facies*
Faces, (to make) *vultus ducere*
Facility, s. *facilitas*, 3 d.
Fact, s. *factum*, 2 d. n. *gestum*, 2 d. n.

Fact, (in) adv. *rēvērà*
Faculties, s. pl. *facultates*, 3 d. pl.
Fade, v. n. *ēvānescĕre*, 3 c.
Fail, v. a. *deficĕre*, 3 c.
Failure, s. *defectus*, *conturbatio*
Faint, v. n. *dēfĭcĕre*, 3 c.
—— away, v. *animo linqui*
Fair, adj. *pulcher*
—— (a market) s. *nundĭnæ*, *ārum*, pl. f.
Fair copy, (a) *callĭgrăphia*, 1 d. f.
Fairly, adv. *venustè*, *æquè*, *probè*
—— (to copy), *transcribĕre*, 3 c.
Fair wind, s. *ventus favens vel secundus*
Faith, s. *fides*, 5 d. f.
Faithful, adj. *fidus*, *fidelis*
Faithfully, adv. *fidè*, *fideliter*
Fall down, v. *cadĕre*, 3 c.
Fallen, p. p. *lapsus*
False, adj. *falsus*
—— hood, s. *mendacium*, *dolus*
Falsely, adv. *falsò*
Fame, s. *fama*; 1 d. f. *rumor*, 3 d. m.
Family, s. *familia*, *domus*
Famous, adj. *clarus*, *insignis*
Fanciful, adj. *levis*, *inconstans*
Fancy, s. *imaginatio*, 3 d. f.
—— fashion, *modus*, *consuetudo*
—— v. *effingere*, *imaginări*
Far, adv. *longè*
—— how, *quousquè*
Fare, s. *victus*, 4 d. m.
—— (coachman's) *vectūra*, *æ* f.
Farewell, *vale*
Farm, s. *fundus*, 2 d. m. *prædium*, 2 d. n.
Farmer, s. *agricola*, 1 d. m. *villicus*, 2 d. m.
Farrier, s. *hippocomus*, 2 d. m.
Fashion, s. *modus*, *forma*, *usus*, *mos*
—— (after the French), *more Gallico*
Fashionable, adj. *concinnus*
Fast, (quick) adj. *celer*
—— (quickly), *celeriter*
Fasten, v. a. *astringĕre*, 3 c.
Fasten gates, (to) *portas obdere*
Fat, adj. *pinguis*. *obesus*
Fatal, adj. *fatalis*
Fate, s. *fatum*, 2 d. n. *sors*, 3 d. f.
Father, s. *pater*, 3 d.
—— in law, *socer*, 2 d.
—— (grand), *ăvus*, *i* 2 d.
—— (God), *susceptor*, 3 d. m.
Fatigue, v. *fatigāre*, *delassāre*
Fault, s. *culpa*, 1 d. f.
—— (to find) *culpāre*, 1 c.
Favour, s. *favor*, 3 d. *gratia*, 1 d. f.
Favoured, p. p. *carus*
Favourite, s. *gratiosus*
Fear, s. *metus*, 4 d. m. *timor*, 3 d. m.
—— v. *timēre*, 2 c.
Feather bed, *culcĭta plumea*
February, *Februarius*, 2 d. m.
Feed, v. *pascĕre*, 3 c. *pasci*, 3 c. dep.
Feel, v. *sentīre*, *tangĕre*
—— (the pulse), *venam tentare*
Feelings, *sensus*, 4 d. m.

Feet, s. *pedes*, 3 d. f.
Felix, adj. *felix*
Fell, (he) *cecidit*
Fellow, (comrade) *sŏdālis*, 3 d. c g.
—— (a good for nothing), *homo nequam, nĕbŭlo*
Felt, part. *sensus, a, um*
—— his pulse, (he) *tetigit illi jam arteriam*
Fence, v. *sepes*, 3 d.
Fern, s. *fīlix, icis*, f.
Ferry boat, s. *ponto, ōnis*, m. *navigium*
Fetch, v. *portare*, 1 c.
Fever, s. *febris*, 3 d. f.
—— (scarlet) *febris purpurea*
Few, adj. *pauci*, pl.
—— people, *perpauci homines*
—— boys are careful enough, *pauci pueri satis sunt diligentes*
—— (very), *perpauci*
—— play things, *crepundia pauca*
Fickle, adj. *inconstans*
Fickleness, *levitas*
Fiddle, *fĭdes vel fidis*, 3 d. f.
—— stick, *plectrum*, 2 d. n.
—— strings, *fidium chordæ*
Fiddler, s. *fĭdĭcen, ĭnis*, m.
Fie! for shame! *vah!* interj.
Field, *ăger, agri*, m.
Fifteen, *quindecim, quindeni*
Fifth, *quintus, quintanus*
Fiftieth, *quinquagesimus, a, um*
Fifty, *quinquaginta, quinquageni*
Fig, s. *ficus, i* f.
Figure, s. *figura, forma*, 1 d.
Fill, v. a. *implēre*, 2 c.
Filthiness, s. *immunditia*, 1 d. f.
Find, v. *invenīre*, 4 c.
—— out, *reperīre*, 4 c. *expiscāri*, 1 c. dep.
Fine, adj. *cultus, bellus*
—— v. *mulctāre*, 1 c.
—— s. (a penalty), *mulcta, multa*, 1 d. f.
Finer, comp. of fine, *elegantior*
Finest, sup. of ditto, *nĭtĭdissimus*
Finely, adv. *scitè, bellè*
Finger, s. *dĭgĭtus*, 2 d. m.
Fingering, (in music) *tactus, ûs*, m. *executio*, 3 d. f.
Finish, v. *absolvere*
Fire, s. *ignis*, 3 d. m.
—— arms, s. pl. *arma ignivoma*
Fire-engine, *machina ad ignem extinguendum*
Firmness, s. *constantia*, 1 d. f. *firmĭtas*, 3 d. f.
First, *primus*
—— (at) *primùm, principio*
Fish, v. a. *piscāri*, 1 c. dep.
—— s. *piscis, is*, m.
Fisherman, s. *piscator*
Fish - market, *forum piscarium*
Fish pond, *piscīna*, 1 d. f.
Fisher, (at cards) *motæ*
Fishing, s *piscatus*
—— boat, s. *navĭgium piscatorium*
Fist, s. *pugnus, i* m.
Fit, adj. *conveniens, aptus, idoneus*
—— v. *aptāre*, 1 c.

Fit me, (they do) *vestes mihi benè aptantur*
Fits, (to be in) *animo linqui*
Five, *quinque*
Flat, adj. *planus*
—— (in music), *gravis tŏnus vel sonus*
Flea, s. *pulex*, 3 d. m.
Fleet, adj. *velox*
Flesh, s. *caro*, 3 d. f.
Flew, (he) pret. *volavit*
Flight, s. *fuga*, 1 d. f.
Flint, s. *silex*, 3 d.
Flock, s. *grex*, 3 d. m.
Floor, s. *tabulatum, pavimentum*
Flooring, *contabulatio*, 3 d. f.
Flower, *flos*, 3 d. m.
—— casket, *cistula floribus*
—— pot, s. *olla floribus*
Flown away, *volatus*, part.
Flour, s. *farina*, 1 d. f.
Flute, s. *tibia*, 1 d. f.
Fly, v. *volāre*, 1 c.
—— s. *musca*, 1 d. f.
Fog, s, *nebula*, 1 d. f.
Foible, s. *vitium*, 2 d. n.
Follow, v a. *sĕqui*, 3 c. dep.
Folly, s. *stultitia*, 1 d. f.
Fond, adj. *cupidus, indulgens*
—— (to be), *diligĕre*, 3 c.
—— of the country? (are you) *tu-ne rus amas?*
Food, s. *cibus*, 2 d. m. *victus*, 4 d. m.
Fool, s. *stultus*, 2 d. m.
Foolish, adj. *ineptus, stultus, a, um*
Foolishness, *stultitia*, 1 d. f.
Foot, s. *pes*, 3 d. m.
—— (sore), s. *pes exulceratus*
—— ball, *pila pedalis*
—— pad, *latro*, 3 d.
Fop, s. *nugator*, 3 d. m.
For, conj. *nam*
—— prep. *de, præ, pro*
—— me, *pro vel propter me*
—— writing so often, *quod tam sæpe scripseras*
—— in the sense of because, *quòd, quia*
—— I have no money, *quippe omnino pecuniâ careo*
—— all that, *neque illo secius*
—— one hundred pounds, *pro centum libris pecuniæ*
—— what, *pro quo*
Forbid, v. a. *vetāre*, 1 c.
Force, v. a. *cogĕre*, 3 c. *impellĕre*, 3 c. *adigĕre*, 3 c.
Forehead, s. *frons, tis*, f.
Foresee, v. *prævidēre*. 2 d.
Forest, s. *saltus, ûs*, m.
Forget, v. *oblivisci*, 3 c. dep.
Forgive, v. a. *ignoscĕre*, 3 c.
Fork, s. *furca*, 1 d. f.
—— (pitch), s. *bidens*, 3 d. m.
Former, adj. *prior*
Formerly, adv. *antehàc*
Fort, s. *castellum*, 2 d. n.
Fortnight, s. *quatuordecim dies*
—— (this day), *in quatuordecim diebus*
Fortunate, adv. *fortunatus, faustus*
Fortunately, adv. *faustè*
Fortune, s. *fortuna*, 1 d. f.
Forty, adj. *quadraginta*
Forward, adj. *audax, promptus, præcox*
Fought, (the battle was) *prælium commissum fuit*
Found, p. p. *inventus, repertus*

Four, adj. *quatuor*
Fourteen, adj. *quatuordecim*
Fourth, adj. *quartus*
Fox, s. *vulpes*, 3 d. f.
Frail, adj. *fragilis*
Franc, s. *decem asses*
France, s. pr. *Gallia*, *æ* f.
Frank, adj. *ingenuus, a, um*
Frederic, s. pr. *Fredericus*
Free, adj. *liber, era, erum*
—— from, *emancipatus ex*
Freedom, s. *libertas, immunitas*
Freely, adv. *spontè*
Freeze, v. *gelāre, congelare*, 1 c.
French, adj. *Gallicus*
—— beans, s. pl. *phaseoli*, 2 d. m.
—— man, *Gallus*, 2 d.
—— language, *lingua Gallica recentior*.
Frequent, adj. *creber, frequens*
Frequently, adv. *crebrò, frequenter*
Fresh, adj. *frigidulus, novus*
Friday, s. *dies Veneris*
Friend, s. *amicus*, 2 d. m. *amica*, 1 d. f.
Friendship, s. *amicitia*, 1 d. f.
Friendly, adv. *amicè, benevolè*
Frighten, v. a. *terrēre*, 2 c.
Frightful, adj. *terribilis*
Frill, s. *fimbria*, 1 d. f. *lacinia*, 1 d. f.
Frog, s. *rāna*, *æ* f.
From, prep. *a, ab, e, ex, de*
Frost, s. *gelu*, n. indec.
Front of a house, *frons ædis*
Fruit, s. *fructus*, 4 d. m.
Fruitful, adj. *ferax*
Full, adj. *plenus, a, um*
Fulfil, v. a. *peragĕre*, 3 c.
Fully, adv. *plenè*
Fund, s. *cumulus*, 2 d. m.
Funnel, s. *infundibulum*, 2 d. n.
Fur, s. *pellis*, 3 d. f. *villus*, 2 d. m.
Further, adv. *ultrà, longiùs*
Furniture, s. *sŭpellex, ctilis*, f. no pl.
Future, (for the) *in futurum*
—— adj. *futurus*
—— s. *tempus futurum*

G

Gain, s. *lucrum*, 2 d. n.
Gain, v. *lucrāri*, 1 d. dep.
Gains, (it) (of a clock), *nimis prŏpĕrat*
Gait, s. *incessus*, 4 d. m.
Gambler, s. *āleātor, ōris*, m.
Gambling, s. *lusio pro nummis*
Game, s. *lusus*, 4 d. m.
Gamester, s. *addictus lusibus*
Game, (animals) s. *præda*
Gaming, s. *aleam jactare, lusio*
Garden, s. *hortus*, 2 d. m.
Gardener, s. *hortulanus*, 2 d. m.
Gate, s. *janua*, 1 d. f.
Gather, v. a. *carpĕre*, 3 c. *stringĕre*, 3 c.
Gave, (I) v. *dedi*
Geese, s. *anseres*

Gem, s. *gemma*, 1 d. f.
General, s. *dux, imperator*
Generally, adv. *plerumque, generaliter*
Generous, adj. *generosus*
Geneva, *Geneva*
Genial, adj. *genialis*
Genteel, adj. *honestus, venustus*
Gentleman, s. *homo comis vel generosus*
Geography, s. *geographia, æ*
Geometry, s. *geometria, æ* f.
George, pr. n. *Georgius*
German, s. *Germanus*, 2 d.
Germany, s. *Germania, æ* f.
Get up, v. *surgĕre*, 3 c.
—— wet, v. *humidum esse pluviâ*
—— on, v. *conscendĕre*, 3 c.
—— rid of, *se expedire à*
Getting late, (it is) *vesperascit*
I shall not get any thing by it, *nihil ego faciam lucri ex eâ re*
Get, v. *acquirĕre*, 3 c.
—— into a carriage, *ascendere in vehiculo*
Giant, s. *gigas*, 3 d. m.
Giddiness, s. *vertigo*, 3 d. f.
Giddy, adj. *ineptus, inconstans*
Gift, s. *munus*, 3 d. n. *donum*, 2 d. n.
Gilliflower, s. *caryophyllum*, 2 d. n.
Gilt, part. *inauratus*
Gimblet, s. *terebra, æ* f.
Girl, s. *puella, æ* f.
Give, v. *dare*, 1 c. irr. *donāre*
—— an answer, *respondĕre*, 2 c.
Give up to, (to) *concedĕre*, 3 c.
Glad, adj. *lætus, a, um*
—— of it, (I am) *gaudeo propter hoc*
Glass, s. *vitrum, speculum*
—— (wine) *scyphus*, 2 d. m. *calix vitreus*
Glitter, v. *coruscāre*, 1 c.
Glove, s. *mănĭca, æ* f.
Gnat, s. *culex*, 3 d.
Gnaw, v. a. *rodĕre*, 3 c.
Go, (to) v. n. *īre*, irr. *vadĕre*, 3 c.
— (shall I) *visne ut eam*
— (they) *eunt*
— there, (obliged to) *necesse est illuc aggredi*
— to meet, (to) *obviam ire*
— directly, (to) *statim abire*
— over to France, (to) *transire in Galliam*
— elsewhere, (to) *alicubi vadere*
— up, (to) *ascendĕre*, 3 c.
— down, (to) *descendĕre*, 3 c.
— in, (to) *introīre*, 4 c.
— out, (to) *exīre*, 4 c.
— away, (to) *abīre*, 4 c.
—— half-a-mile, (to) *grădi quingentos passus*
God, s. *Deus*, 2 d.
—— daughter, *filia lustrica* f.
—— father, *pater lustricus*
—— son, *filius lustricus*
—— save the king, *vivat rex*
Goes, (he, she, or it) *it*
Going to leave, (are you) *an tu abscedes?*

Going out for a week, (they are), *abibunt illi per hebdomadam*
—— was, (he) *abibat*
—— to sing, (he was) *tunc cogitabat canere*
Gold, s. *aurum*, 2 d. n.
—— finch, *carduēlis, is* f.
—— watch, *chronometer auri*
Gone to Paris, (he is) *Lutetiam profectus est*
—— (he is) *abscessit*
—— to meet, *obviam itus*
Good, adj, *bonus, a, um*
—— (you are so), *tam bonus es*
—— for nothing fellow, *nĕbŭlo, ōnis*, m.
—— bye, *vale et salve*
Goodness, s. *benevolentia, bonitas*
Goose, s. *anser*, 3 d.
Gooseberries, s. pl. *grosŭlæ*, 1 d. f.
Gospel, (the) *evangelium*, 2 d. n.
Got safe home, (we) *tuti domum redivimus*
Govern, v. a. *gubernāre*, 1 c.
Governess, s. *præceptrix, īcis, gubernatrix, īcis*
Gown, s. *stola, toga, vestis*
Grammar, s. *grammatica*, 1 d. f.
Grand-daughter, s. *neptis*, 3 d. f.
—— father, s. *avus*, 2 d. m.
—— son, s. *nepos*, 3 d. m.
Grant, v. a. *concedĕre*, 3 c.
Grapes, s. pl. *uvæ*, 1 d. f.
Grasshopper, *cĭcāda, æ* f.
Grass, *herba*, 1 d. f. *gramen*, 3 d. n.
Gratis, adv. *gratis*
Gratitude, s. *gratitudo*, 3 d. f.
Grave, s. *tumulus, sepulchrum*
—— adj. *severus, gravis*
Gravel, s. *sabulum*, 2 d. n.
Gravy, s. *succus*, 2 d. m. *jus*, 3 d. n.
Greasing, (the wheels want) *rotæ axungiā carent*
Great, adj. *magnus*
—— many, *plures*
Greater, adj. *major, vastior*
Greatly, adv. *valdè, maximè*
Greek, adj. *Græcus, a, um*
—— language, *lingua Græca*
Green, adj. *viridis*
—— house, s. *conservatorium*, 2 d. n.
Grey, adj. *cinereus, a, um*
Grief, s. *mæror*, 3 d. m.
Groan, s. *gemitus*, 4 d. m.
Grocer, s. *aromatopola*, 1 d. m.
Groom, s. *ăgāso, ōnis*, m.
Grove, s. *nemus*, 3 d. m.
Ground, s. *solum*, 2 n. *humus*, 2 d. f.
Grow, v. n. *crescĕre*, 3 c.
Growing, part. *crescens*
Grub, s. *chrysălis, dis*, f.
Grumble, v. *murmurāre*, 1 c.
Grumbling, s. *murmuratio*, 3 d. f.
—— (I am), *murmuro*
Guard, s. *sătelles, ĭtis*, m. *custodia*, 1 d. f.
Guardian, s. *tutor*, 3 d. m.
Guess, v. *conjicĕre*, 3 c. *conjectare*, 1 c.
Guildhall, s. *curia municipalis*
Guilty, adj. *sons, nocens*

Guinea, s. *viginti unus solidi*
Gum, s. *gummis*, 3 d. f. *gummi*, n. indec.
Gun, (canon), *tormentum bellicum*
Gun powder, *nitrum*, *i* n.
—— s. (small arms),* *scloppus*, 2 d. m.

H

Habit, (a lady's) *vestis equestris*
—— custom, *mos*, 3 d. m.
Hack-horse, *equus conductitius*
Hackney coach, *currus mercenarius*
Had no master, (I) *præceptorem non habui*
—— you rather go thither, *an cupis magis eò proficisci?*
—— you spoken? *num tu locum fueras*
—— (if you) *si feceris tu*
—— come, (if you) *si tu venisses*
—— rather not, (I) *nolo equidem*
—— it not been for me, *si ego non interfuissem*
Hair, s. *coma*, 1 d. f. *cæsaries*, 5 d. f. *capillus*, m.
—— dresser, *tonsor*
Half-way, s. *dimidio vitæ*
Half-past four, *semihora post quartam*
Hall, (a large house) *aula*, 1 f.
—— s. *locus concilii*
—— s. *armus porci*
Hamlet, s. *vīcus*, 2 d. m.
Hammer, s. *tŭdes*, 3 d. m. *malleus*, 2 d. m.
Hand, s. *manus*, 4 d. f.
—— v. a. *per manus tradere*
Hands, (of a clock) *indices*, 3 d. c. g.
Handkerchief, s. *sūdārium*, 2 d. n.
Handle, s. *manubrium*, 2 d. n.
Handsome, adj. *venustus*, *pulcher*
Handsomer, comp. *pulchriar*
Handsomest, sup. *pulcherrimus*
Happen, v. n. *contingere*, 3 c.
Happier, adj. comp. *felicior*
Happiness, s. *fēlīcĭtas*, 3 d. f.
Happy, adj. *fēlix*
Harbour, s. *portus*, 4 d. m.
Hard, adj. *durus*
Harden, v. n. *obdurescĕre*, 3 c. m.
Hardly, adv. *vix*
—— ever, *vix omninò*
Hare, *lepus*, 3 d. m.
Harriet, pr. n. *Henrietta*, 1 d.
Harmonious, adj. *modulatus*
Harshness, s. *asperitas*, *acerbitas*
Hart, s. *cervus*, 2 d. m.
Has, (he) *habet*, *fecit*
—— he not? *nonne fecit?*
Haste, (make) *festina*, *move te ocyùs*

* The student is aware that there is difficulty in chusing classical words for the modern inventions: such as *playing cards*, *printing*, and *fire-arms*.

Haste, (in) *festīnè*
—— (let us make) *festinemus*
Hat, s. *pileus*, 2 d. m. *galē-rus*, 2 d. m.
Hate, v. a. *odisse*, defect.
Hatred, s. *odium*, 2 d. n.
Have, v. *habēre*, 2 c.
—— been there, (I) *ibi fui*
—— some, (I) *habeo*
—— that (we shall not) *id nos non habebimus*
—— done, *cessa*
Hay, *fœnum*, 2 d. n.
—— market, *forum pro fœno*
He, she, it, pron. *ille, a, ud; is, ea, id*
— fills, *ille implet*
— loves, *is amat*
Head, s. *caput*, 3 d. n.
Headach, s. *dolor capitis*
———— I have the, *caput mihi dolet*
Head dress, s. *ornatus pro capite*
Health, s. *valetudo*, 3 d. f. *salus*, 3 d. f.
Healthy, adj. *sanus, validus*
Hear, v. *audire*, 4 c.
——? (do you) *audisne?*
Hearer, s. *auditor*, 3 d.
Hearing, s. *auditus*, 4 d. m.
Harken, v. n. *auscultāre*, 1 c.
Heart, s. *cor*, 3 d. n.
Heartily, adv. *ex animo, toto pectore*
Heat, s. *calor*, 3 d. m.
Heath, s. *erica*, 1 d. f.
Heaven, s. *cœlum*, 2 d. n.
Heavy, adj. *gravis*
——— road, *via lutosa*
Hedge, s. *sepes*, 3 d. f.
Heel, s. *calx*, 3 d.

Height, s. *altitudo*, 3 d. f.
Help, v. a. *juvāre*, 1 c.
Helter skelter, adv. *confusè*
Hem, (a) *fimbria*, 1 d. f.
Hemp. s. *cannăbis*, 3 d. f.
Hen, s. *gallīna*, 1 d.
—— house, *aviarium*, 2 d. n.
Hence, *abhìnc*
——— do they proceed from, *an illi abhinc decedunt*
Her, (who taught) *quis illam docuit*
—— for, *pro illâ*
—— I see, *eam video*
—— away, (I give) *illam ex manibus do*
—— a ring, (I gave) *illi annulum dedi*
—— mother, *mater sua*
—— brother, *frater suus*
Here, *hìc*
—— they are, *adsunt*
—— (come) *hùc veni*
—— after, *posthàc*
Hesitate, v. n. *dubitāre*, 1 c.
Hesitation, s. *hæsitatio*, 3 d. f.
High, (ten feet) *altus decem pedum*
—— deeds, *res gestæ*
——— merit, *meritum præstantissimum*
——— road, *via, æ* f.
——— life, *ordo clarissimus, conditio illustrior*
Higher, adj. *altior, excelsior*
Highest, adj. *altissimus, excelsissimus*
Highly, adv. *excelsè, altè*
——— necessary, *valdè necessarium*
Highwayman, s. *fur, latro*
Hill, s. *collis*, 3 d. m.

Him, pro. acc. *eum, illum*
—— (I know), *illum novi*
—— (I write to) *ad eum scribo*
—— (I take) *illum prehendo*
Himself, pro. *ipse*
Hinder, v. a. *impedīre*, 4 c. *prohibēre*, 2 c.
Hinge, s. *cardo*, 3 d.
Hint, s. *admonitio*, 3 d.
Hire, v. *condūcĕre*, 3 c.
—— s. *merces, stipendium*
His, pro. pos. *suus, a, um*
Hiss, s. *sibilum*, 2 d. n.
History, s. *histŏria, æ* f.
Hog, s. *porcus*, 2 d. m. *sus*, 3. d. c. g.
—— sty, *suile*, 3 d. n. *hara*, 1 d. f.
Hogshead, s. *dōlium*, 2 d. n. *cadus*, 2 d. m.
Hold, v. a. *tenēre*, 2 c.
—— your tongue, *tace*
Hole, s. *fŏrāmen*, 3 d.
Holidays, s. *dies festi*
Home, s. *dŏmus*, 2 d. f.
—— (at) *domi*
—— (from) *domo*
Hone, s. *cos*, 3 d. f.
Honest, adj. *probus, honestus*
Honesty, s. *probitas, integritas*, f.
Honey, s. *mel*, 3 d. n.
—— suckle, *pĕriclymĕnos, i* f.
Honor, s. *hŏnor vel hŏnos*, 3 d. m.
Honor, v. a. *honorāre*, 1 c.
Honors, s. *hŏnōres*
Honorable, adj. *hŏnōrābĭlis*
Hoop, s. *circulus*, 2 d. m.
Hop, s. plant, *lŭpŭlus*, 2 d. m.
Hope so, (I) *ita spero*

Horn, s. *cornu*, n. indec.
Horse, s. *equus*, 2 d. m.
—— (saddle) s. *equus*
—— (carriage) *bijuges*, s. pl. m. *equi bĭjuges*
—— back, *equester*, adj. *eques*, s.
—— radish, *răphănus rusticanus*
Hosier, s. *călĭgārius*, 2 d. m.
Hot, adj. *calidus*
—— (red) *ardens*
—— (it is) *calet, æstuat*
Hound, s. *cănis venaticus*
Hound, (pack of) *cănes*
Hounds, s. *hora, æ* f.
House, (country) *villa*, 1 d. f.
—— (mansion) *domus, ædes*
—— of Lords, *Domus Parium*
—— (at your) *domi tuæ*
—— (at our) *domi nostræ*
—— (from my) *à domo meâ*
—— (dove) *columbarium*, 2 d. n.
—— (hot and green) *vaporarium, hypocaustum*, 2 d. n.
—— (coach) *stabulum rhedarium*
—— (brew) *zythepsarium*, 2 d. n.
—— (bake) *pistrinum*, 2 d. n.
—— (play) *theatrum*, 2 d. n.
—— (wash) *lăvăcrum*, 2 d. n.
—— (cow) *bŏvīle, is* n.
—— (brick) *domus lateribus structa*
—— hold, s. and adj. *familia*, 1 d. f. *familiaris*, adj.

How, adv. *quomodò, quàm*
—— ever great, *quàm magnum sit*
—— bad, *quàm pravus*
—— much, *quantum*
—— pretty she is! *ut sit formosa!*
—— far is it, *quantò distat, quantùm abest*
—— do you do? *quomodò vales?*
—— so, *quid ità*
—— many, *quot, quam multi*
—— long since, *quampridem*
—— can I do it, *quà possem id facere*
Human, adj. *hūmānus, a, um*
Humane, adj. *comis, benignus*
Humble, adj. *hŭmĭlis, supplex*
Humbly, adv. *humilitèr*
Hundred, a. *centum*
Hundred and twenty five (one) *centum viginti quinque*
Hunger, s. *fames*, 3 d. f.
Hungry, adj. *esuriens*
—— (I am) *esurio*
Hunt, v. a. *venāri*, 1 c. *venatum ire*
Hunter, (man) *venator*, 3 d.
—— (horse) *equus venator*
Hunting, *venatio*, 3 d. f.
Hurricane, s. *turbo*, 3 d. m.
Hurt, v. a. *lædĕre*
—— oneself, *se lædere*, 3 c.
Hurtful, adj. *nocens*
Hush, *tace*
Husband, s. *vir*, 2 d. *maritus*, 2 d.
Husbandman, s. *agricola*, 1 d. m.
Hyacinth, *hyăcinthus*, 2 d. m.

I

I, (pron. pers.) *ego*
Jack, (spit) *veruversorium*, 2 d. n.
Jade, (of horses) *equus ignavus*
James, *Jacobus*, 2 d.
Jane, *Johanna*, 1 d.
January, *Januarius*, 2 d. m.
Idiom, s. *idiōma*, 3 d. n.
Idiomatical, *idiomati pertinens*
Idle, adj. *otiosus, ignāvus*
Idleness, s. *ignāvia*, 1 d. f.
Jealous, adj. *suspiciosus*
Jelly, s. *gelatum jus*
Jessamine, s. *jessaminum*, 2 d. n.
Jest, s. *jocus*, 2 d. m. *facetia*, 1 d. f.
Jewels, s. *gemmæ*, 1 d. f.
Jeweller, *gemmarius*, 2 d.
If, (conj.) *si*
— he should come, *si ille veniret*
— she comes, *si veniat*
— he likes, *si velit*
— you please, *se velis*
— so, *sin ita*
Ignorance, s. *inscientia*, f. *ignorantia*, f.
Ignorant, *inscius, ignarus*
Ill, s. *malum*, 2 d. n.
— adj. *malus, a, um*
— manners, *pravitas, mores pravi*

Ill breeding, *mores asperi*
— omen, *malum augurium, portentum sinistrum*
— nature, *indoles morosa, ingenium immite*
— treat, v. a. *lædĕre*, 3 c.
— (to be) v. n. *ægrotāre*, 1 c.
Illness, s. *morbus*, 2 d. m.
Illumination, s. *illuminatio*, 3 d. f.
Imagine, v. *existimāre*, 1 c. *imaginări*, 1 c. dep.
Imitate, v. a. *imitări*, 1 c. dep.
Immediately, adv. *statim*
Immense, adj. *immensus, a, um*
Immoderate, adj. *immoderatus, profusus*
Impart, (to) v. *impertīre vel impertīri*
Imperceptibly, adv. *mĭnūtātĭm*
Impertinently, adv. *insulsè*
Implements, s. *instrumenta*, s. pl. n.
Impossible, adj. *impossibilis*
Improve, v. *proficĕre*, 3 c.
Improvement, s. *fructus*, 4 d. m.
Impudent, adj. *impŭdens*
Inattention, s. *negligentia*, 1 d. f.
In Paris, *Lutetiæ*
— (prep.) *in*
— the fire, *in flammis, in igne*
— the house, *in domo*
— my name, *meo nomine*
— London, *Londini vel Londino*
— his eyes, *ejus æstimatione*
— learning, *discendo*

In order to, *ut, ut meliùs*
— France, *in Galliâ*
— the year one thousand eight hundred and eleven, *A. D. millesimo octingentesimo et undecimo*
Incessant, adj. *constans*
Incessantly, adv. *assiduè*
Inclination, s. *propensio*, 3 d. f.
Incline, v. *inclināre*, 1 c.
Inclined, (to be) v. *propendēre*, 2 c.
Inconvenience, s. *incommodum*, 2 d. n.
Inconvenient, adj. *incommodus, intempestivus*
Incorrigible, adj. *incorrigibilis*
Indebted, adj. *ŏbærātus, devinctus*
——— to you for, *obstrictus tibi sum quòd*
Indeed, interj. *profectò, itane verò*
Indian-rubber, *gummi Indicum*
——— adj. *Indicus*
Indies, (East), *India, æ f.*
Indisposed, adj. *æger, ægrotus*
Indisposition, s. *ægritudo*, 3 d. f.
Induce, v. a. *allicĕre*, 3 c. *persuadere*, 2 c.
Industry, s. *industria*, 1 d. f.
Inestimable, adj. *inæstimabilis*
Infant, s. *infans*, 3 d. c. g.
Infer, v. *inferre, colligĕre*
Infinite, adj. *infinitus, immensus*
Infinitely, adv. *ad infinitum*

Infirmities, s. pl. *infirmitates*
Inform, v. a. *certiorem facere*
Information, s, *informatio, delatio*, 3 d. f.
Ingenious, adj. *ingeniosus, a, um*
Inhabitant, s. *incola*, 1 d. c. g.
Injure, v. a. *nocēre*, 2 c. *lædĕre*, 3 c.
Injured, p. p. *læsus*
Ink, s. *atramentum*, 2 d. n.
— bottle, *atramenti phiala*
— stand, s. *atramentarium*, 2 d. n.
Inn, s. *diversorium*, 2 d. n.
—— keeper s. *caupo*, 3 d. m.
Innocent, adj. *innocens, insons*
Innumerable, adj. *innumerus, infinitus*
Inquire, v. *quærĕre, inquirĕre*
Inquiry, s. *inquisitio*, 3 d. f.
Inquisitive, *curiosus, a, um*
Insist, v. *urgēre*, 2 c.
Inspection, s. *inspectio*, 3 d. f.
Instant, s. *instans, præsens*
——— on the tenth, *die decimo mensis instantis*
Instead, adv. *loco, vice*
Instep, s. *mons pedis*
Institution, s. *institūtio*, 3 d. f.
Instruct, v. *erudīre*, 4 c. *docēre*, 2 c.
Instruction, s. *institutio, eruditio*
Instrument, s. *instrumentum*, 2 d. n.
———— (used for a harp) *cĭthăra, lyra*
Insult, s. *insultatio*, 3 d. f.
Insure, v. a. *præstare damna*

Intelligent, adj. *intelligens*
Intelligible, adj. *intelligĭbĭlis*
Intend, (I) *statuo, volo*
Intention, s. *consilium*, 2 d. n.
Intent, s. *propositum*, 2 d. n.
Interest, s. *emolumentum*, 2 d. n. *fœnus*, 3 d. n.
Interesting, adj. *amabilis*
Intermix, v. *intermiscēre*, 2 c.
Interrupt, v. a. *interrumpĕre*, 3 c.
Into, prep. *in cum*, acc.
Intoxicate, v. a. *inebriāre*, 1 c.
Intreat, v. a. *obsecrāre*, 1 c.
Intreaty, s. *supplicatio*, 3 d. f.
Introduction, s. *exordium*, 2 d. n. *introductio*, 3 d. f.
Invite, v. a. *vocāre*, 1 c.
Invoice, s. *bonorum recognitio*
Joiner, s. *faber lignarius*
Joke, s. *jŏcus*, 2 d. m.
Joking, (she is) *ipsa illudit*
Jonquil, *asphŏdĕlus, i* m.
Journey, s. *ĭter*, 3 d. n.
Joy, s. *lætitia*, 1 d. f. *gaudium*, 2 d. n.
Ireland, s. pr. *Hibernia, æ* f.
Irish, *Hibernicus*
—— man, *Hibernicus*
Iron, s. *ferrum*, 2 d. n.
—— wire, s. *netum ferreum*
—— gate, s. *porta ferrea*
Island, s. *insŭla, æ* f.
Is, aux. v. *est*
— it? *est ne?*
—— not? *nonne est?*
—— so? *itane est?*
It rains, *pluit*
— (I thank you for) *gratias id propter tibi ago*

It is, *est*
—— true, *verum est*
—— a man, *homo est*
— (that is) *id est*
Italian, adj. *Italicus*
Italy, s. pr. *Italia, æ* f.
Judge, s. *jūdex, ĭcis,* m.
—— v. *jūdĭcāre,* 1 c.
Judgment, s. *jūdĭcium,* 2 d. n.
Judicial, adj. *jūdĭciālis*
Jug, s. *cantharus,* 2 d. m.
July, (month) *Julius,* 2 d. m.
Jump, (to) v. *saltāre*
Jump, s. *saltus, subsultus*
June, (month) *Jūnius,* 2 d. m.
Juniper, (tree) *jūnĭpĕrus, i* f.
Just, adj. *justus, æquus*
—— so, *sic est*
—— left, *modo profectus*
—— dined, (I have) *modo prandi*
Justice, s. *justĭtia, æ* f.
—— (to do) *reddere justitiam*
Juvenile, adj. *jŭvĕnīlis*
Ivory, s. *ebur,* 3 d. n.

K

Keen, adj. *acutus, acer*
Keep. s. *custodia, æ* f.
—— v. *servāre,* 1 c.
—— an establishment, *tenēre domum lautum*
—— horses, *habēre equos*
—— any, (I never) *nunquam equos servo, vel habeo*
—— at home, *domi se continere*
—— good house, *tempestive domum redire*
—— a carriage, *habere essedum*
—— this, *hoc serva*
—— time in music, *certam legem temporum servare*
Keeping us, (the means of) *ratio nos detinendi*
Kettle, (great) *caldarium,* 2 d. n.
Key, s. *clavis,* 3 d. f.
Kid, s. *hædus,* 2 d. m.
—— adj. *hædinus, a, um*
Kill, v. *occidere,* 3 c. *interficere,* 3 c.
Kill, two birds with one stone, *absolvĕre uno labore ærumnas duas*
—— him, *illum interfice*
Kind, adj. *benignus, humanus*
Kindly, adv. *blandissimè*
Kind, s. *species,* 5 d. f.
Kindness, s. *benignitas, beneficium*
King (God save the) *vivat rex*
Kingdom, s. *regnum,* 2 d. n.
Kinsman, s. *cognatus, propinquus,* 2 d. m.
Kiss, v. *osculāri,* 1 c. dep.
Kitty, *Catharina*
Kitchen, s. *culina, coquina*
—— garden, *hortus culinarius*
Kite, (the bird) s. *milvus,* 2 d. m.
Knave, *nĕbŭlo,* 3 d. m.
—— (at cards) *miles, eques*
Knavery, *fraus,* 3 d. f.
Knee, s. *gĕnu,* n. indec.
Knife, s. *culter,* 2 d. m. *cultellus,* 2 d. m.

Knife, (pen) s. *scalpellum*, 2 d.
Knight, s. *eques*, 3 d. m. *eques auratus*
Knock, v. a. *pulsāre*, 1 c.
——— s. *verber*, 3 d. n.
——— there is a, *aliquis pulsat portas*
Knocker, s. *cornix*
Know, (let me) *fac me certiorem*
Know a person, (to) *novisse aliquem*
——— a thing, (to) *cognoscere aliquid*
——— (I do not) *nescio*
——— my father (you) *novisti patrem meum*
Knowledge, s. *scientia*, *peritia*, *eruditio*
——— without, *ignarus*, *insciens*

L

Laborious, adj. *lăboriōsus*, *a*, *um*
Labour, s. *lăbor vel lăbos*, 3 d. m.
Lace, s. *fimbria*, 1 d. f.
Lad, s. *puer*, 2 d.
Lady, s. *domina*, *hera*
—— (young) *virgo nobilis*, *puella*
Lake, s. *lacus*, 2 d. f.
Lame, adj. *claudus*, *mancus*
Lament, v. *lugēre*, 2 c.
Lamp, s. *lampas*, 3 d. f. *lucerna*, 1 d. f.
Land, s. *ager*, *terra*
—— (arable) *ager arabilis*, m.
—— v. n. *appellĕre*, 3 c.
Landing, *ad terram appulsus*
Landlord, *prædii dominus*
Lane, s. *angiportus*, 4 d. m. *diverticulum*, 2 d. n.
Language, s. *lingua*, 1 d. f. *sermo*, 3 d. m.
Lantern, s. *lāterna*, 1 d. f.
Larch-tree, s. *lărix*, *īcis* f.
Large, adj. *lātus*
Larger, adj. *amplior*, *latior*
Lark, s. *alauda*, 3 d. f.
Last, adj. *ultimus*, *novissimus*
Last night, *nox ultima*
—— time, *tempore postremo*
—— year, *anno ultimo*
Lasting, part. *stabilis*
——— (ever) *sempiternus*
Latch, s. *obex*, 3 d.
Lately, adv. *nupèr*, *modò*
Late, adj. *serus*, *tardus*
Later, adj. *recentior*
Latin, adj. *Lătīnus*, *a*, *um*
Laugh, v. n. *ridēre*, 2 c.
Laughter, s. *risus*, 4 d. m.
Law, s. *lex*, 3 d. f.
—— (father in) *socer*, 2 d.
—— (brother in) *frater mariti*
Law (sister in) *soror mariti*
—— (son in) *gener*, 2 d.
—— (daughter in) *nurus*, 4 d.
—— expenses, *impensæ*
—— proceedings, *controversia judiciaria*
Lawn, (stuff) s. *sindon*, *carbasus*
Lawsuit, s. *actio*, 3 d. f. *causa*, 1 d. f. *lis*, 3 d. f.
Lawyer, s. *causidicus*, *jurisconsultus*, 2 d. m.
Lay, (a bet) *pignus deponĕre*

Lay, v. a. *ponĕre*, 3 c.
—— the cloth, (to) *mensam sternere*
—— or set a trap, *lăqueum tendere, insidias struere*
Laziness, s. *pigritia, segnitia*, 1 d. f.
Lazy, adj. *piger*
—— bones, *erro, ōnis*, m.
Lead, (of a house) *tecti plumbum*
—— (for plumbers) *plumbum*
—— (at cards) *ducere*
Lean, adj. *macer, macilentus*
Leap, v. *salio*, 4 c. *salto*, 1 c.
—— year, *annus bissextilis*
Learn, (to) v. *discĕre*, 3 c.
Learned, part. *doctus, a, um*
Learning, s. *doctrina*, 1 d. f.
——— French, (I am) *disco linguam Gallicam*
Lease, s. *instrumentum fundī elocandi*
Least, adj. *minimus, a, um*
——— (at) *certè*
Leave, s. *licentia, potestas, venia*
——— v. *relinquĕre, deserĕre*, 3 c.
——— (to give) *veniam dare*
——— off, (to) *desinĕre*, 3 c. *desistĕre*, 3 c.
——— (to take) *decēdĕre*, 3 c.
——— me alone, *ne sic mihi molestus esto*
——— off crying, *desine lugēre*
Leaves, s. pl. *paginæ*, 1 d. f.
Lecture, s. *prælectio, lectio*
Leech, s. *hirudo*, 3 d. f. *sanguisuga*, 1 d. f.
Leek, (a plant) *porrum*, 2 d. n.

Left off, (I have) *jam destĭti*
—— adj. *reliquus, orbatus*
—— hand, s. *manus sinistra, manus læva*
——— handed, *scævus*
Leg, s. *crus*, 3 d. n. *tibia*, 1 d. f.
—— of mutton, *coxa ovina*
Lemon, s. *malum citreum*
Lend, v. *dare mutuum, commodo*
Lent, s. *quadragesima, jejunium quadragesimale*
Leopard, *leŏpardus*, 2 d. m
Less, adv. *minŭs*
—— adj. *minor*
Lesson, s. *lectio*, 3 d. f.
Let, v. *elocāre*, 1 c.
—— him speak, imperat. *loquatur, loquitor*
Letter, s. *lĭtĕra*, 1 d. f.
——— to a friend, *lĭtteræ*, s. pl. *epistola*, 1 d. f.
—— paper, *charta literis scribendis*
Lettuce, *lactūca*, 1 d. f.
Lewis, s. pr. *Ludovicus*, d. m.
Liar, s. *mendax, mendosus*
Liberty, s. *lĭbertas*, 3 d. f.
Library, s. *bibliotheca*, 1 d. f.
Lieutenant, s. *optio, præfectus*
Life, s. *vita*, 1 d. f.
Lift up, v. *tollĕre*, 3 c.
Light, s. *lumen*, 3 d. n.
—— (day) *lux*, 3 d. f.
—— (before day), *ante lucem, antĕlūcānus*
Light horse, s. *velites*, pl. m.
Like it, (because I) *quia id mihi gratum est*
———(if you) *si tibi placeat*

Like, (the) *similis, e*
——— (as you) *ut placet, ut libet*
——— (he is not) *haud similis est*
——— like me, *mihi similis*
——— v. a. *diligĕre,* 3 c.
——— (to be) *similem esse*
Liked, (he is not) *non est popularis vel laudatus*
Likely, adv. *probabliter*
——— adj. *probabilis*
Likeness, s. *similitudo,* 3 d. f.
Lily of the valley, *lilium convallium*
Limb, s. *membrum,* 2 d. n.
Limit, s. *terminus,* 2 d. m. *limes,* 3 d. m.
Line, s. *līnea,* 1 d. f.
—— (string) *funiculus,* 2 d. m.
Linen, (cloth) *linteum,* 2 d. n. *sindon,* 3 d. f.
Lion, s. *leo,* 3 d. m.
Listen, (to) v. *auscultāre,* 1 c.
Listening, s. *auscultatio,* 3 d. f.
Litigious, adj. *lītīgiōsus*
Little, adj. *parvus, a, um*
—— adv. *parum,*
—— and little, *paulatim*
Live, v. *vivĕre,* 3 c.
—— in a house, *habitāre in domo*
Living, (church) *beneficium ecclesiasticum*
Livery, s. *vestis domestici*
Load, s. *onus,* 3 d. n.
—— of coals, *vehes carbonum*
—— of hay, *carrus fœni*
—— of wood, *carrus lignorum*
Loaded, adj. *onustus, oneratus*

Loaf, s. *panis,* 3 d. m.
—— of sugar, *sacchari meta*
Lobster, s. *astacus,* 2 d. m.
Lock, s. *sera,* 1 d. f.
—— v. *serāre,* 1 c. *obserāre,* 1 c.
—— up, *in carcerem conjicĕre*
Lodging, s. *ædium pars conducta*
London, s. pr. *Londinium vel Londinum,* 2 d. n.
Long ago, adv. *jamdudum*
—— adj. *longus, prolixus*
Long to see him, (I) v. *eum videre cupio*
—— time, adv. *diù*
—— as (as) *quamdiù*
—— as my arm, (as) *per longitudinem brachii*
Look at, (to) *vidēre,* 2 c. *inspicĕre,* 3 c.
—— for that, *id quærĕre*
Looking for you, (I am) *te ipsum quæro*
Look at that, *hoc aspice*
——— me, *me vide vel intuēre*
——— upon yourself, *te ipsum considera*
——— here, *hìc inspice*
——— like, *similem esse*
——— after, *curāre,* 1 c.
——— well, *benè valere*
——— (air or appearance) s. *vultus, persona, species*
Looked over, *inspectus, lectus*
Looking-glass, *speculum,* 2 d. n.
Loss, s. *damnum,* 2 d. n.
Lord, s. *dominus,* 2 d.
—— mayor, s. *prætor urbanus*
Lordship, *dominatus, principatus*

Lordship, or manor, *ditio, onis*, f.
Lose, v. *perdĕre, amittĕre*
Lost, p. p. *perditus, amissus*
Loud, adj. *clarus, vocalis*
—— (so) *ita concitatus*
—— (aloud) *altâ voce*
Love, (to) v. *amāre*, 1 c. *diligĕre*, 3 c.
—— you, (I) *te amo*
Loved, *amatus*
Love, s. *amor*, 3 d. m.
Lovely, adj. *amabilis*
Lovelier, adj. *formosior*
Low, adj. *humilis*
—— (to) v. *mugīre*, 4 c.
Lowest price, (at the) *minimo pretio*
Luck, s. *fortuna*, 1 d. f. *successus*, 4 d. m.
Lucky, adj. *prosper, faustus*
Lump, (swelling) s. *tuber*, 3 d. n.
—— of earth, *gleba*, 1 d. f.
Lunch, s. *frustum*, 2 d. n. *merenda*, 1 d. f.
Luncheon s. *merenda, æ* f.

M

Machination, s. *māchĭnātio, conspiratio*
Mad, adj. *insanus, vesanus, demens*
Made, p. p. *factus*
—— (well) *venustus, pulchrè factus*
Madam, *domina*, vocat.
Mad-dog, s. *canis rabidus*
Maggot, *galba, termes, lendix*
Magistrate, *măgistrātus, præfectus*
Magpie, *pica*, 1 d. f.
Maid, s. *virgo*, 3 d.
—— (chamber) *ancilla*, 1 d.
—— (servant) *ancilla*
Majesty, s. *măjestas*, 3 d. f.
Maintain, v. *affirmāre*, 1 c.
Major, *lĕgātus*, 2 d.
Make, (to) v. a. *facĕre*, 3 c.
Make (we) a point of, *insistĕre*
—— use, (we) *utimur*
—— faces, *vultus ducĕre*
—— a noise, *strepĕre*, 3 c.
Make a pen, *pennam acuĕre*
—— up, *redire in gratiam*
—— haste, *festināre*, 1 c.
Malady, s. *morbus*, 2 d. m.
Mallows, s. *malvæ*, pl.
Malt, s. *brasium*, 2 d. n.
Man, s. *homo*, 3 d.
—— cook, *coquus*, 2 d.
—— kind, *genus humanum*
—— servant, *famulus, domesticus*
Management, s. *administratio*, 3 d. f.
Mane, s. *juba*, 1 d. f.
Manner, s. *mos*, m. *mŏdus*, m.
—— (in a) *quodammodò, ùt*
Mansion, s. *domus*, 4 d. f.
—— house, (the) *prætorium urbanum*
Mantua-maker, s. *sartrix*, 3 d. f.
Manure, s. *stercus*, 3 d. n. *fimus*, 2 d. m.

Manuscript, s. *liber manuscriptus*
Many, adj. *plures, multi, complures*
—— accidents, *căsus frequentes*
—— (several) *plurimi*
—— professors, *complures doctores*
—— ? (how) *quot ?*
Marble, s. *marmor,* 3 d. n.
March, (month) *Martius,* 2 d. m.
Mare, s. *equa,* 1 d. f.
Marigold, s. *caltha,* 1 d. f.
Mark, v. *notāre,* 1 c. *signāre,* 1 c.
—— s. *signum,* 2 d. n.
Market, s. *forum,* 2 d. *mercatus,* 2 d. m. *emporium,* 2 d. n.
—— fish, *forum piscarium*
—— hay, *forum fœni*
Marriage, s. *nuptiæ,* s. pl. f.
Marrow, s. *mĕdulla,* 1 d. f.
Marry, v. *uxorem ducere*
—— (the office of a priest) *connubio jungere*
Married, (he is) *uxorem duxit*
Marsh, s. *palus,* 3 d. m.
Masculine, adj. *masculinus*
Mask, s. *larva, æ* f.
Masked, p. *larvātus, a, um*
Mast, s. *malus,* 2 d. m.
Master, s. *herus,* 2 d. *dominus,* 2 d.
—— (teacher) *præceptor, magister*
—— (French) *præceptor, linguæ Gallicæ*
Matt, s. *matta,* 1 d. f. *teges,* 3 d. f.
Match, s. *nuptiæ,* f. *connubium,* 2 d. n.
Match, (to light a) *sulphuratum accendĕre*
Mate. s. *socius,* 2 d. m. *collega,* 1 d. m.
Material, adj. *corporeus*
Mathematics, *măthēmătĭca,* s. pl. n.
Matrimony, s. *matrĭmōnium,* 2 d. n.
Matter, s. *mātĕria,* 1 d. f.
—— ? (what is the) *quid rei est ?*
—— (it does not) *parùm refert*
Matter with you ? (what is the) *quid tibi vis ?*
—— (what was the) *quid erat ? quæ res evēnit ?*
Mattress, s. *culcita lanea*
Maxim, *axioma,* 3 d. n. *præceptum,* 2 d. n.
May, (month) *Maius,* 2 d. m.
—— from verb to be, *the present tense potential and subjunctive, includes, in the inflections of Latin verbs the power of* can *or* may.
—— (I) *possum*
—— (in order that I) *ut possim*
—— speak, (you) *potes loqui*
—— you like it, *velim ut placeat tibi*
—— go, (we) *nos ne possimus abire ?*
—— I go out, *licetne mihi exire ?*
—— be, (it) *potest esse*
Mayor, s. *prætor urbanus*
Me, pers. pro. *me,* acc. c.
—— (of) *mei*
—— (near) *prope me*
—— (without) *sine me*

Me, (he speaks of) *de me loquitur*
—— (they love) *me diligunt*
—— (for) *pro me*
—— (before) *ante me*
—— (they see) *me vident*
—— (they speak to) *mihi loquuntur*
Meadow, s. *pratum*, 2 d. n.
—— land, *pascuum, pascua*, pl.
Meal, (repast) s. *cibus, cœna*
Mean, adj. *abjectus, mĕdiocris*
Mean no offence, (I) *nolo offendĕre*
—— (what do you) *quid vis dicere?*
—— (when do you) *quando intelligis?*
Mean, (we) *volumus, proponimus*
Meaning, s. *sensus*, 4 d. m. *ănĭmus*, 2 d. m.
Means, s. plu. *facultates, opes*
—— (by all) *prorsùs*
—— (by no) *nullo modo, nequaquam*
Measles, s. *rubiolæ*, s. pl. f.
Measure, v. *metīri*, 4 c.
—— s. *mensūra*, 1 d. f. *mŏdus*, 2 d. m.
Meat, s. *cĭbus*, 2 d. m. *căro*, 3 d. f.
—— (roast) *caro assa*
—— (boiled) *caro cocta*
—— (sweet) *tragemata*, s. pl. n.
Meddle, v. *se immiscere rei*
Mediterranean, adj. *mĕdĭterrāneus, a, um*
Medlar, s. *mespĭlum*, 2 d. n.
Meet, (to go and) *ire obviam*
Meet, v. *occurrĕre*, 3 c.
—— me at home, (you will) *me invenies domi*
——, to assemble, v. *congrĕdi*, 3 c. dep.
Meeting, s. *conventus*, 4 d. m. *congregatio*, 3 d. f.
Member of Parliament, *senator*, 3 d.
—— s. *membrum*, 2 d. n.
Memorandum, s. *memorandum*, 2 d. n. *memoranda*, pl. n.
Men, s. *homines*, 3 d.
Mend, v. *rĕficĕre*, 3 c.
Mention, v. *mĕmŏrāre*, 1 c.
Mentioned, p. p. *mĕmŏrātus commemoratus*
Merchant, (wine) s. *œnopola*, 1 d. m. *vinarius*, 2 d. m.
Merciful, adj. *mĭsĕricors, clemens*
Merit, s. *mĕrĭtum*, 2 d. n.
—— v. *mĕrēre*, 2 c.
Merrily, adv. *festivè*
Merry, adj. *hilaris, lepidus*
Meshes, s. pl. *rētis măcŭlæ*
Met, p. p. *obventus*
Method, s. *ratio*, 3 d. f. *mĕthŏdus*, 2 d. f.
Mews, (for horses) *stăbŭla*, pl. 2 d. n.
Mice, *mures*, pl. 3 d. m.
Michaelmas, *festum sancti Michaëlis*
Middle, s. *mĕdium*, 2 d. n.
Midnight, s. *media nox*
Midsummer, s. *solstitium æstivum*
Might, s. *potentia*, 1 d. f.
—— do, (I) *facerem*
—— (with all his) *totis viribus*

Might have done it, (I) *hoc potuissem facere*
Milan, s. pr. *Mediolanum*, 2 d.
Mild, adj. *mitis*
Mile, s. *mille passus*
Mile stone, s. *milliāre, is*, n.
Milk, s. *lac*, 3 d. n.
—— pot, *canthărus*, 2 d. m.
Mill, s. *mŏla*, 1 d. f. *pistrīna*, 1 d. f.
—— (paper) *mola chartaria*
—— (wind) *mola vento agitata*
Miller, s. *mōlĭtor*, 3 d. m.
Million, s. *decies centena millia*
Minced meat, *minūtal*, 3 d. n.
Mind, s. *mens*, 3 d. f.
—— v. *curāre*, 1 c. *respicĕre*, 3 c.
—— (never) *ne respicias*
Mine, (it is) *meus est*
—— (a friend of) *amicus meus*
—— (a book of) *liber meus*
Minister, s. *mĭnister*, 2 d. m.
———— priest, *ecclesiæ pastor, clericus, minister*
Mint, s. *officina nummorum regia*
—— (a herb) s. *mentha*, 1 d.
Minute, (every) *mōmentāneus*
Mischief, s. *mălum*, 2 d. n.
Mischievous, adj. *mălignus, a, um*
Miser, s. *avarus, miser*
Misery, s. *mĭsĕria, paupertas*
Misfortune, *infortunium*, 2 d. n.
Miss, (a title) *hera, æ* 1 d.
—— v. *prætermittĕre*, 3 c.
Missing p. *amissus, a, um*
Mislay, v. *extra locum ponere*
Mist, s. *nebula*, 1 d. f.
Mistake, s. *error*, 3 d. m. *erratum*, 2 d. n.
——— v. *falli*, 3 c. *errāre*, 1 c.
Mistaken, (you are) *erras*
Moat, s. *fossa, æ* f.
Mob, s. *turba, æ* f.
Mock, v. *deludĕre, ludificāre, dērīdēre*
Mocker, s. *derisor*, 3 d. m.
Mocks me, (he) *me derīdet*
Modern, adj. *recens, hodiernus*
Modest, adj. *mŏdestus, pudicus*
Modesty, s. *mŏdestia*, 1 d. f.
Monday, s. *dies, lunæ, feria secunda*
Money, s. *argentum, nummus*
——— box, s. *arca nummorum*
Month, s. *mensis, is* m.
Moon light, s. *lunaris lampas*
—— shines, (the) *luna splendet*
More, adj. *plus*
—— than, *plus quàm*
—— than once, *sæpiùs*
—— (no) *non plus*
Moreover, adv. *insuper*
Morning, s. *māne*, n. *tempus matutinum*
——— gown, *toga cubicularis*
Morrow, (the day after to-) *perendiè*
Mortal, s. *mortālis*
——— adj. *lethalis*
Mortgage, s. *hypotheca*, 1 d. f.
Moss, s. *muscus*, 2 d. m.

Most obedient, *obsequentissimus*
—— adv. *maximè*
—— people, *plurimi*
Mother, s. *māter*, 3 d.
—— of pearl, *concha Persica*
Motive, s. *incitamentum*, 2 d. n
Move, v. *movere*, 2 c.
Moves, (he) *movet*
Mouldy, adj. *mūcĭdus*
Moult, v. *plumas exuere*
Mount, s. *collis*, 3 d. m.
Mountebank, s. *circulator*, 3 d. m.
Mourning, (to be in) *atratus vel pullatus*
Mouse, s. *mus*, 3 d. m.
—— trap, s. *muscĭpŭla*, 1 d. f.
Mouth, s. *os*, 3 d. n.
Much, adj. *multus, a, um*
—— (very) *plurimus, a, um*
—— (how) *quantus, a, um*
Mud, s. *lutum*, 2 d. n.
Muff, s. *manica villosa*
Mulberry, s. *mōrum* 2 d. n.
—— tree, *mōrus*, 2 d. f.
Mule, s. *mūlus*, 2 d. m. *mūla*, 1 d. f.
Murder, *homicidium*, 2 d. n. *cædes*, 3 d. f.
Museum, s. *mūsæum*, 2 d. n.
Music, s. *mūsĭce, es* f. *mūsĭca, æ* f.
Music master, *magister vel instructor musices*
Musk, s. *muscus, moschus*, 2 d. m.
Muslin, s. *nebula linea*
Must go, (I) *īre debeo*
—— do, (they) *facĕre debent*
—— come back) (you) *revenīre te oportet*
—— converse, (you) *loqui vel colloqui debes*
—— have, (we) *habere debemus*
—— come, (you) *venire te oportet*
—— (I) see you to-morrow, *te videre cras debeo*
—— be quiet, (I) *tacendum est, silere debeo*
—— finish, (they) *finiunto*, imper.
—— learn, (he) *discat, discito*, 3 p. imperat.
—— mind, (you) *attende, attendito*, 2 p. imperat.
Mustard, s. *sĭnāpis, is* f. *sĭnāpe, is* n.
Mutton, s. *caro ovina*
Myrtle, s. *myrtus*, 2 d. f.
Myself, pron. *ipse ego*
Mystery, s. *mysterium, arcanum* n.
My, pron. *meus, a, um*
— daughter, *filia mea*
— father, *pater meus*
— brothers, *fratres mei*

N

Nail, of iron, *clavus*, 2 d. m.
—— (finger) *unguis*, 3 d. m.
—— v. *clavis pangĕre, suffigĕre*
Naked, adj. *nūdus*
Name, s. *nōmen*, 3 d. n.
Namely, adv. *nōmĭnātĭm*

Napkin, s. *mappa*, 1 d. f. *linteolum*, 2 d. n.
Naples, *Neāpŏlis, is* f.
Narcissus, s. *narcissus*, 2 d. m.
Narration, s. *narrātio*, 3 d. f.
Narrow, adj. *arctus, angustus*
Nation, s. *gens*, 3 d. f. *natio*, 3 d. f.
National, adj. *gentīlis*,
Native, adj. *nātīvus*
——— land, *patria, æ* f.
Natural, adj. *nātūrālis, e*
Nature, s. *natura, æ* f.
Naughty, adj. *malus, a, um*
Near, prep. and adv. *juxta, secundum, prope*
Nearer, comp. *propior*
Nearly, *propè, parcè*
Neat, adj. *nĭtĭdus*
Neatly, adv. *nĭtĭdè*
Neatness, s. *nĭtor*, 3 d. m.
Necessary, adj. *opus*, indec. adj.
Necessity, s. *nĕcessĭtas*, 3 d. f.
Neck, s. *collum*, 2 d. n.
—— cloth, s. *collare*, 3 d. n.
—— lace, s. *mŏnīle*, 3 d. n.
Nectarine, s. *nŭcĭpersĭca*, 1 d. f.
Need, s. *egestas*, 3 d. f. *inedia*, 1 d. f.
Needful, adj. *ŏpus*, adj. *opus est*
Needle, s. *ăcus, ūs*, f.
——— case, *ăcuum theca*
Neglect, v. *neglĭgĕre*, 3 c.
——— s. *neglectus*, 4 d. m. *negligentia*, 1 d. f.
Negro, s. *ethiops*, 3 d. *maurus*, 1 d. m.

Neighbour, s. *vīcīnus*, 2 d. m.
Neighbourhood, s. *vīcīnia*, 1 d. f. *vicinitas*, 3 d. f.
Neighbouring, adj. *proxĭmus, vīcīnus*
Neither, conj. *nec, neque*
Nephew, s. *fratris vel sororis filius*
Nerve, s. *nervus*, 2 d. m.
Nest, s. *nīdus*, 2 d. m.
Net, s. *rēte*, 3 d. n.
Netherlands, s. p. *Belgicæ Provinciæ*
Nettle, s. *urtīca*, 1 d. f.
Never, adv. *nunquam*
——— mind, *tranquillo sis animo*
Nevertheless, adj. *nĭhĭlomĭnŭs*
New, adj. *novus, a, um*
—— bread, *panis mollis vel recens*
News, *rumōres*, 3 d. m.
—— paper, *nouvellæ scriptæ*
New year's day, *calendæ Januarii*
—— laid eggs, *ōva recentia*
Next, adj. *proxĭmus*
—— to me, (he is sitting) *mihi proxĭmus sĕdet*
—— day, *postrīdiè*
—— month, *mense proximo*
—— adv. *deinceps, deinde*
—— prep. *secundum, juxta*
—— room, (in the) *in camerâ proximâ*
—— year, *annus proximus*
Nib, s. *rostrum*, 2 d. n. *cuspis*, 3 d. f.
Nice, adj. *delicatus*
Niece, s. *fratris vel sororis filia*
Night, s. *nox*, 3 d. f.

Night, (last) *postremâ nocte*
—— cap, *pileus nocturnus*
—— (I heard a noise in the) *audivi strepitum nocte*
—— all, *totâ nocte*
Nightingale, s. *luscinia*, 1 d. f. *philŏmela*, 1 d. f.
Nimble, adj. *agilis, celer*
Nimbleness, s. *agilitas*, 3 d.
Nine, *nŏvem*
Nineteen, *novendecim, undeviginti*
Nineteenth, *undevigesimus*
Ninety, *nōnāginta*
Ninth, *nonus*
No, *non*, adj. *nullus*, adj.
— not yet, *nondùm*
— longer, *ne diutius*
— where, *nusquam*
— more, *nihil amplius*
— matter, *nihil rĕfert*
— means, (by) *nullo modo, nequaquàm*
— one, *nullus*
Nobility, s. *nobĭlĭtas*, 3 d. f.
Noble, adj. *nōbĭlis, e*
Nobody, s. *nemo*, 3 d. c. g.
Noise, s. *sonitus, ûs* m. *strepitus, ûs* m.
None, pron. *nullus*
—— (I have) *nullos habeo*
Nonsense, s. *absurdus sermo*
Noon, s. *mĕrīdies, ei* m.
—— after, s. *tempus pōmĕrīdiānum*
Nor, conj. *nec, neque*
North, s. *septentrio*, 3 d. m.

Nose, s. *nāsus*, 2 d. m.
Nosegay, s. *fasciculus florum*
Nostrils, (s. plu.) *nares*, pl. f.
Not, adv. *non, haud, ne*
—— yet, *nondum*
—— (I have) *non habeo*
Note, s. *nota, annotatio, tenus, epistola*
Notice, v. *observāre*, 1 c.
Nothing, s. *nihil*, n. indec.
——— but play, (you do) *nihil facis nisi ludere*
——— but laugh, (he does) *ridet tantùm*
Notwithstanding, adv. *attamen, nihilominus*
Novel, adj. *novus*
—— s. *historia amœna vel novella*
Novelty, *novitas*, 3 d. f.
November, s. *November*, 3 d. m.
Nourish, v. a. *nutrīre*, 4 c.
Now, adv. *nunc*
—— and then, *nonnunquam*
Number, s. *numerus*, 2 d. m.
Numerous, adj. *numerosus*
Nurse oneself, (to) *se curāre sedulò*
Nursery, (room) *cubiculum nutrici appropriatum*
——— for trees, *seminarium*, 2 d. n.
Nut, s. *nux*, 3 d. f.
Nutmeg, *nux moschata*
Nut tree, *nux, nŭcis* f.

O

Oak, s. *rōbur*, 3 d. n. *quercus*, 4 d. f.
Oar, s. *rēmus*, 2 d. m.
Oats, s. *ăvēna*, 1 d. f.

Oath, s. *juramentum*, 2 d. n.
Obedient, (most) *obsequentissimus*

Obey, v. *obsĕqui*, 3 c. dep. *obedīre*, 4 c. *parēre*, 2 c.
Obeys him, (he) *huic paret*
Object, s. *res*, 5 d. f. *objectum*, 2 d. n.
Oblige, v. a. *cogĕre*, 3 c. *benè merēri*, dep.
Obliged, (to be) *devinctum esse*
——— to you, (I am very much) *valdè tibi sum devinctus*
Obliging, *blandus*, *bĕnĕfĭcus*
Obscure, adj. *tenebrosus*, *difficilis*
Observation, s. *observātio*, 3 d. f.
Observe, v. *notāre*, 1 c. *observāre*, 1 c.
Obstacle, s. *impedimentum*, 2 d. n.
Obstinacy, s. *contumacia*, 1 d. f.
Obstinate, adj. *pertĭnax*, *obstinatus*
Obtain, v. *obtinēre*, 2 c.
——— an opinion, *sententiam alicujus obtinere*
Occasion, s, *occāsio*, 1 d. f. *causa*, 1 d. f.
——— (there is no) *non ŏpus est*
Occupy, (to) v. a. *occupāre*, 1 c.
Occur, v. *occurrĕre*, *obvenīre*
O'clock ? (what is it) *quotâ est horâ ?*
——— (before six) *ante sextam horam*
October, s. *October*, 3 d. m.
Odd, adj. *lĕvis*, *inusitatus*
Oddity, s. *rārĭtas*, 3 d. f. *insolentia*, 1 d. f.
Oddness, *raritas*
Odious, *odiosus*

Of, prep. *de*, *ex*, *à* &c.
Off, (to take) *abhinc auferre*
Offence, s. *offensio*, 3 d. f. *culpa*, 1 d. f.
Offend, v. *offendĕre*, 3 c.
Offer, s. *condĭtio*, *propōsitum*
——— v. *præbēre*, 2 c. *prōponĕre*, 3 c.
Office, s. *mūnus*, 3 d. n. *offĭcina*, 1 d. f.
Officer, s. *præfectus*, *lēgātus*, &c.
Often, adv. *sæpè*
Oil, s. *ŏleum*, 2 d. n.
Old, adj. *vĕtus*, *antĭquus*
— age, *sĕnecta*, 1 d. f. *sĕnectus*, 3 d. f.
— man, *senex*, 3 d. m.
— woman, *vĕtŭla*, 1 d. f. *ănus*, 4 d. f.
Omen, s. *ōmen*, 3 d. n.
Omit, v. *omittĕre*, 3 c.
On, prep. *sŭper*, &c.
On account, *eâ causâ*
— purpose, *consultò*
— my part, *meâ parte*
— the table, *sŭper mensam*
— foot, *pedester*
— horseback, *equester*
— the left, *ad sinistram*
— a sudden, *sŭbĭtò*
— the contrary, *è contrario*
— on the wrong side, *ăliorsŭm*
— Sunday, *die Dominicâ*
— Tuesday, *die Martis*
— Monday next, *die proximâ Lunæ*
Once, adj. *semel*
One, adj. *ūnus*, *a*, *um*
——— (every) *quisque*, pron.
——— (any) *quivis*
Only, adv. *tantùm*
Open, adj. *apertus*, *a*, *um*

Open it, imper. *id aperi*
Opening, s. *apertio, hiatus*
Openly, adv. *apertè*
Openness, s. *candor*, 3 d. m.
Opera, s. *ŏpĕra, fabula musicis modis decantata*
Opinion. s. *ŏpīnio*, 3 d. f.
Opportunity, s. *opportunitas*, 3 d. f.
Oppose, (to) v. a. *oppōnĕre*, 3 c.
Opposite, adj. *adversus, ex adverso*
Opposition, s. *oppositio*, 3 d. f.
Oppress, v. a. *opprimĕre*, 3 c.
Opulent, adj. *dives, opulentus*
Or, conj. *sīve, &c.*
Orange, s. *malum aureum, aurantium*
Orchard, s. *pomarium*, 2 d. n.
Order, v. a. *jubēre*, 2 c.
—— s. *ordo, inis*, 3 d. m.
—— (placed in) *ordine*
—— (in) *ut*
Ordinary, adj. *usitatus*
Organ, s. *orgănum, i* n.
—— music, *organa musica*
Ornament, s. *ornamentum*, n. *ornatus*, m.
Orthography, s. *orthographia*, 1 d. f.
Ostler, s. *stabularius*, 2 d. m.
Other, adj. *alius, a, ud*
Otherwise, adj. *aliusmodi*
Other side, (on the) *è contrario, alterâ ex parte*
Oven, s. *furnus*, 2 d. m.
Overcome, v. a. *vincĕre*, 3 c. *superāre*, 1 c.
Over, prep. *super, supra, &c.*
—— (to look) *inspicĕre*, 3 c.
Over again, (to read) *iterùm legere*
—— (it is all) *actum est*
—— the door, *sŭper vel supra portam*
—— against, *ex adverso*
—— flow, s. *exundāre*, neut. *inundāre*, act.
—— flowing, s. *inundātio*, 3 d. f.
Overrun, v. a. *vastāre*, 1 c. *depopulāri*, dep.
Overseer, s. *inspector*, 3 d. m.
Oversight, s. *incūria*, 1 d. f.
Overtake on the road, *assĕqui*
Overturn, v. a. *evertĕre, subvertĕre*
Ought, (he) *dēbet*
—— not, (I) *non dēbeo*
—— to shun vice, (men) *hŏmĭnes vĭtium fugere dēbent*
Ounce, s. *uncia*, 1 d. f.
Our, ours, pron. *noster, tra, trum*
Ourselves, *nos*
—— (we have hurt) *nosmet ipsos læsimus*
Out, prep. *è, ex, extra, &c.*
— (he is) *abest*
Outside, s. *sŭperfĭcies*, 5 d. f.
Out, (the fire is) *ignis extinctus est*
—— (the candle is) *candēla est extincta*
Outlaw, *exul, ŭlis*, c. g.
Out buildings, *appendĭces ædis*
— of order, *confusus*
— of vanity, *ex superbiâ seu vānĭtāte*
Outrage, *injuria atrox*

Owe, v. *dēbēre*, 2 c.
Owing, p. *dēbĭtus, a, um* p. p. *dēbens*, act.
——— to, *propter*
Own, adj. *proprius, a, um*
——— (to) v. *fatēri*, 2 c. dep.
Owl, s. *noctua*, 1 d. f. *strix*, 3 d. f.
Owner, s. *possessor*, 3 d.
Ox, s. *bos*, 3 d. m.
Oxen, s. *boves*, pl.
Oyster, s. *ostrea*, 1 d. f.
——— woman, *ostrearia*, 1 d.
——— shell, *testa*, 1 d. f.

P

Pack, s. *fascis*, 3 d. m.
——— up, v. *sarcĭnāre*, 1 c.
Packer, s. *suffarcinator*, 3 d.
Pack of cards, *fasciculus chartarum*, 2 d. m.
——— of dogs, *grex canum*
——— of fools, *grex stultorum*
Paddock, s. *septum*, 2 d. n.
Padlock, s. *sera*, 1 d. f.
Page to the king, *ĕphebus honorarius*
——— of a book, *pāgĭna*, 1 d. f.
Paid attention, (he) *attendit*
——— your bill, (have you) *solvistine hoc debitum*
Pail, s. *situla*, 1 d. f.
Pain, s. *dolor*, 3 d. m. *pœna*, 1 d. f.
——— v. n. *dolēre*, 2 c. *cruciāre*, 2 c.
Pains me, (it) *dolet mihi*
Painter, s. *pictor*, 3 d.
Painting, s. *pictūra*, 1 d. f. *ars pingendi*
Pair, s. *par*, 3 d. n.
Palace, s. *palatium*. 2 d. n. *regia*, 1 d. f.
Palate, s. *pălātum*, 2 d. n.
Pale, adj. *pallidus, a. um*
Paleness, s. *pallor*, 3 d. m.
Palm, s. *palma*, 1 d. f.
——— tree, *palma, æ*
Pane of glass, *quadra vitri*, 1 d. f.
Pantry, *pānārium*, 2 d. n.
Papa, *pāter*, 3 d.
Parcel, *fascĭcŭlus*, 2 d. m.
Pardon, s. *venia*, 1 d. f.
——— v. *condonāre*, 1 c. *ignoscĕre*, 3 c.
Pare one's nails, *ungues resecāre*
Parents, s. *parentes*, 3 d.
Paris, s. pr. *Lutetia, æ* f.
Parish, s. *părochia, æ* f.
Parishioner, s. *părŏchus*, 2 d. m.
Park, s. *vivarium*, 2 d. n.
Parliament, s. *senatus*, 4 d. m.
Parlour, s. *triclinium*, 2 d. n.
Parrot, s. *psittăcus*, 2 d. m.
Parsley, s. *apium*, 2 d. n.
Parsnip, s. *pastĭnāca*, 1 d. f.
Parson, s. *pastor*, 3 d. *clericus*, 2 d.
Part, s. *pars*, 3 d. f.
——— for my, *quod ad me attinet, ego autem*
Partake, v. *participāre*, 1 c.
Partial, adj. *iniquus*
Partiality, s. *favor*, 3 d. m.
Particular, adj. *particularis, singularis*

Partner, s. *socius*, 2 d.
Partnership, s. *societas consociatio*, 3 d. f.
Partook, (I) *participavi, interfui*
Parties, (state) s. *factiones*, 3 d. f.
Pass, v. *transīre*, 4 c.
—— a joke, *irridēre*, 2 c.
Passage, s. *transĭtus*, *ûs* m.
—— at sea, *trajectus*, *ûs*, m.
Passed, p. p. *prætĕrĭtus*, *a*, *um*
Passing, acc. p *transiens*, *præteriens*
Passions, s. *animi affectus*
—— (in a) *irâ*, 1 d. f.
Passionate, *ĭrăcundus*, *a*, *um*
Past, p. p. *præteritus*, *transactus*
Paste, (dough) s. *farina aquâ subacta*
—— (to fasten) s. *gluten ex farinâ*
Pastime, *ludus*
Pastry, s. *placentæ*, 1 d. f.
Pasture, s. *pascuum*, 2 d. n.
Patent, s. *diplomă*, 3 d. n.
Path, s. *sēmĭta*, 1 d. f.
Patience, s. *pătientia*, *æ* f.
Patient, s. *æger vel ægra*
—— adj. *pătiens*
Patiently, adv. *pătientèr*
Patron, s. *patrōnus*, 2 d. m.
Pattern, s. *exemplar*, 3 d. n.
Paul, s. *Paulus*, 2 d.
Pave, v. *sternĕre*, 3 c. *pavīre*, 4 c.
Pavement, (the) s. *păvimentum*, 2 d. n.
Paw, s. *ungŭla*, 1 d. f.
Pay, s. *stipendium*, 2 d. n.
Pay, v. *solvĕre*, 3 c.
—— a visit, *visĕre*, 3 c.
—— attention, *adhibēre diligentiam*
Pea, s. *pīsum*, 2 d. n.
Peas, (green) *pisa viridia*
Peace, s. *pax*, *cis* f,
Peacefully, adv. *tranquillè*, *pācātè*
Peach, s. *mālum Persĭcum*
—— tree, s. *malus Persicus*
Pear, s. *pyrum*, 2 d. n.
—— tree, s. *pyrus*, 2 d. f.
Pearl, s. *margarita*, 1 d. f.
Peasant, s. *rustĭcus*, 2 d. m.
Pebble, s. *calculus*, 2 d. m.
Peculiar, adj. *pĕcūliāris*, *proprius*
Pedlar, s. *mercator circumforaneus*
Peel, (orange) s. *tunica aurantii*
—— v. *decorticare*
Peer, s. *patrĭcius*, *i* m.
Peevish, adj. *morosus*
Peevishness, s. *morositas*, 3 d. f.
Pen, s. *calamus*, 2 d. m. *stylus*, 2 d. m. *penna*, 1 d. f.
Pence, s. *denarii*, pl. m.
Pencil, s. *pēnĭcillum*, 2 d. n.
Pen knife, s. *scalpellum*, 2 d. n.
Penmanship, s. *scriptura*, 1 d. f.
Penny, s. *denarius*, 2 d. m.
Pension, s. *pensio*, 3 d. f.
People, s. *pŏpŭlus*, 2 d. m.
—— were discoursing, (some) *aliqui loquebantur*
—— are suffering, (the) *populus angitur miseriâ*

People, in the sense of many persons, *quamplures homines*
——— were playing, (some) *quidam ludebant*
——— (many) *multi, plurimi*
——— (were there many) *an plures adfuerint?*
Pepper, s. *pĭper*, 2 d. n.
Per cent, *per centum*
Perceive, v. *sentīre*, 4 c. *cernĕre*, 3 c.
Perfect, adj. *perfectus, pĕrītus*
Perfection, s. *perfectio*, 3 d. f.
Perfectly, adv. *perfectè*
Perform, (on an instrument) v. *ludĕre*, 3 c.
——— (to accomplish) *perficĕre*, 3 c. *peragĕre*, 3 c.
——— (on the stage) *ludos scenicos agĕre*
——— (one's duty) *officium facere*
Performance, s. *opus*, 3 d. n. *actio*, 3 d. f.
Perhaps, adv. *fortassè*
Peril, s. *pĕrīcŭlum*, 2 d. n.
Perilous, adj. *pĕrīcŭlōsus*
Perish, v. n. *perīre*, 4 c.
Perjury, s. *perjūrium*, 2 d. n.
Permit, v. *permittĕre*, 3 c.
Pernicious, adj. *perniciōsus*
Person, s. *persōna*, 1 d. f. *quidam vel quædam*
Personally, adv. *persōnālĭtèr*
Persuade, v. a. *persuādĕre*
Peruse, v. a. *perlĕgere*
Peter, (St.) *Sanctus Petrus*, 2 d.
Petition, s. *pĕtītio*, 3 d. f.
Petticoats, s. *vestes mŭlĭĕris*
Pew, s. *subsellium septum*
Pewter, s. *stannum*, 2 d. n.
Pheasant, s. *phāsiānus vel phāsiāna*
Phial, s. *phiăla*, 1 d. f.
Philosopher, *phĭlŏsŏphus*, 2 d. m.
Philosophy, s. *philŏsŏphia*, 1 d. f.
Phrase, s. *locutio*, 3 d. f. *phrasis*, 3 d. f.
Physician, s. *medicus*, 2 d. m.
Physic, s. *medicina*, 1 d. f.
Pick, (to choose) v. *legĕre*, 3 c. *eligĕre*, 3 c.
—— axe, s. *bipennis*, 3 d. f.
Pickled pork, *porcina salita*
Picture, s. *tabella, æ* f. *pictura*, 1 d. f.
Pie, s. *artocrea*, 1 d. f.
Piece, s. *portio*, 3 d. f.
Pier, s. *pila*, 1 d. f. *agger*, 3 d. m.
Pierce, v. a. *penetrāre, terebrāre*, 1 c.
Piety, s. *piĕtas*
Pig, s. *porcus, porcellus*
— sty, *suile*, 3 d. n.
Pigeon, s. *cŏlumbus, cŏlumba*
——— house, *cŏlumbārium*, 2 d. n.
——— pie, *columbæ crusto incoctæ*
Pillow, s. *pulvīnar, cervical*, 3 d. n.
Pimple, s. *lentīgo*, 3 d. f.
Pin, s. *acicula*, 1 d. f.
Pine-tree, s. *pinus, i* f. *pinus, ûs* f.
Pink, (flower) s. *căryophyllum*, 2 d. n.
Pine apple, s. *nux pinea*
Pipe, s. *tŭbŭlus*, 2 d. m.

Pipe (in music) s. *fistula,* 1 d. f.
Pit, s. *fossa,* 1 d. f. *fovea,* 1 d. f.
— of a playhouse, *orchestra,* 1 d. f.
Pitch fork, *merga,* 1 d. f.
Pitcher, s. *amphora*
Pitiful, adj. *miserabilis*
Pity, v. *misereri,* 1 c.
—— on him, (have) *miseresce, illius*
—— s. *misericordia,* 1 d. f.
Place, s. *locus,* 2 d. m.
—— (situation) *munus,* 3 d. n.
—— (to take) v. *accidĕre,* 3 c.
Placid, adj. *placidus, a, um*
Plague, s. *pestis,* 3 d. f.
—— v. *vexāre,* 1 c.
Plain, (even) adj. *planus, æquus*
—— (ugly) *deformis*
Plan, s. *exemplar,* 3 d. n.
Plant, v. *plantāre*
—— s. *planta,* 1 d. f. *virgultum,* 2 d. n.
Plaster, s. *emplastrum,* 2 d. n.
Plate, s. *pătĭna, discus*
Play, s. *lusus,* 2 d. m. *ludus,* 2 d. m.
—— (drama) *comœdia,* 1 d. f. *fabula,* 1 d. f.
—— house, *theatrum,* 2 d. n.
Played, p. p. *lusus*
Play time, *tempus ludendi*
Player, s. *lusor,* 3 d. m. *histrio,* 3 d. m.
Plea, s. *plăcĭtum,* 2 d. n.
Plead, v. *causas agere*
Pleader, s. *orator,* 3 d. m. *advocatus,* 2 d. m.
Pleading, s. *causæ defensio*
Pleasant, adj. *amœnus*
Please, v. *oblectāre,* 1 c.
—— every one, *satisfacere unicuique*
Pleased, p. p. *dēlectātus, oblectatus*
Pleasure, s. *vŏluptas,* 3 d. f. *dēlectātio,* 3 d. f.
Pledge, s. *depositum,* 2 d. n. *pignus,* 3 d. n.
Plot, s. *conspīrātio,* 3 d. f.
—— of ground, *agellus,* 2 d. m.
—— (to) v. *conjurāre,* 1 c.
Plough, s. *ărātrum,* 2 d. m.
Ploughshare, s. *vōmer,* 3 d. m.
Ploughing, s. *aratio,* 3 d. f.
Plum, s. *prunum,* 2 d. n.
—— tree, s. *prunus,* 2 d. f.
Plunge, v. *immergĕre,* 3 c.
Pocket, s. *loculus, sacculus,* 2 d. m.
Poet, s. *poēta,* 1 d. m. *vates,* 3 d. m.
Point, s. *punctum,* 2 d. n.
Pointer, s. *canis subsidens*
Poison, s. *venenum,* 2 d. n.
Poker, s. *ferrum ad ignem excitandum*
Polished, p. p. *pŏlītus, excultus*
Polite, adj. *urbānus, comis*
Political, adj. *pŏlĭtĭcus*
Pond, (fish) s. *piscīna,* 1 d. f.
Poney, s. *ĕquulus,* 2 d. m.
Poor, adj. *inops, pauper*
Populous, adj. *populo frequens*
Pope, s. *Pāpa,* 1 d. m.
Poplar, s. *pōpŭlus,* 2 d. f.
Poppy, s. *păpaver,* 3 d. n.
Pork, s. *caro suilla*
Porridge, s. *jusculum,* 2 d. n.

Port, (sea) s. *portus, ûs* m.
—— wine, s. *vinum rubrum*
Porter, (a servant) s. *janitor,* 3 d. *ostiarius,* 2 d.
—— (beer) s. *cerevisia, æ* f.
Portion, s. *portio,* 3 d. f.
—— (marriage) s. *dos, tis* m.
Possess, v. a. *possĭdēre,* 2 c.
Possessions, s. *possessiones,* 3 d. f.
Possible, adj. *possĭbĭlis*
Post, (a situation) s. *munus,* 3 d. n.
—— (a stake) *postis,* 3 d. m.
—— horses, *veredi,* 2 d. m.
—— man, s. *tăbellārius,* 2 d. m.
—— chaise, *rheda, æ* f.
—— up, *publicè proponere*
Postpone, v. *postponĕre,* 3 c.
Pot, s. *olla,* 1 d. f.
— lid, *operculum,* 2 d. n.
Potatoes, s. *battata,* pl. n.
Poverty, s. *paupertas,* 3 d. f.
Poultry, s. *pullĭties,* 5 d. f.
—— yard, *gallinarium,* 2 d. n.
Pound, (weight) s. *libra,* 1 d. f. *as,* 3 d. m.
—— (money) *mina, libra, viginti solidi*
Pour, v. *fundĕre,* 3 c.
Pouring, (it is) *depluit*
Powder, s. *pulvis,* 3 d.
—— (gun) s. *pulvis nitratus*
Power, s *potentia,* 1 d. f.
Powerful, adj. *vălĭdus, potens*
Pox, (small) *vărĭŏlæ,* pl. f.
Practice, s. *usus,* 4 d. m.
Practise, v. *exercēre,* 2 c.
Praise, v. *laudāre,* 1 c.
—— s. *laus,* 3 d. f.
Praise, (worthy of) *dignus laude*
Prattle, v. n. *garrīre,* 5 c.
Prattler, s. *garrītor,* 3 d. m.
Pray, v. *orāre,* 1 c. *precāri,* 1 c. dep.
—— do that, *oro ut hoc făcias*
Prayed, p. p. *orātus*
Prayer, s. *obtestatio,* 3 d. f. *prĕcis,* gen. sing.
Prayers, plur. *prĕces, cum*
Prayer, (the Lord's) *oratio Dominica*
Prayers, (book of) *liber precum*
Preach, *prædicāre,* 1 c.
Preacher, s. *prædĭcātor,* 3 d. m.
Precarious, adj. *precarius*
Precedency, s. *jus præcedendi*
Precious, adj. *pretiosus*
—— stones, s. pl. *gemmæ,* 1 d. f.
Prefer, v. n. *præferre,* 3 c. *præpōnere,* 3 c.
Preferable, adj. *præfĕrendus, a, um*
Premises, (property) s. pl. *fundi,* m. *prædia,* pl. n.
—— (spoken) *præmissa,* n. pl.
Prepare, v. *præparāre, parāre,* 1 c.
Preparation, s. *præpărātio,* 3 d. f.
Preposition, s, *præpŏsĭtio,* 3 d. f.
Prescribe, v. *præscrībĕre,* 3 c.
Prescription, s. *præscriptio,* 3 d. f. *rĕcĭpe,* imperat.
Presence, s. *præsentia,* 1 d. f.
Present, adj. *præsens*
—— v. *donāre,* 1 c.

Presently, adv. *mox, statim*
Preserve, v. a. *tuēri*, 2 c.
——— (fruits) *saccharo condire*
Presume, v. n. *arrogāre*, 1 c. *conjicĕre*, 3 c.
Pretend, v. *simulāre*, 1 c.
Pretext, s. *species*, 5 d. f. *simŭlātio*, 3 d. f.
Pretty, adj. *formosus, a, um*
Prevent, v. *impedīre*, 4 c. *prævenīre*, 4 c.
Previously, adv. *primùm*
Prey, s. *præda*, 1 d. f. *spolium*, 2 d. n.
Pride, s. *fastus, ûs, superbia, æ*
Priest, s. *săcerdos*, 3 d.
Prince, s. *princeps*
Principal, adj. *præcĭpuus, princĭpālis*
Print, s. *sculptūra, æ* f. *impressio*, 3 d. f.
—— (to) v. *typis imprimĕre*, 3 c.
Printing, s. *typis impressio, typographia, æ*
Printer, s. *typographus*, 2 d. m.
Prison, s. *carcer*, 3 d. m.
Prisoner, s. *captivus, vinctus*
Private, adj. *prīvātus*
——— (in) adv. *prīvātìm, secretò*
Privateer, s. *navis prædatoria*
Privilege, s. *prīvĭlĕgium*, 2 d. n.
Prize, s. *palma, præmium, navis capta*
Probable, adj. *prŏbābĭlis*
Proceedings at law, s. pl. *controversiæ judiciariæ*
Process, s. *lis*, 3 d. f. *actio* 1 d. f.
Procure, v. *acquirĕre*, 3 c.
Prodigal, s. *nepos, prŏdĭgus*
Prodigy, s. *ostentum, portentum, prodĭgium*, 2 d. n.
Produce, v. a. *producĕre, prōferre*
Profession, s. *quæstus*, 4 d. m. *ars*, 3 d. f.
Profess, v. *exercēre*, 2 c.
Professor, s. *prŏfessor*, 3 d. m.
Profit, s. *lucrum*, 2 d. n. *fructus*, 4 m
Profitable, adj. *lucrosus*
Profound, adj. *prŏfundus, doctus*
Profuse, adj. *prŏfusus*
Project, s. *conatus*, 4 d.
Progress, s. *progressus, ûs* m.
Promise, v. *prōmittĕre, pollicēri*, dep.
Promised, p. p. *prōmissus, pollicitus*
Prompt, adj. *paratus, promptus*
Prompted, p. *excitatus, monitus*
Prompter, s. *monitor*, 3 n.
Pronounce, v. a. *enunciāre, recitāre*
Pronunciation, s. *elocutio, rĕcĭtātio*
Proof, s. *dŏcŭmentum, testimonium*, 2 d. n.
Proper, adj. *aptus, idoneus*
Properly, adv. *propriè*
Proposal, s, *propositio*, 3 d. f.
Proposition, s. *propositio*, 3 d. f.
Proud, adj. *superbus, a, um*
Prove, v. a. *probāre, affirmāre*

Proverb, s. *proverbium, adagium.*
Provide, v. a. *providēre, parāre.*
——— (for) *parāre, prospicēre.*
Provided that, *eâ conditione.*
Providence, s. *providentia, æ f.*
Provision, s. *victus, ûs, alimentum, i*
Prudent, adj. *prūdens.*
Prudence, s. *prūdentia, æ f.*
Prunes, s. *prūna,* 2 d. n. pl.
Pruning knife, s. *falx,* 3 d. f.
Public, adj. *communis, publĭcus*
——— house, s. *pŏpīna, caupona,* f.
Publish, v. a. *edĕre,* 3 c.
Pudding, s. *fartum,* 2 d. n.
Puff up oneself, v. *tumefacĕre,* 3 c. *se inflāre,* 1 c.
Pull, v. *vellĕre, retrahĕre*
——— off, (to) *detrahĕre*
——— down, *diruĕre, demolīri*
Pulled, p. p. *vulsus, retractus*
Pulpit, s. *rostrum, pulpitum,* 2 d. n.
Pulse, s. *pulsus, ûs,* m.
——— to feel, *pulsum vel venam tentare*
Pump, s. *antlia* 1 d. f.
Pumps, s. *calcei choreis apti.*
Pumpion or pumpkin, s. *pĕpo,* 3 d. m.
Punctual, adj. *accuratus, tempestivus.*
Punctual, adv. *accuratè, certo temporè*
Punish, v. a. *punīre,* 4. c.
Punished, p. p. *punitus*
Punishment, s. *supplĭcium,* 2 d. n.
Punition, s. *pœna,* 1 d. f.
Pupil, s. *discĭpŭlus, pupillus,* 2 d.
Purchase, v. *emĕre,* 3 c.
Purchased, p. p. *emptus*
Purchase, s. *res empta*
Pure, adj. *pūrus, castus*
Purple, s. *purpŭra, æ f.*
Purpose, s. *prŏposĭtum,* 2 d. n.
Purposely, adv. *cogitatò*
Purse, s. *crŭmena,* 1 d. f. *marsupium,* 2 d. m.
Push, v. *pellĕre, impellĕre,* 3 c.
Put, v. a. *collŏcāre,* 1 c. *pōnĕre,* 3 c.
— oneself in a passion, (to) *se valde iratum præbere*
— on, *induĕre,* 3 c.
— on your gloves, *indue manicas*
— by, *seponĕre*
— off, *differre, procrastināre*
— out, *dislocāre, luxāre,* 1 c.
— up, *tollere,* 3 c.
— up for sale, *venāle proponere, hastæ subjicere*
— horses to, *ĕquos jugo subjicĕre*
— up on the road, *diversorium petere*
Puzzle, v. *confundĕre*

Q

Quack, s. *empiricus*
Quadruped, s. *quadrŭpes,* 3 d.
Quail, s. *cŏturnix,* 3 d. f.
Quaker, s. *tremulus fanaticus,* 2 d.

Qualification, s. *acquisitio, conditio, dos*
Qualify, v. a. *facere idoneum*
Quality, s. *quălĭtas*, 3 d. f. *ordo*, 3 d. m.
Quantity, s. *quantĭtas*, 3 d. f.
Quarrel, s. *jurgium*, 2 d. n.
——— v. *rixāri*, dep. *jurgāri*, dep.
Quarrelsome, adj. *litigiosus, a, um*
Quarry s. *fodina lapidum*
Quartern, s. *quarta pars*
Quaver, s. *mŏdŭlātio*, 3 d. f.
Queen, s. *regīna, æ* f.
Quench, v. a. *extinguĕre*, 3 c.
Question, s. *quæstio, interrogatio,*
Question, v. *interrogāre*, 1 c.
——— to ask a, *quæstionem proponere*
Quick, interj. *festina*
Quickly, adv. *citò*
Quiet, adj. *quiētus, tranquillus*
Quietly, adv. *tranquillè*
Quill, s. *penna*, 1 d. f.
Quire of paper, s. *papyri vel chartæ scapus*
Quit, v. *relinquĕre*, 3 c.
Quite, adv. *omninò, tōtus*
—— safe, *tutò*
—— the contrary, *contrarius omninò*
Quiver, s. *phăretra*, 1 d. f.

R

Rabbit, s. *cŭnīcŭlus*, 2 d. m.
Rabble, s. *turba*, 1 d. f.
Race, s. *cursus, ûs*, 4 d. m.
—— horse, *equus cursor*
Rack, s. *fālisca*, 1 d. f.
Radish, *răphănus*, 2 d. m.
——— (horse) *raphanus agrestis*
Rain, v. *pluĕre*, 3 c.
—— s. *imber*, 3 d. m. *pluvia*, 1 d. f.
—— bow, s. *iris*, 3 d. f. *arcus pluvius*
Raise, v. *elevāre*, 1 c.
Raisins, s. pl. *uvæ siccatæ*, 1 d. f.
Ram, s. *aries*, 3 d. m.
Rampart, s. *agger*, 3 d. m. *vallum*, 2 d. n.
Random, (at) adv. *inconsultò*
Rank, s. *ordo*, 3 d. m. *series*, 5 d. f.
Rapture, (in) *effusus lætitiâ*
Raspberry, s. *Idæi rubi bacca*
Rascal, s. *furcĭfer*, 2 d.
Rash, adj. *tĕmĕrārius*
Rashness, s. *tĕmĕrĭtas*, 3 d. f.
Rat, s. *sōrex*, 3 d. m.
Rate, (at any) *ullo modo*
Rather, adv. *magis*
——— (to have) v. *malle*
——— (I had) *malo*
Raven, s. *corvus*, 2 d. m. *corax*, 3 d. m.
Raw, adj. *crūdus, incoctus*
Ray of the sun, *rădius*, 2 d. m.
Reach, v. *attingĕre*, 3 c. *assĕqui*, 3 c. dep.
Read, v. *lĕgĕre*, 3 c.
Readily, adv. *citò*
Reading, s. *lectio*, 3 d. f.
Ready, adj. *præpărātus, a um*

Real, adj. *vērus, a, um*
Really, adv. *reverà, certè*
Reap, v. *mĕtĕre,* 3 c.
Reaper, s. *messor,* 3 d.
Reason, s. *rătio,* 3 d. f.
Rebel, v. n. *rebellāre, res novas tentare*
Rebuke, v. *exprobāre, increpāre*
Rebuild, v. *reædĭfĭcare,* 1 c.
Receipt, s. *acceptilatio,* 3 d. f.
Receive, v. a. *accipĕre, recipĕre*
Recess, s. *rĕcessus,* 4 d. m.
Reckon, v. *numerāre,* 1 c.
——— upon, v. *confidĕre,* 3 c.
Recollect, v. dep. *rĕcordāri*
Recommend, v. a. *commendāre,* 1 c.
Recommendation, s. *commendātio,* 3 d. f.
Recommence, v. a. *rursus incipĕre*
Recompence, s. *præmium,* 2 d. n.
Reconcile, v. a. *reconciliāre,* 1 c.
Reconciliation, s. *concĭliātio,* 3 d. f.
Record, v. *in acta referre*
Records, s. *annāles,* s. *pl.* m.
Recover one's health, (to) *convalescĕre, revalescere*
——— she will not, *ex morbo non convalescet*
Recovery, s. *rĕcŭpĕrātio,* 3 d. f. *allĕvātio,* 3 d. f.
Recourse, (to have) *rĕcurrĕre,* ad.
Rector, s. *rector, clĕrĭcus*
Red, adj. *rŭber, bra, brum*
Reduce, v. a. *reducĕre,* 3 c. *redigĕre,* 3 c.
Reed, s. *ărundo,* 3 d. f.
Re-establish, v. a. *restituĕre,* 3 c.
Reflect, v. *considerāre,* 1 c.
Refresh, v. *relaxāre,* 1 c. *renovāre,* 1 c.
Refuse, v. *recusāre,* 1 c.
Regarding, prep. *de*
Regent, s. *regni procurator*
Regiment, s. *legio,* 3 d. f.
Regret, v. a. *ægrè ferre*
Regular, adj. *usitatus, ex ordine*
Regularly, adv. *certo, ex ordine*
Reign, v. n. *regnāre,* 1 c.
Rein, s. *habena* 1 d. f. *lorum,* 2 d n.
Rejoice, v. *lætāri,* 1 c. dep. *gaudēre,* 2 c.
Relate, v. a. *narrāre,* 1 c.
Relation, s. *narrātio,* 3 d. f.
Relations, (kindred) *consanguinei, parentes*
Relieve, v. a. *succurrĕre,* 3 c. *consolāri,* 1 c.
Religion, s. *rĕlĭgio, pietas*
Religious, adj. *rĕlĭgiōsus, pius*
Rely upon, v. *confīdĕre,* 3 c.
Remain, v. n. *manēre,* 2 c. *remanēre,* 2 c.
Remainder, s. *rĕsĭduum,* 2 d. n.
Remark, s *observātio,* 3 d. f.
Remedy, s. *rĕmĕdium,* 2 d. n.
Remember, v. *memini, rĕcordāri*
Remembrance, s. *rĕcordātio, memoria*
Remit, v. a. *rĕmittĕre,* 3 c. *absolvĕre,* 3 c.
Remnant, s. *residuum,* 2 d. *rĕlĭquum,* 2 d. n.
Render, v. a. *reddĕre,* 3 c.

Renew, v. a. *renovāre, integrāre*
Renown, s. *gloria, celebritas*
Rent, s. *reditus, ûs* m. *vectigal*, 3 d. n.
Repast, s. *refectus, ûs* m. *cibus*, 2 d. m.
Repeat, v. *iterāre*, 1 c. *repetĕre*, 3 c.
Repel, v. *repellĕre*, 3 c.
Repent, v. n. *rĕsĭpiscĕre, pænitēre*
Repetition, s. *repetitio*, 3 d. f.
Reply, v. *respondēre*, 2 c.
—— s. *responsio*, 3 d. f.
Report, s. *rumor*, 3 d. m.
—— v. *nunciāre, narrāre*
Represent, s. *repræsentāre, ostendĕre*
Reprimand, s. *objurgātio*, 3 d. f.
—— v. *objurgāre*
Repress, v. a. *reprimĕre, coërcēre*
Reproach, v. a. *exprobrāre, conviciāri*
Reproved, p. p. *objurgatus, reprehensus*
Reptile, s. *animal repens*
Republic, s. *respublica*, f.
Reputation, s. *existimatio*, 3 d. f.
Request, s. *petitio*, 3 d. f.
——, v. *rogāre, supplicāre*, 1 c.
Require, v. *exigĕre*, 3 c.
Resemble, v. *referre, comparare*
Reside, v. n. *habitāre, commorāri*
Resolve, v. *statuĕre*, 3 c.
Resolved, p. p. *statutus, decretus*
Respect, s. *respectus, reverentia*
——, v. *respicĕre, reverēri*
Respectful, adj. *officiosus*
Rest, s. *quies*, 5 d. f. *cessatio*, f.
—— in music, *pausa*, 1 d. f.
Restore, v. a. *restaurāre, reddĕre*
Resume, v. a. *resumĕre*, 3 c.
Retain, v. a. *detinēre, retinēre*
Retake, v. a. *rursus sumĕre vel capĕre*
Return, v. n. *redīre*, 4 c. *revertĕre*, 3 c.
Reward, s. *præmium*, 2 d. n.
Rewarded, p. p. *compensatus*
Ribbon, s. *vitta*, 1 d. f.
Review, s. *inspectio*, 3 d. f.
Rice, s. *oryza*, 1 d. f.
—— soup, s. *jusculum cum oryzâ*
Rich, adj. *dives, locuples*
Riches, s. pl. *ŏpes*, 3 d. f. pl.
Richly, adv. *lautè, copiosè*
Rid of, to be, *se liberāre vel expedīre*
Riddle, s. *ænigma*, 3 d. n.
Ride (to) *equitāre*
Ridiculous, adj. *ridiculus, a, um.*
Riding, *equitans*, p. *equitatio*, 3 d. f.
—— in a coach, *vectio*, 3 d. f.
Right, s. *jus*, 3 d. n. *æquum*, 2 d. n.
—— (is it?) *num fas est?*
—— (it is,) *æquum est*
—— (to the,) *dextrâ manu*
—— down gamblers, *aleatores*
—— (to be in the,) *rectè fecisse*
—— (I am,) *rationem habeo*

Right, (you are,) *tu rectè dicis*
Righteous, adj. *æquus, justus*
Ring, s. *annulus*, 2 d. m.
—— (to) v. *tinnīre*, 4 c. *sonāre*, 1 c.
—— the church bells (to), *campanas modulatè pulsare*
—— the bell, *tinni, sona*, imper.
Rinse, v. a. *lavāre*
Ripe, adj. *maturus, a, um*
Ripen, v. a. *maturāre*, 1 c.
—— v. n. *maturescĕre*, 3 c.
Rise, v. *orīri*
Rising sun, s. *Sol oriens*
—— the sun is, *Sol oritur*
Risk, v. *periclitāri*, dep. *experīri*, dep.
—— s. *discrimen*, 3 d. n. *periculum*, 2 d. n.
River, s. *flumen*, 3 d. n. *amnis*, 3 d. m.
Road, s. *via*, f. *iter*, 3 d. n.
Roads for ships, *sinus, ûs*, 4 d. m.
Roar, v. *rŭgīre*, 4 c.
Roaring (lion's), *rŭgītus, ûs*, m.
Roast, v. *assāre*, 1 c.
—— meat, *caro assa*
—— beef, *bovilla assa*
Rob, v. *latrocināri*, dep. 1 c.
Robber, s. *fur*, 3 d. c. g.
Robbery, s. *latrocinium*, 2 d. n.
Robert, s. *Robertus*, 2 d.
Rock a cradle, *cunas agere*
—— s. *rupes*, f. 3 d. *petra*, 1 d. f. *cautes*, f. 3 d.
Rockets, s. *ignea missilia*
Rod, s. *virga*, 1 d. f.
Roe-buck, s. *capreŏlus*
Rogue, s. *scelestus*
Roll, s. *crustulum panis*

Roman, s. *Romanus*, 2 d.
—— adj. *Romanus, a, um*
Rome, s. pr. *Roma*, f.
Roof, s. *tectum*, 2 d. n.
Room, s. *camera*, 1 d. f. *conclave*, 3 d. n.
—— dining, *cœnaculum*, 2 d. n. *triclinium*, 2 d. n.
—— next, *cubiculum proximum*
—— bed, *cubiculum*, 2 d. n.
—— drawing, *penetrale*, 3 d. n.
—— (space) *locus, spatium*
Root, s. *radix*, 3 d. f.
Rope, s. *fūnis*, 3 d. m. *restis*, 3 d. f.
Rose, s. *rŏsa, æ* f.
—— bud, s. *alabastrus*, 2 d. m.
Rotten, p. *putridus, corruptus*
Rough, adj. *asper, a, um*
—— unpolite, *rudis*
—— sea, *fretum tempestuosum*
Round, adj. *rŏtundus, globosus*
—— all the year, *toto anno*
Row, s. *series, ordo*
Royal, adj. *rēgius, rēgālis*
Rub, v. *fricāre*, 1 c.
Rub out, *defricāre*, 1 c.
Rubbish, s. *rudus*, 3 d. n.
Ruby, s. *carbunculus*, 2 d. m.
Rudder, s. *gŭbernācŭlum*, 2 d. n.
Rude, adj. *rudis, impĕrītus*
Rudeness, s. *inurbanitas*, 3 d. f.
Rug, s. *gausăpe*, 3 d. n.
Ruin, s. *ruina*, 1 d. f.
—— v. *diruĕre*, 3 c. *demolīri*, 4 c.
Rule, s. *dominatio*, 3 d. f.
—— or ruler, *rēgŭla, æ*, f.

Ruler, s. *gubernator*, 3 d.
Run, v. n. *currere*, 3 c.
—— away, *fugĕre*, *aufugĕre*, 3 c.
—— to the assistance of, *auxilium ferre*
Rush, v. n. *ruĕre*, 3 c.
Russia, *Sarmătia*, *æ* f.
Rust, s. *rūbigo* 3 d. f.
Rusty, adj. *rūbīginōsus*
Rut, s. *vestigium*, *rotæ*
Rye, s. *sĕcāle*, 3 d. n.
—— bread, *pānis sĕcālicus*

S.

Sack, s. *saccus*, 2 d. m.
Sacrifice, s. *sacrĭficium* 2 d. n.
Sacred, adj. *săcer*, *sanctus*
Sad, adj. *tristis*, *mœstus*
Saddle, s. *ephippium*, 2 d. n.
——— cloth, s. *instratum equestre*
——— horse, *equus vectarius*
Saddler, s. *ephippiorum opifex*
Safe, (quite) *sospes*, *tutus*, *incolumis*
—— for meat, *cella pĕnāria*
Safely, adv. *tūtò*, *securè*
Safety, s. *salus*, 3 d. f.
Saffron, s, *crocus*, 2 d. m.
Sage, s. *sapiens*, *phĭlŏsŏphus*
—— (herb), *salvia*, *æ*, f.
Said, (he) *ipse dixit*
Sail, v. n. *navigāre*, 1 c.
—— s. *velum*, 2 d. n. *navis*, f.
Sailing, s. *navigātio*, 3 d. f.
Sailor, s. *nauta*, *æ*, m.
Saint, s. *sanctus vel sancta*
Sake, (for my) *meâ causâ*
Salad, s. *ăcētāria*, s. pl. n.
Salary, s. *stipendium*, 2 d. n. *salarium*, 2 d. n.
Sale, s. *venditio*, 3 d. f.
Salmon, s. *salmo*, 3 d. m.
Salt, s. *sal*, 3 d. m.
—— v. *salire*, 4. c. *sale condere*
Saltpetre, s. *nitrum*, 2 d. n.
Salute, v. *sălūtāre*, 1 c.
Same, (the) *idem*, *ipse*
Same manner, (in the) *tali modo*, *eodem modo*
Sand, s. *săbŭlum*, 2 d. n. *arena*, 1 d. f.
Sash, s. *cingulum*, 2 d. n.
Satire, s. *satyra*, 1 d. f.
Satisfaction, s. *sătisfactio* 3 d. f.
Satisfactory, adj. *satisfaciens*, *gratus*
Satisfy, v. *satifăcere*
Satisfied, *contentus*, *satiatus*
Saturday, s. *dies Saturni*
Sauce, s. *condĭmentum*, 2 d. n.
Saw, s. *serra*, 1 d. f.
—— v. *serrĕre*, 3 c.
—— from to see, *vidi*, *vidisti*, *vidit*
Say, v. a. *dicĕre*, 3 c.
—— (what do you) *quid dicis?*
—— (that is to), *id est*
—— (they used to) *homines dicebant*, *solebant dicere*
Saying, s. *dictum*, 2 d. n.
———, part. *dicens*
Scabbard, s. *vagina*, 1 d. f.
Scaffold, s. *locus supplicii editior*
Scale, of fish, s. *squāma*, 1 d.f.
Scales, s. *trutina*, 1 d. f.

Scanty, s. *contractior,*
Scar, s. *cicātrix,* 3 d. f.
Scarce, adj. *rarus*
Scarcely, adv. *vix, ægrè*
Scarcity, s. *cāritas,* 3 d. f. *inopia,* 1 d. f.
Scarf, s. *mitella, fascia,* 1 d. f.
Scarlet, adj. *ostrum,* 2 d. n.
——— fever, *febris purpurea*
School, s. *schŏla,* 1 d. f.
——— fellow, *condiscĭpŭlus,* 2 d. m.
Science, s. *scientia,* 1 d. f.
Scissars, *forfex, ĭcis,* f.
Scold, v. *mulier rixosa*
Scorn, s. *contemptus,* 4 d. m.
Scotland, *Scotia, Caledonia*
Scots, (the) *Scoti,* pl.
Scoundrel, s. *homo nequam, nebulo*
Scourge, s. *flagellum,* 2 d. n.
Scratch, s. *levis incisura*
——— *scalpĕre, scabĕre*
——— as a cat, *unguibus lacerare*
Screen, s. *umbraculum,* 2 d. n.
Screw, s. *cochlea,* 1 d. f.
Scull, s. *cranium,* 2 d. m.
Sculler of a boat, *cymbŭla, æ* f.
Scythe, s. *falx, cis,* f.
Sea, s. *măre, is,* n.
—— man, *nauta, æ* m.
—— coast, *ora, æ* f. *littus,* 3 n.
—— port, *portus, ûs,* m.
—— weed, *alga,* 1 d. f.
Seal, s. *phŏca,* 1 d. f.
—— or signet, *sigillum, signum,* 2 n.
—— v. *epistolam signāre*
Sealing wax, *cera,* 1 d. f.
Seam, s. *sūtūra,* 1 d. f.
Search, v. *inquirĕre,* 3 c.
——— s. *inquisitio,* 3 d. f.

Season, s. *tempestas,* 3 d. f.
Seat, s. *sedes,* 3 d. f.
——— of arts, *sedes lĭbĕrālium artium*
——— of a nobleman or gentleman, *suburbanum, villa, prætorium*
Second, adj. *secundus, a, um*
——— v. a. *adjuvāre,* 1 c.
Secondly, adv. *secundò*
Secret, s. *arcanum,* 2 d. n.
Secretly, adv. *clam, furtim*
Secretary, s. *ămănuensis, scrība*
See, v. *vidēre,* 2 c.
—— them, (I do not) *illos non video*
—— one's way, (to) *viam invenire*
Seed, s. *sēmen,* 3 d. n.
Seek, v. *quærĕre,* 3 c.
Seem, v. n. *vidēri,* 2 c.
Seems, (it) *videtur*
Seen, p. p. *visus, a, um*
See-saw, s. *motus reciprocus*
Seize, v. a. *occupāre, căpĕre,* 3 c.
Seldom, adv. *rarò*
Self, pron. *ipse, a, ud*
—— love, s. *amor sui*
Selfish, adj. *illĭbĕrālis*
Selfishness, s. *amor sui*
Sell, v. a. *vendĕre,* 3 c.
Semibreve, s. *nota semibrevis*
Send, v. *mittĕre,* 3 c.
—— back, *remittĕre,* 3 c.
Sense, s. *ratio, judicium, sensus*
Sensible, adj. *sensĭlis*
——— people, s. *homines sapientes*
Sentence, s. *sententia, phrăsis*
Sent, p. p. *missus*
—— for, *accersitus, vocatus*

Sentiment, s. *sensus, sententia*
Sentry, s. *excŭbiæ*, s. pl. f.
——— box, s. *spĕcŭla*, 1 d. f.
September, s. *September*, 3 d. m.
Sequel, s. *consĕquentia, exitus*
Serious, adj. *gravis, e*
Seriously, adv. *gravitèr*
Sermon, s. *concio*, 3 d. f.
Serpent, s. *serpens, anguis*
Service, s. *servĭtium*, 2 d. n.
Set sail, v. *vela dare*
— fire to, *accendĕre*, 3 c.
— off or out, *proficisci*, 3 c. dep. n.
— down, *scriptarâ committere*
— out, *exponĕre*, 3 c.
Settle, v. *sedem figere*
——— a bill, *solvĕre debitum*
Settlement, s. *sedes*, 3 d. f.
Seven, adj. *septem*
Seventh, adj. *septimus*
Seventeenth, adj. *septemdecim*
Seventy, adj. *septuaginta*
Several, adj. *plures*
——— times, *sæpè*
Severe, adj. *sĕvērus, durus*
Severely, *sĕvērè, asperè*
Sew, (to) v. *suĕre*, 3 c.
Sex, adj. *sex*
Sexton, s. *sacrista*, 1 d. m.
Shade, s. *umbra, æ* f.
Shadow, s. *umbra*, 1 d.
Shake, v. *quatĕre, concutĕre*
——— s. *concussio, motus*
——— in music, *mŏdŭlātio*, 3 d. f.
Shall I do it? *faciamne?*
——— have, (I) *habeo*, f.
——— do it, (he) *hoc faciet*
——— speak, (I) *loquar*
——— I have some? *num habebo?*
——— not be, (I) *non ero*
Shall be, (you) *eris*
Shame, s. *pŭdor*, 3 d. m.
Shameful, adj. *turpis, fœdus*
Shamefully, adv. *turpiter*
Shame! (for) *pro pudor!*
Shape, s. *figura, forma*, 1 d. f.
——— (her) *sua forma*
Share, s. *portio, pars*, 3 d. f.
——— v. *partiri*, 4 c. *dividĕre*, 3 c.
——— (plough,) s. *vomer*, 3 d. m.
Sharp, adj. *acutus*
——— (in taste) *acidus*
——— (note in music) *tonus acutus*
Sharpen, v. *acuĕre*, 3 c.
Sharpened, p. p. *exăcūtus, cuspidatus*
Shave, v. *radĕre*, 3 c. *tondĕre*, 2 d.
She, pers. pro. *illa, ipsa, ea*
Sheath, s. *vagina*, 1 d. f.
Shed, s. *appendix ædificii*
Sheep, s. *ovis*, 3 d.
Sheet of paper, *folium*, 2 d. n.
——— (for a bed) *lodix*, 3 d. f.
Shelf, s. *abacus*, 2 d. m.
Shell, s. *testa*, 1 d. f.
Shepherd, *pastor*, 3 d. m.
Sheriff, s. *vicecomes*, 3 d. m.
———'s officer, *appăritor*, 3 d. m.
Shew, v. *monstrāre*, 1 c.
Shield, v. *defendĕre*, 3 c.
——— s. *scūtum*, 2 d. n. *clypeus*, 2 d. m.
Shilling, s. *sŏlĭdus*, 2 d. m.
Shine, s. *fulgĕre*, 2 c. *splendĕre*, 2 c.
Shines, (moon) *luna refulget, splendet, dat lucem*
——— (sun) *sol fulget vel refulget*

Shining characters, *homines illustres*
Ship, s. *nāvis*, 3 d. f.
Shipwreck, s. *naufrăgium*, 2 d. n.
Shire, s. *provincia*, f. *comitatus*, m.
Shoe, s. *calceus*, m. *solea*, f.
—— (horse) *equi calceus*
—— maker, s. *sūtor*, 3 d. m.
Shoot, v. n. *germināre*, 1 c.
—— v. a. *displodĕre, petere*
—— (kill) v. a. *necāre, occidĕre*
Shooting party, *venatio*, 3 d. f.
Shop, s. *tăberna, officina*, 1 d. f.
—— (next) *taberna proxima*
—— keeper, *tăbernārius*, 2 d. m.
Shore, s. *littus*, 3 d. n.
Short, adj. *brevis, curtus*
—— time, (in a) adv. *brevi tempore*
Shorten, v. a. *contrahĕre*, 3 c. *decurtāre*, 1 c.
Shorter, adj. *brevior, compendiosior*
Shortly, adv. *brevì, mox*
Shot, s. *pilulæ plumbeæ*
—— *displosio*
—— (canon) *glandes ferreæ*
Shovel, s. *lĭgo*, 3 d. m.
Should, v. *possem, potuerim*
—— speak, (I) *loquerer*
—— have, (I) *haberem*
—— we see? *nosne videremus?*
Shoulder, s. *hŭmĕrus*, 2 d. m.
—— of an animal, *armus*, 2 d. m.
Show, s. (a spectacle) *spectaculum*, n. *pompa*, f.
Show, v. *monstrāre*, 1 c.
Showed, p. p. *monstrātus*
Shower, s. *imber*, 3 d. m.
Shrimp, s. *squilla parva*
Shroud, s. *amiculum ferale*
Shrub, s. *arbuscula*, 1 d. f.
Shrubbery, s. *fruticetum*, 2 d. n.
Shudder, v. *tremĕre, horrēre*
Shuffle, s. *mistura*, 1 d. f.
Shun, v. a. *devitāre, fugĕre*
Shut, v. a. *claudĕre*, 3 c.
—— up, *intercludĕre*, 3 c. *incarcerāre*, 1 c.
Shutter, s. *claustrum*, 2 d. n.
Shuttle-cock, s. *suber pennatum*
Shy, adj. *cautus*
Sick, adj. *æger, ægrotus*
—— people, *ægroti*
Sickle, *falx messoria*
Sickness, s. *morbus*, 2 d. m.
Side, s. *lătus*, 3 d. n.
—— (sea) *littus*, 3 d. n.
—— (on the other) *è contrario*
Sides, (on all) *undiquè*
Sieve, s. *cribrum*, n.
Sigh, s. *suspīrium*, n. *gemitus*, m.
—— v. n. *gemĕre, suspīrāre*
Sight, s. *visus*, 4 d. m.
—— (by) *visu, primâ facie*
Sign, s. *signum*, 2 d. n.
—— v. a. *signāre*, 1 c. *obsignāre*
Signify, v. *signĭfĭcāre, valēre*
Silence, s. *sīlentium, taciturnitas*
Silent, adj. *tacitus*
Silk, s. *sērĭcum, bombyx*, 3 d. m.
—— worm, *bombyx*, 3 d. m.
Silliness, s. *insulsĭtas*, 3 d. f.

Silly, *ineptus*
—— (fellow) *stultus*
Silver, s. *argentum*
—— smith, s. *faber argentarius*
—— plate, *vasa argentea*
Simple, adj. *simplex*
Simpleton, s. *fatuus*, 2 d. m.
Sin, s. *peccatum* 2 d. n.
— v. *peccāre*, 1 c.
Since, adv. *quum*
—— in the sense of because, *quia*
—— you are willing to hurt me, *cum mihi nocere velis*
Sincere, *sincērus, a, um.*
Sincerely, *sincērè*
Sing, v. *canĕre*, 3 c.
Singer, *cantor*, 3 d. m.
Singing-master, *musices professor*
Single, adj. *ūnĭcus, a, um.*
—— man, *cælebs, ĭbis*, c. g.
—— woman, *cælebs*, 3 d.
Singular, adj. *singŭlāris, e*
Sink, v. *sidĕre, imminuĕre*
—— s. *latrina*, f. *sentina*, f.
Sinner, s. *peccator*, m.
Sir, *Domine, voc.*
Sister, s. *sŏror*, 3 d. *germana*, 1 d. f.
Sit, v. *sedēre*, 2 c.
— still, *sede tranquillè*
— down, *decumbĕre*, 3. c.
Sittings, s. *sessio*, 3 d. f.
Situated, p. p. *sĭtus, pŏsĭtus*
Situation, s. *pŏsĭtio*, 3 d. f.
Six, adj. *sex*
Sixth, adj. *sextus*
Six hundred, adj. *sexcenti*
Sixteen, adj. *sexdĕcim*
Sixteenth, adj. *decimus sextus*
Sixty, adj. *sexaginta*

Size, s. *magnitudo*, 3 d. f.
Skate, v. *per glaciem ire ferreis instrumentis*
—— (fish) *raia lævis, squatina*
Sketch, s. *delineatio*, 3 d. f.
Skies, praised to the, *laudatus ad nubes*
Skilful, adj. *pĕrītus, a, um.*
Skill, s. *pĕrītia, æ* f.
Skin, s. *cutis, pellis*, 3 d. f.
Skip, s. *saltus*, 4 d. m.
Sky, *cælum*
—— light, *fenestra cæli supposita*
Slack, adj. *laxus, a, um.*
Slain, adj. *cæsus, occisus*
Slander, v. *calumniārī*, 1 c. dep.
—— s. *calumnia* 1 d. f.
Slate, s. *tegula, æ* f. *palimpseston*, n.
Slave, s. *servus*, 2 d. m.
—— trade, *mercatus servorum*
Slavery, s. *servitium*, 2 d. n.
Slaughter, s. *cædes*, 3 d. f.
—— house, s *lănĭēna, æ*
Sledge hammer, s. *malleus major*
Sleep, v. n. *dormīre*, 4 c.
—— s. *somnus*, 2 d. m.
Sleepy, adj. *somnolentus, somniculosus*
Sleeves, *mănĭcæ*, f.
Slept (he) pret. *dormivit*
Slice, s. *offula, assula*, f.
Slide, v. n. *labi*, 3 c. dep.
Sliding, part. *lābens*
Slight, adj. *lĕvis*
Slightly, adv. *negligenter, lĕvĭter*
Slip, v. n. *labi*, 3 c.

Slip down, *cadĕre, decidĕre*
—— of paper, *charta exigua*
Slipper, s. *crepida*, 1 d. f.
Slippery, a. *lubrĭcus*
Sloven, s. *homo sordidus*
Slow, adj. *piger, tardus*
Slowly, adv. *lentè, tardè*
Sluggard, s. *pĭger, dormitator*
Sluggish, adj. *segnis, ignavus*
Sly, adj. *văfer*
Small, adj. *parvus, a, um*
—— pox. *variolæ*, s. pl. f.
Smell, v. *ŏdōrāri, olfacĕre, olēre*
—— s. *ŏdor*, 3 d. m.
Smelling, s. *ŏdōrātus*, 4 d. m.
Smile, s. *rīsus, ūs*, 4 d.
Smith, s. *faber ferrarius*
Smoke, s. *fūmus*, 2 d. m.
—— v. *fumāre, tabaci fumum exhaurire*
Smooth, v. *complanāre*, 1 c.
—— adj. *lævis, æquus*
Snail, s. *testudo*, 3 d. f.
Snake, s. *anguis*, 3 d. *coluber*, 2 d.
Snare, s. *laqueus*, m. *insidiæ*, s. pl. f.
Sneeze, v. n. *sternuĕre*, 3 c.
Snipe, *gallĭnāgo minor*
Snow, s. *nix*, 3 d. f.
—— v. n. *ningĕre*, 3 c.
Snuff, s. *sternūtāmentum*, 2 d. m.
—— of a candle, *myxa*, 1 d. f.
—— v. *emungĕre*
—— box, *pyxidicula pulveris sternutatorii*
Snuffers, s. *ēmunctōrium*, 2 d. n.
So, adv. *ita*
— do I, *et ego quoque*
— it was, *sic erat*
So much, *adeo*
—— the worse, *tanto pejus*
— good, *tam bonus*
— that, *modò, dummodò*
— much the better, *tanto melius*
— large, *tam magnus*
— I am, *ita quidem ego sum*
Soap, s. *săpo*, 3 d. m.
Society, s. *sŏciĕtas*, 3 d. f.
Socket, s. *scăpus*, 2 d. m.
Sock, s. *pedale*, 3 d. n. *soccus*, 2 d. m
Sofa, s. *torus*, 2 d. m.
Soft, adj. *mollis, e*
Soften, v. *emollīre*, 4 c.
Softened, p. p. *mollitus, emollitus*
Sold, p. p. *vendĭtus*
—— (he) *vendidit*
Soldier, s. *mīles, ĭtis*, 3 d.
Solicit, v. *sōlĭcĭtāre*, 1 c.
Solon, s. pr. *Solon, is* 3 d.
Some, *quidam, nonnullus*
—— bread, *panis*
—— meat, *caro*
—— people, *nonnulli, aliqui*
—— time, *paulum temporis*
—— times, *ălĭquandò*
—— one, *ălĭquis*
—— of it, *pars*, 3 d. f.
—— (I want) *partem alĭquam desidero*
—— of it, (give me) *da mihi partem*
—— (I have sold) *vendĭdi partem ălĭquam*
—— thing, *res ălĭqua*
—— where, *alicubi, uspiam*
—— else, *aliò*
—— (I have) *habeo*
—— (he buys) *emit*
Son, *filius*

Son, (God) *filius lustricus*
—— in law, *gener*, 2 d. m.
Song, s. *carmen*, 3 d. n. *canticum*, 2 d. n
Soon, adv. *citò*
—— (too) *præmātūrè*
Sooner, comp. *citius*
Soonest, sup. *citissimè*
Soot, s. *fūligo*, 3 d. f.
Sophia, s. pr. *Sophia*, *æ* f.
Sore throat, *fauces ulceratæ*
Sorrel-horse, s. *equus helvinus*
Sorrow, s. *mæror*, 3 d. m. *tristitia*
Sorrowful, adj. *tristis*, *mæstus*
Sorry, adj. *tristis*, *vilis*
—— for it, (I am) *pœnitet me*, *doleo ĭdeò*
Sort, s. *gĕnus*, 3 d. n.
Sovereign, s. *rex*, *gis*, 3 d.
Soul, s. *anima*, f. *animus*, m.
Soup, s. *decoctum*, *sorbillum*, 2 d. n.
Sour, adj. *acidus*, *acerbus*
South, s. *Meridies*, 5 d. m. *auster*, 2 d. m.
Sow, s. *sus*, 3 d. f.
—— s. *serĕre*, 3 c.
Spade, s. *ligo*, 3 d. m.
——— at cards, *vomerculus*, 2 d. m. *lĭgo*, 3 d. m.
Spain, s. pr. *Hispania*, *æ* f.
Spanish, gent. *Hispanicus*
Spare, v. *cedĕre*, *parcĕre*
—— you, (I cannot) *non possum sine te esse*
Spark, s. *scintilla*, *æ* f.
Sparrow, s. *passer*, 3 d. m.
Speak, v. n. *loqui*, 3 c.
——— to him, *loquere cum illo*
——— the truth, *verum dicito*

Speak, to her mother? (did you) *matri illius an tu locutus sis*
——— yes I did, *imo vero cum illâ locutus sum*
Speech, s. *sermo*, 3 d. m.
Speed, s. *festinatio*, *expeditio*, f.
—— with all, *omni celeritate*
Spelling, s. *orthographia*, *æ* f.
Spend money, v. *expendĕre pecuniam*, *largīri*
—— time, *tempus consumĕre*
Spice, s. *arōma*, 3 d. n.
Spider, s. *ărānea*, 1 d. f.
Split, v. a. *fundĕre*, *effundĕre*
Spin, v. *nēre*, 2 c.
Spinster, s. *lanifica*, *cælebs*, *ibis*
Spirit, s. *spiritus*, 4 d. m. *spectrum*, 2 d. n.
Spit, s. *veru*, n. indcl.
Spite, s. *malitia*, *malevolentia*
—— of him, (in) *illo invito*
Split, v. a. *diffindĕre*, 3 c.
Spoil, v. *corrumpĕre*, 3 c.
—— (or plunder), *devastāre*, *spoliāre*
Sponge, *spongia*, 1 d. f.
Spoon, s. *cochlear*, *āris*, 3 d. m.
Spot, s. *macula*, f. *labes*, 3 d. f. *nævus*, 2 d. m.
Sprain, s. *luxātio*, 3 d. f.
Sprat, s. *sardīna*, *æ* f.
Spread, v. *pandĕre*, *expandĕre*
Spring of water, *fons*, m. *scaturigo*, f.
——— (steel,) *lamina e ferro convoluta*
——— (season), *ver*, 3 d. n.
Sprightly, adv. *vividus*, *alacer*

Spur, s. *calcar*, 3 d. n. *stimulus*, 2 d. m.
Spy, s. *explorator*, *speculator*
—— v. *observāre*, *explorare*
Squadron (of cavalry), s. *turma*, 1 d. f.
———— (of a fleet), *classis*, 3 d. f.
Square, adj. *quadratus*, *a*, *um*
——— s. *quadra*, 1 d. f. *platea*, f.
Squirrel, s. *sciurus*, 2 d. m.
Stab, v. *confodĕre*, 3 c.
Stable, s. *stăbŭlum*, 2 d. n.
Stack, s. *acervus*, *cumulus*
Staff, s. *baculus*, 2 d. m.
—— (of the army), s. *centuriones manentes apud imperatorem*
Stag, s. *cervus*, 2 d. m.
Stage, s. *theatrum*, 2 d. n.
—— coach, *vĕhĭcŭlum mĕrĭtorium*
Stain, s. *macula*, f. *dedecus*, 3 d. m.
Stairs, s. pl. *scālæ*, f. pl.
Stale bread, *panis diu coctus*
Stand, v. *stāre*, 1 c.
—— (music), *adminiculum*, 2 d. n.
Star, s. *stella*, 1 d. f.
Starch, s. *ămylum*, 2 d. n.
Stare at, (to) *obtutu hærere*
—— in the face, (to) *intueri in vultum alicui*
Start, v. *subsilīre*, 4 c.
—— (on a journey), *proficisci*, dep.
—— s. *motus*, *saltus*
Starve, v. *fame enecare*
State, s. *conditio*, f. *status*, m.
Stationer, s. *chartopola*, 1 d. m.
Statuary, s. *sculptor*, 3 d.
Stay, v. *manere*, 2 c.
—— s. *mora*, *mansio*, f.
Stays, (ladies), s. pl. *thorax nexilis*
Stead, (in) *loco*, abl.
Steady, adj. *constans*, *stabilis*
Steadiness, s. *firmitas*, *stabilitas*
Steal, v. a. *fūrāri*, *latrocināri*
Steel, s. *chălybs*, 3 d. m.
Steep, adj. *præceps*, *præruptus*
Steer, v. a. *gubernāre*, *cursum dirigĕre*
Steeple, s. *templi turris*
Step, s. *passus*, *gradus*
—— father, s. *vitrĭcus*, 2 d. m.
—— mother, s. *nŏverca*, 1 d. f.
Sterling, adj. *legalis moneta*
Steward, s. *curator domesticus*, *famulus*
Stick, s. *fustis*, *baculus*
Stiff, adj. *rigidus*, *rigens*
—— neck, s. *collum rigens*
Still, adj. *tranquillus*
—— adv. *adhūc*
Sting, s. *ăculeus*, 2 d. m.
—— v. *pungĕre*
Stir up the fire, *focum excitāre*
Stirrup, s. *stapes*, 3 d. m.
Stocking, s. *caliga*, 1 d. f. *tibiale*, 3 d. n.
Stolen, adj. *surreptus*, *subductus*
Stole, (he) *fūrātus est*
Stone, s. *lapis*, 3 d. m.
——— house, *domus lapidea*
Stool, (foot) *scăbellum*, 2 d. n.
Stoop, v. *inclināre*
Stop, v. *prohibere*, *impedire*

Storm, s. *procella*, 1 d. f.
Story, s. *historia, æ* f.
——— teller, *homo mendax*
Stove, s. *văpōrārium*, 2 d. n.
Stout, adj. *strenuus*
—— man, *homo robustus, homo fortis*
Strait, s. *frĕtum*, 2 d. n.
——— adj. *arctus, angustus*
Straight, adv. *citò, statim*,
Strange, adj. *mīrabilis, alienus*
Stranger, s. *peregrinus, hospes*
Straw, s. *stramen, culmus, palea*
——— bed, *lectus stramineus*
——— hat, *galerus stramineus*
Strawberry, *frāgum*, 2 d. n.
Strawberry beds, *areolæ arbuteæ*
Street, s. *vicus*, 2 d. m. *platea*, 1 d. f.
Strength, s. *robur*, 3 d. n. *vires*, s. pl. f.
Strike, v. a. *ferīre*, 4 c. *cædere*, 3 c.
String, s. *fūnĭcŭlus*, 2 d. m.
Strong, adj. *vălĭdus, a, um*
Stronger, adj. *robustior, us*
Strongest, *firmissimus*
Struck, p. p. *percussus, sonitus*
Stud, s. *equarum armentum*
Study, v. *studēre*, 2 c.
——— s. *meditatio*, f. *studium*, n.
Stuff, s. *pannus*, 2 d. m.
—— linen, *linteum*, 2 d. m.
Stupid, adj. *stŭpĭdus, a, um*
Style, s. *stȳlus*, 2 d. m.
Subdue, v. a. *domāre*, 1 c.
Subject, s. *argumentum*, n. *civis*, c. g.
Submit, v. n. *submittĕre, cedĕre*
Subscribe, v. a. *subscrībĕre*, 3 c.
Subscriber, s. *subscriptor*, 3 d. m.
Subscription, s. *subscriptio*, 3 d. f.
Succeed, v. *succedĕre*
Success, s. *successus*, 4 d. m.
Succory, s. *cichorium*, 2 d. n.
Such, adj. *talis*
Sudden, adj. *rĕpentīnus*
Suddenly, adv. *ĭnŏpīnātò*
Suffer, v. *păti*, dep. 3 c.
Sugar, s. *sacchărum*, 2 d. n.
——— (loaf), *sacchari, meta*
——— (brown), *saccharum crudum*
Suit, v. *respondēre, congruĕre*
—— at law, *actio*, f. *causa*, f.
—— at cards, *genus*, 3 d. n.
—— of clothes, *vestītus*, 4 d. m.
Sulky, adj. *mōrōsus, a, um*
Sultry, adj. *torridus, fervĭdus*
Sum, s. *summa pecunia*
Summer, s. *æstas*, 3 d. f.
Sun, s. *sol*, 3 d. m.
—— dial, *sōlārium*, 2 d. n.
—— shines, (the) *sol refulget*
—— is rising, (the) *sol exoritur*
Sunday, *dies Dominica*
Sung, p. p. *cantatus*
Supper, s. *cœna*, 1 d. f.
Suppose, v. *supponĕre, opināri*
Support, v. *sustentāre*
Sure, adj. *certus, a, um*.
Surely, adv. *profectò*
Surgeon, s. *chīrurgus*, 2 d. m.
Surpass, v. *præstāre*, 1 c.

Surprise, v. *de improviso supervenire*
——— s. *superventus*
Surveyor, s. *inspector*, 3 d. m.
Surveyor, (land), s. *metator*
Suspect, v. *suspicāri*, 1 c. dep.
Suspicion, s. *suspĭcio*, 3 d. f.
Swallow, s. *hirundo*, 3 d. f.
——— v. a. *sorbēre*, *vorāre*
Swarm, s. *examen*, 3 d. n.
Swam, (he) *natavit*
Swear, v. *jurāre*, *maledīcere*
Sweden, s. p. *Suedia*, *æ* f.
Swedes, (the) *Suēvi*, *ōrum*
Sweep, v. a. *verrĕre*, *purgāre*
Sweet, adj. *dulcis*, *e*
Sweetbread, s. *pancreas*, 3 d. n.
Sweetly, adv. *suāvitĕr*
——— (to sing more) *canĕre dulcius*
——— meats, s. *bellaria*
Swell, v. n. *tumēre*, *turgēre*
Swelling, s. *tumor*, 3 d. m.
Swift, adj. *celer*, *velox*
Swim, v. n. *năre*, *natāre*
Swiss, (the) *Helvētii*, *ōrum*
Switzerland, s. pr. *Helvētia*, *æ* f
Swimming, s. *natatio*, 3 d. f.
Swimmer, s. *nătātor*, 3 d. m.
Sword, s. *gladius*, 2 d. m.
——— cutler, s. *faber gladiorum*
System, s. *systēma*, 3 d. n.
Syrup, s. *syrupus*, 2 d. f.

T

Table, s. *mensa*, *æ*, f.
——— cloth, *mappa*, *æ*, f.
Table-beer, *cerevisia cibaria*
Tail, s. *vestis tractus*, *cauda*
Tailor, s. *sartor*, *vestiarius*
Take, v. a. *capĕre*, 3 c.
—— leave, *valedicere*
—— care, *cavēre*, *curāre*
—— blood, *venam incidĕre*
—— place, *evenīre*
—— away, *auferre*
—— in, *recipĕre*
—— a walk, *deambulāre*
—— one's pleasure, *indulgere genio suo*
—— off, *sumĕre*, *ex.*
—— a lesson, *lectionem audire*
—— any thing to, *ferre*, ad.
—— cold, *frigus contrăhĕre*
—— up any one, *căpĕre*, *prĕhendĕre*
—— to, *incipĕre*, 3 c.
Take out, *seligĕre*
—— pains, *moliri*, *laborare*
—— down, *demĕre*, 3 c.
Tale, s. *fabula*, 1 d. f.
Taking, part. *ducens*
——— s. *assumptio*, 3 d. f.
Talent, s. *facultas*, *dos*, f.
Talk, v. *confabulāri*, *lŏqui*
—— nonsense, *nugas dicĕre*
Tall, adj. *procerus*, *altus*
Taller, adj. *celsior*
Tallow, s. *sebum*, 2 d. n.
——— chandler, *candelarum venditor*
Tame, adj. *mitis*, *mansuetus*
—— v. *domāre*, 1 c.
—— one's passions, *reprimere motus animi*
Tankard, s. *canthărus*, *i*, m.
Tan, s. *cortex ad coria inficienda*
Tap, v. a. *levitĕr percutĕre*
—— a cask, v. *dolium relinere*
Tar, (a sailor), s. *nauta*, *æ*

Target, s. *scutum*, n. *clypeus*,
Tart, s. *scribīta*
—— apple, s. *scribīta pomis repleta*
Tartish, adj. *acidus*
Task, s. *pensum*, 2 d. n.
Taste, s. *gustus*, *ûs*, *gustatus*, *ûs*, m.
—— v. *gustāre*, 1 c.
Taught. p. p. *doctus*
Tax, s. *tributa*, *census*
Tea, s. *thea*, f.
Teach, v. *docēre*, 2 c.
Tear, v. *lacerāre*, *scindĕre*
Tears, (to shed) *flēre*, 2 c.
Tease, v. *vexāre*, 1 c.
Tedious, adj. *molestus*
Teeth, s. *dentes*, *ium*, m.
Tell, v. *dicĕre*, 3 c.
Tell tale, s. *dēlātor*, 3 d. m.
Temerity, s. *tĕmĕrĭtas*, 3 d. f.
Temper, s. *indoles*, f. *ingenium*, n.
Ten, adj. *dĕcem*
Tender, adj. *tĕner*, *mollis*
Tenderly, adv. *mollĭtèr*
Tenderness, s. *tĕnĕrĭtas*, f.
Tenth, adj. *dĕcĭmus*
Term, s. *verbum*, 2 d. n.
Terrier, s. *canis indagans animalia subterranea*
Thames, *Thamesis*, 3 d.
Than, conj. *quàm*
—— rather, *potiùs quàm*
Thank, v. *grătĭas ăgĕre*
Thankful, adj, *gratus*, *a*, *um*
Thanks, s. pl. *gratiæ*, *ārum*, f.
That, pron. *is*, *ea*, *id*; *ille*, *illa*, *illud*; *iste*, *ista*, *istud*
—— way, *illàc*
—— which, *id quod*
—— one, *hic*, *hæc*, *hoc*
—— is, *id est*
—— (in order) *ut*, *ideo*

Thatch, s. *culmus*, m. *stipula*, f.
Thatched-house, *casa culmis tecta*
Thaw, v. *regelāre*, *solvi*
Theatre, s *theatrum*, 2 d. n.
Thee, pron. *te*, acc.
Theft, s. *furtum*, 2 d. n.
Their, *eorum*, *illorum*
Theirs, *ipsorum*
Them, *eos*, *illos*, acc.
—— (I speak to), *illis loquor*
—— (against) *contra eos*
Them, (to) *illis*
Themselves, *se*, *seipsos*
Then, adv. *tum*, *tunc*
—— (now and) *nonnunquam*, *subinde*
—— (for therefore) *ergo*, *igitur*
Thence, adv. *illīnc*, *indè*
Thenceforth, *deincèps*
There, adv. *ibì*, *illic*
—— is too much already, *jam nimis est*
Therefore, *ergo*
There is, *est*
—— are, *sunt*
—— was, *fuit*
—— were, *fuerunt*
—— will, be, *erit*, sing. *erunt*, pl.
—— would be, *esset*, s. *essent*, pl.
Thereabouts, adv. *circiter*, *circa*
Thereby, *indè*, *eò*
Therein, *in eo*
Thereupon, *exindè*, *posteà*
There, demons. pro. *hi*, *hæ*, *hæc*
They, pron. *ii*, *eæ*, *ea*, plur.
They alone, *ipsi soli*, pl.

They who were there, *qui adfuerunt*
Thick, adj. *densus, spissus*
Thief, s. *fur*, 3 d.
Thigh, s. *femur*, 3 d. n.
Thimble, s. *digitāle*, 3 d. n.
Thine, pos. pr. *tuus, a, um*
Thing, (any) *quidque, quidnam*
——— (some) *aliquid*
Think, v. *putāre*, 1 c.
——— of it, *cogita de eo*
Third, adj. *tertius*
Thirst, s. *sitis*, 3 f.
Thirsty, adj. *sitiens*
Thirteenth, *decimus tertius*
Thirtieth, adj. *tricesimus*
Thirty, *triginta*
This, pron. *iste, hic*
Thistle, s. *carduus*, 2 d. m.
Thither, adv. *eò*
——— I am going, *illuc nunc eo*
Thorn, s. *spīna, æ* f.
Thorough, *per*
Those, dem. pron. *hi vel qui*
——— of my country, *hi patriæ meæ*
——— of my father, *hi patris mei*
——— who love their children, *qui liberos suos amant*
——— who laughed at me, *qui de me riserunt*
Thou, p. pr. *tu*
——— art fair *tu es formosa*
——— I give thee, *tibi dò*, dat.
——— I accuse thee, *te accuso*, acc.
——— with thee, *tecum*
Though, conj. *etsi*
Thought, s. *cōgĭtātio*, 3 d. f.
Thousand, s. *mille*
——— eight hundred, (In the year one) *anno millesimo octingentesimo*
Translate, v. *vertĕre*, 3 c.
Thread, s. *filum*, 2 d. n.
Threaten, v. *minări*, 1 c. dep.
Three, adj. *tres*
——— times, *ter*
Threshold, s. *limen*
Thrive, v. *vigēre, valēre*
Throat, *guttur, jugulum*
Throne, s. *thronus*, 2 d. m. *solium*, 2 d. n.
Through, *per*
——— the body, *transfigĕre*
Throw, v. *jactāre*, 1 c.
Thrown, p. p. *jactatus, a, um*
Thrush, s. *turdus*, 2 d. m.
Thumb, s. *pollex*, 3 d. m.
Thunder, s. *tŏnĭtru*, n.
Thunder bolt, *fulmen*, 3 d. n.
Thursday, s. *dies Jovis*
Thus, adv. *ità*
Thy, pos. pron. *tuus*
Thym, s. *thymum*, 2 d. n.
Tiber, s. pr. *Tĭber vel Tĭbĕris*
Tide, s. *æstus maris*
Tidings, s. *nuncius*, m. *rumor*,
Tidy, adj. *concinnus, mundus*
Tie, v. *alligāre*, 1 c.
——— s. *vinculum*, n. *nexus* m.
Tight, adj. *arctus, strictus*
Title, s. *titulus*, 2 d. m.
Tile, s. *tĕgŭla*, 1 d. f.
Till the ground, v. a. *colĕre, subigĕre agrum*
——— now, *donèc, anteà*
——— I read, *dum f. legam*
Timber, s. *materia*, f. *lignum*, n.
——— (not cut) *arbores*
Time (in) *tempŏre*, abl. c.
——— will you go (at what) *quo tempore abibis?*

Times, s. (six) *sexiès*, adv.
——— several, *sæpĕnŭmĕrò*
Timely, adv *tempestivè*
Timorous, adj. *timĭdus*
Tin, s. *stannum*, 2 d. n.
Tinder, s. *igniārium*, 2 d. n.
——— box, s. *pyxidula continens igniarium*
Tippet, s. *fascia*, 1 d. f.
Tiresome, adj. *fatigans*
Tit for tat, *dens pro dente*
To, prep. *ad*
— day, *hodie*
— morrow, *cras*
— night, *hac nocte*
Toast, s. *panis tostis*
Together, *simùl*, *unà*
Told, p. p. *nunciātus*, *dictus*
——— (he) pret. *dixit*
Tom-tit, s. *parus*
Tone, s. *tonus*, 2 d. m.
Tongs, s. pl. *forceps*, 3 d.
Tongue, s. *lingua*, 1 d. f.
Too, adj. *etiam*
——— long, *nimis longus*
——— good, *nimis bonus*
——— much, *nimis*
——— many, *nimis multi*
Took (I) *cepi*
Tool, s. *instrumentum*, 2 d. n.
Tooth, s. *dens*, 3 d. m.
——— ach, s. *dolor dentium*
Toss, s. *apex*, 3 d. m. *culmen*, n.
Top to bottom (from) *de fastigio ad imum*
Torment, s. *tormentum*, n. *cruciatus*, m.
——— v. *cruciāre*, *vexāre*
Torn, p. p. *lăcĕratus*
Touch, s. *tactus*, 4 d. m.
Towards, prep. *adversùs*, *versùs*
Towards the south, *versùs meridiem*
Towel, *mantile* n. *mappa*, f.
Tower, s. *turris*, f. *arx* f.
Town, s. *oppĭdum*, 2 d. n.
Toys, s. *crepundia*, pl. n.
Trade, s. *quæstus*, *mercatus*, 4. d.
Translate, v. a. *vertĕre*, 3 c.
Translation, s. *versio*, *translatio*, 3 d. f.
Trap, s. *laqueus*, m. *decipulum*, n.
Travel, v. *peregrinări*
——— ten miles a day, *decem millia itineris die facĕre*
Travels, s. *peregrinatiōnes*
Tread upon, v. a. *conculcāre*, 1 c.
Treasure, s. *gaza*, f. *thesaurus*, m.
Treatise, s. *dissertātio*, 3 d. f.
Treat, s. *ĕpŭlæ*, pl. f.
——— v. *convivio accipĕre*
Treble, s. *triplus*, *triplex*
Tree, s. *arbor*, 3 d. f.
Trefoil, s. *trifolium*, 2 d. n.
Trick, s. *dolus*, m. *fallacia*, f.
——— at cards, *vices*, *unæ*, *duæ*
——— (machination) *dŏlus*
Trifle, s. *nugæ*, *ārum*, pl. f.
Trifling, *frivolus*, *levis*
Trigger, *sufflamen*, 3 d. n.
Troop, s. *caterva*, f. *turma*, f.
Trouble, s. *molestia*, *tristitia*, f.
——— v. *vexāre*, *angĕre*
Troublesome, adj. *molestus*, *a*, *um*
Trough, s. *alveus*, 2 d. m.
Trout, s. *truta*, 1 d. f.
Truce, s. *indūciæ*, pl. f.
True, adj. *verus*, *a*, *um*
Truly, adv. *veerè*

Trump at cards, s. *charta index*
Trunk, s. *arca*, 1 d. f.
——— of a tree, *truncus*, 2 d. m.
Truss of hay, *fœni manipulus*
Trust (to) v. *merces fide vendere*
—— or confide in, *fidem habere*
—— s. *fiducia*, 1 d. f.
Trusty, adj. *fidelis, fidus*
Truth, s. *veritas, fides*, f.
——to speak, *veritatem dicĕre*
Try, v. *experīri*, 4 c. *aggrĕdi*
Tub, s. *cădus*, 2 d. m.
Tuesday, s. *dies Martis*
Tulip, s. *tulipa, æ* f.
Tumble, s. *saliator*, 3 d. m.
Tun, s. *dōlium*, 2 d. n.
Tune, v. a. *aptè fidiculas contendĕre*
—— s. *numeri*, pl. n. *modulatio*, f.
Tuner of instruments, *mŏdŭlātor*, 3 d. m.
Turf, s. *cespes*, 3 d. m.
Turk, s. *Turcus, i*
Turkey, a fowl, *gallina Numidica*
Turn, v. a. *flectĕre*, 3 c.
Turn one's self, *vertĕre*, 3 c.
—— back, *revertĕre*, 3 c.
Turnip, s. *rāpum*, 2 d. n.
Turpentine, s. *tĕrĕbinthĭna*, 1 d. f.
Turtle, s. *testudo*, f.
——— dove, *turtur*, m.
Tuscany, s. pr. *Etruria, æ, Tuscia*
Twelfth, adj. *duodecimus*
——— night, *vespera epiphaniæ*
Twelve, adj. *duodecim*
——— o'clock at night, *nox media*
——— at noon, *mĕrīdies*, 5 d. f.
——— (till) *usque ad meridiem*
Twenty, adj. *viginti*
Twentieth, adj. *vicesimus*
Twice, adj. *bis*
Twilight, s. *crĕpuscŭlum*, 2 d. n.
Twins, s. pl. *gemini, gemelli*, pl.
Two, adj. *duo, bini*
—— pence, *duo denarii*
——— —— a pound, *duo denarii pro librâ*

U

Ugly, adj. *dēformis, e*
Ugliness, s. *dĕformĭtas*, 3 d. f.
Unanimous, adj. *unănĭmus*
Unable, adj. *infirmus, impotens*
Uncertain, adj. *dubius, incertus*
Uncle, s. *patruus, avunculus*
Uncommonly, adv. *rarò*
Undeceive, v. a. *errore liberare*
Understand, v. *intelligĕre*, 3 c.
Understanding, s. *intellectus, ûs*, m.
Under, prep. *sub, subter*
——— him, *infra illum*

Under the necessity, *obligatus*
—— eleven pence, *minus undecim denariis*
—— cook, *coquus adjutans*
—— them, *infra illos*
Undertake, v. *tentāre*, 1 c.
Underling, *alteri subditus*
Undress, v. *exuĕre vestes*
Unfortunate, adj. *infelix*
Unfruitful, adj. *sterilis, infructuosus*
Ungrateful, adj. *ingratus*
Unhurt, adj. *illæsus*
University, s. *universitas*, f. *academia* f.
Unmarried, adj. *cælebs*
Unpardonable, adj. *irremissibilis*
Unpolite, *rudis, impolitus*
Until, *donec, usque dum*
—— Tuesday (not) *non ante diem Martis*
Unwholesome, adj. *insalubris*
Unwell, adj. *ægrotus, infirmus*
Unworthy, adj. *indignus*
Upholsterer, s. *lectorum fabricator*
Upon, prep. *super, supra*
—— it or them, *super id, vel illos*
Upright, adj. *probus, erectus*
Up, *sursùm*
— stairs, *sursùm, desuper*
— ? (are you) *surrexistine ?*
Upwards, *sursùm*
Us, pron. *nos*
Use, v. *uti, dep*
—— s. *usus, consuetudo*
—— (for the) *in usu*
—— (we make) *utimur*
Used, p. p. *usĭtātus*
—— by most masters, *in manibus plerumque magistrorum*
Useful, adj. *utilis, e*
Usually, adv. *plerumquè*
Utility, s. *utilitas*, 3 d. f.

V

Vacation, s. *dies festi, otium*
Vain, adj. *vanus, superbus*
Variety, s. *varietas*, 3 d. f.
Varnish, s. *vernix*, 3 d. f.
Vanity, s. *vanitas, inanitas*
Vat, s. *dolium*, n. *cupa*, f.
Veal, s. *caro vitulina*
Vegetables, s. *olera, um*, 3 d. n.
Veil, s. *velum*, 2 d. n.
Vein, s. *vena*, 1 d. f.
Velvet, s. *velvetum*, 2 d. n.
Venice, s. p. *Venĕtiæ* f.
Venerable, adj. *venerandus, venerabilis*
Vengeance, *ultio*, 3 d. f.
Venus, *Vĕnus, ĕris*
Verb, s. *verbum*, 2 d. n.
Verdict, s. *judicium, veredictum*
Vermilion, s. *minium*, 2 d. n.
Very well, *optimè*
—— handsome, *formosior, formosissimus*
—— lately, *nuper, recentiùs*
—— word, (the) *verbum ipsum*
Vicar, s. *vicarius*, 2 d.
Vicarage, *vicariatus*, 4 d. m.
Vice, s. *vitium*, 2 d. n.

Vicious, adj. *pravus, vitiosus*
Vicinity, s. *vicinitas*, 3 d. f.
Vienna, *Vienna, æ* f.
View, s. *prospectus*, 4 d. m.
Vile, adj. *vilis, e*
Village, s. *pagus, vicus*, 2 d. m.
Vine, s. *vitis*, 3 d. f.
Vineyard, s. *vīnētum*, 2 d. n.
Vinegar, s. *acetum*, 2 d. n. *vīnea*, f.
Vintage, s. *vindemia*, 1 d. f.
Violet, (colour) s. *violaceus*
——— (flower) s. *viola*, 1 d. f.
Violin, s. *fides*, f.
Viper, s. *vipera*, 1 d. f.
Virtue, s. *virtus, tis* f.
Virulency, s. *acerbitas*, 3 d. f.
Visage, s. *facies*, 5 d. f.
Visit, s. *officiosus aditus*
—— v. *visĕre, visitāre*
Visitor, s. *salutator*, 3 d. m.
Vivacity, s. *vivacitas*, 3 d. f.
Voice, s. *vox, cis* f.
Void, s. *vacuum*, 2 d. n.
Volume, s. *volumen*, 3 d. n. *tomus*, 2 d. m.
Vowel, s. *litera vocalis*
Vulgar, adj. *vulgaris, e*
——— s. (the) *plebs*, 3 d. f. *vulgus*, 2 d. m.

W

Wafer, s. *crustulum signatorium*
Wag, s. *homo lepidus*
Wager, s. *pignus*, 3 d. n.
——— v. *pignus opponĕre*
Wager, s. *stipendium*, 2 d. n.
Waggon, s. *rheda*, f. *plaustrum*, n.
Waggoner, *rhedarius*, 2 d.
Waist, s. *cinctura*, 1d. f.
Wait upon, v. *inservīre*, 4 c.
—— at table, *inservīre cœnâ*
—— for, *expectāre*, 1 c.
—— on a friend, *invisĕre amicum*
Waiter, s. *puer, assecla*
—— (silver) *discus argenteus*
Walk, s. *ambulatio*, 3 d. f.
—— v. n. *ambulāre*, 1 c.
—— fast, *ambulāre celeritèr*
—— slowly, *ambulāre lentè*
—— in (pray) *oro ut venias intrò*
Walk out to, *exīre*
—— for pleasure, *deambulāre, expatiāri*
Wall, s. *murus*, 2 d. m.
—— flower, *parietaria*, 1 d. f.
Walls, (the) *mœnia*, pl. n.
Wales, s. pr. *Wallia, æ* f.
Walnut, s. *nux juglans*
——— tree, s. *arbor juglans*
Walter, s. p. *Gualterius*
Wander, v. *vagāri*, dep.
Want, s. *inopia*, 1 d. f.
—— of sleep, *insomnia, æ* f.
—— v. *egēre, indigēre*
—— a hat, (I) *galerum cupio emere*
Wants to see you, (he) *te videre vult*
Wanting, (there are five) *quinque desunt*
War, s. *bellum*, 2 d. n.
—— (man of) *navis bellica*

Warble, (to) v. n. *modulāri*, dep.
Ward, s. *custodia*, 1 d. f. *pupillus*, 2 d. m.
Warden, s. *custos*, 3 d.
Wares, s. *merces*, 3 d. pl. f.
Ware, (earthen) *vasa fictilia*
—— (china) *vasa Sinensia*
—— house, *repositorium*, 2 d. n.
Warm, v. *calefacĕre*, 3 c.
—— (to be) *calēre*, 2 c.
—— (my feet are) *mei pedes calidi sunt*
—— (it is) *calescit*
—— (it was) *caluit*
—— beds, (to) v. *lectos calefacere thermoclinio*
Warming-pan, *thermoclinium*, 2 d. n.
Warn, v. *monēre*, 2 c.
Warning, s. *monitio*, 3 d. f.
Warrant, s. *auctoritas*, f. *jussum*, n.
—— (to apprehend) *warrantum*, n.
—— you, (I) *credo equidem*
Was, imp. and pret. *eram*, *fui*
—— cold, (it) *frigebat*
—— (the weather) *frixit*
Wash oneself, s. *lavāre*, 1 c.
Wash, v. a. *luĕre*, 4 c.
Washed my hands, (I have) *manus meas lāvi*
Wash house, *lavacrum*, 2 d. n.
Washerwoman, *lotrix*, 3 d. f.
Wasp, s. *vespa*, 1 d. f.
Waste, adj. *inutilis*, e
—— v. *consumĕre*
Watch, s. *chronometer*, *automatum ad horas indicandas*
Watchmaker, s. *automatopœus*, 2 d. m.
—— house, s. *custōdia*, æ f.
—— man, s. *excubitor*, 3 d.
Water, s. *aqua*, æ f.
—— colours, *colōres*
—— the flowers, *rigare flores*
—— (to go by) *aquā vadĕre*, *navigāre*
—— man, *remex*, 3 d.
—— mill, *mola aquatilis*
—— pot, *situlus hortensis*
Wave, s. *unda* f. *fluctus*, *ûs*, 4 d.
Wax, s. *cera*, æ f.
—— (sealing) *cera*, 1 d.
—— candle, *cereus*, 2 d. m.
—— chandler, *cerarius*, 2 d. m.
Way, (every) *quāquaversum*, *omni modo*
—— in the same, *eodem modo*
—— of joke, (by) *jocosè*, *per jocum*
We, pron. pers. *nos*
Weak, adj. *debilis*, e
—— side, (his) *in quo sit nimium facilis*
Weaken, v. *debilitāre*
Wealth, s. *opes*, pl. f. *divitiæ*, pl. f.
Wealthy, adj. *dives*, *opulentus*
Weapon, s. *telum*, n. *ferrum*, n.
Wear, v. *vestiri*, dep.
Weary, adj. *lassus*, *fessus*
Weather, s. *tempestas*, 3 d. f.
Web, s. *tela*, 3 d. f.
Wedding, s. *nuptiæ*, pl. f.
Wednesday, s. *dies Mercurii*
Weed, s. *herba inutilis*

Weed, v. a. *sarrire*, 4 c.
Week, s. *hebdomada*, 1 d. f.
—— (last) *hebdomada modo præterita*
—— (next) *hebdomada proxima vel veniens*
Weep, v. n. *flēre*, 2 c.
Weigh, v. *pendĕre*, 3 c.
Weight, s. *pondus*, 3 d. n.
—— (by) *pondĕre*, abl.
Welcome, adj. *optatus, gratus*
Welfare, s. *salus*, 3 d. f.
Well, (very) *optimè factum*
—— and good, *ita benè est*
Went, (he) *ivit*
—— away, (they) *abierunt*
Wept, (he) *plōrāvit*
Were, (plur. of was) *eramus, eratis, erant*
—— so good, (you) *ita comis eras*
West, s. *occidens*, 3 d. m.
—— Indies, *India Occidentalis*
Wet, adj. *humidus*
—— v. *humectāre*
Whale, s. *balæna*, 1 d. f.
—— bone, *os cetuceum*
Wharf, s. *fluminis portus*
What, *qui, quæ, quod*
—— does my brother do? *meus frater quid facit?*
—— ! you are crying? *Hem! lachrymas?*
—— is the matter? *quid rei est?*
—— is it o'clock? *quotâ est horâ?*
—— do you say? *tu quid dicis?*
—— is that? *hoc quid est?*
—— is he? *quis ille est?*
—— are they? *qui sunt?*
What for? *pro quâ?*
—— colour? *qui color?*
—— ever, prom. *qualiscunque*
—— you may ask, *omnia quæ cupis*
—— he may be, *quicunque sit*
Wheat, s. *triticum*, 2 d. n.
Wheel, s. *rota*, æ f.
—— barrow, s. *vehiculum unâ rotâ*
—— rut, *rotæ vestigium*.
When I have done, *quùm finiverim*.
—— I am at home, *ubi domi sum*
Whence, adv. *undè*
—— come you? *undè venis*
Whenever, adv. *quandocunque*
Where, adv. *ubi*
—— are you? *ubinàm es*.
—— were you? *ubi fuisti?*
—— shall you be? *ubi eris?*
Whereas, adv. *cùm, quòd*
Whereby, *quo, per quod*
Wherever, *ubicunque*
Whereupon, *ex quò, undè*
Whet, v. a. *acuĕre*, 3 c.
Whether, conj. *sive, utrùm, an*
Whey, s. *sĕrum*, 2 d. n.
Which, pron. *quis, uter*
—— will you take? *utrum vis habere*
—— in, *utro*
—— way? *quâ viâ, quo modo*
While, a little, *paullispèr, parumpèr*

Whilst, adv. *dum, donec, quoad*
Whim, s. *voluntas sŭbĭta*
Whimsical, adj. *levis, ridiculus*
Whip, s, *scutica,* f. *flagellum,* n.
—— v. a. *flagellāre,* 1 c.
Whirlwind, s. *turbo,* 3 d. m.
Whisker, s. *mystax,* 3 d. m.
Whisper, v. *submissè lŏqui, in aurem dicĕre*
Whist, s. *ludus chartis*
White, adj. *albus*
——— frost, *pruīna,* 1 d. f.
Whiteness, *albor, nitor, candor*
Whiting, (fish) *alburnus,* 2 d. m.
Who, pron. *quis* interrog. *qui* relative
—— (they) *qui*
—— (he) *ille qui*
—— (she) *illa quæ*
—— is there ? *quis adest ?*
—— is it ? *quis est ?*
—— are they ? *qui sunt ?*
—— has it ? *quis illud habet ?*
—— ever, *quicunque, quisquis*
Whole, adj. *totus*
——— sale, *in solidum*
——— some, *saluber, salutaris*
Wholly, *prorsùs, omninò*
Whom, *quem*
Whose, *cujus*
——— coach is that ? *cujus currus est ?*
Whosoever, *quicunque*
Why, adv. *cur*
Wicked, adj. *prāvus*
Wickedness, s. *prāvĭtas*
Wide, (nine feet) *latus pedum novem*
Wide, (seven inches) *latus septēnis unciis*
Widow, s. *vĭdua,* 3 d. f.
Widower, *viduus,* 2 d. m.
Width, s. *lătitūdo,* 3 d. f.
Wife, s. *uxor,* 3 d. *conjux,* 3 d.
Wig, s. *căpillamentum,* 2 d. n.
Wild, adj. *indomitus, dissolutus*
Wilderness, s. *deserta,* pl. n. *solitudo* f.
Will, s. *vŏluntas,* 3 d. f.
—— (testament) *testamentum,* 2 d. n.
—— you have ? *tu cupisne habere ?*
—— he be ? *eritne ?*
—— he have some ? *habebitne ălĭquot*
—— talk of it, (I) *eâ de re colloquar*
—— have them do so, (you) *jubes ut sic faciant*
Willing, adj. *volens, libens*
——— (I am) *sic quidem volo*
——— (he does not seem) *nonvult ut videtur*
William, *Gulielmus*
Willingly, adv. *lĭbentèr*
Willow tree, s. *sălix,* 3 d. f.
Win, v. *lucrari,* 1 c. *consĕqui,* 3 c.
Wind, s. *ventus,* 2 d. m.
Windmill, s. *mola vento agitata*
Wind up (to) *concludere,* 3. c.
————— a watch (to) *torquēre fīlum horarii*

Window, s. *fĕnestra*, 1 d. f.
Windy, adj. *ventōsus*
Wine, s. *vinum*, *merum*, 2 d. n.
—— glass, s. *vinarium vitreum*
Wing, s. *ala*, *penna*, 1 d. f.
Winter, s. *hyems*, 3 d. f.
Wipe, v. *abstergĕre*
Wire, s. *metallum netum*
Wisdom, s. *săpientia*, 1 d. f.
Wise, adj. *săpiens*
Wisely, adv. *sapientèr*
Wiser, comp. *săpientior*
Wisest, sup. *săpientissimus*
Wish, v. *optāre*
Wishes, s. *vota*, 2 d. n.
Wit, s. *ingenium*, 2 d. n. *lĕpor*, *ōris*, 3 d. m. *sales*, pl. m.
Wittily, adv. *lĕpĭdè*
Witch, s. *saga*, *venefica*
With, prep. *cum*
—— you, (we have not been angry) *nos tibi non irati fuimus*
—— me, *mecum*
—— them, *cum illis*
Withdraw, v. *secedĕre*, *recedĕre*.
Within, prep. *intra*, *cis*
—— four days, *intra dies quatuor*
Without it, *sine eo*
—— me, *sine me*
—— them, *sine illis*
—— knowing, *nesciens*
Withstand, v. *resistĕre*, *obluctāri*
Witness, s. *testis*, 3 d. c. g.
—— v. *testāri*
Witty, adj *lĕpĭdus*
Wolf, s. *lupus*, m. *lupa*, f.
Woman, s. *mulier*, 3 d. *femina*, 1 d.
Woman (old,) s. *ănus*, *vetulà*
Won, p. p. *lucrativus*
Wonder, s. *miraculum*, *prodigium*, n.
—— v. *admirāri*, *mirāri*
Wonderful, adj. *prōdigiōsus*
Wonderfully, adv. *mirabilitèr*, *mirè*
Wood, s. *sylva*, 1 d. f. *saltus*, *ûs*, m.
—— (timber) *lignum*, m. *materia*, f.
—— cock, *gallinago*, 3 d. f.
—— house, *lignārium*, 2 d. n.
Wooden, adj. *ligneus*
Wool, s. *lāna*, 1 d. f.
Woollen, adj. *lāneus*
—— cloth, *pannus*, *i. m.*
Word, s. *vox*, 3 d. f. *verbum*, 2 d. n.
Wore (he) pret. *gessit*, *tulit*
Work, s. *opus*, n. *opera*, f.
—— v. *laborare*, *operāri*
Working day, *dies negotiosus*
Work box, *arca operum*
—— man, *opifex vel artifex*, 3 d.
Workmanship, *ŏpĭfĭcium*, 2 d. n.
World, s. *mundus*, 2 d. m.
Worldly, adj. *mundānus*
Worm, s. *vermis*, 3 d. *lumbricus*, 2 d. m.
—— silk, s. *bombyx*, 3 d. m.
—— wood, s. *absinthium*, 2 d. n.
Worn-out, *tritus*
Worship, s. *cultus*, 4. d. m.
Worse, adj. *pejor*, *deterior*
—— and worse, *in pejus ruens*
Worse, (to be) *pessimus a*, *um*.
Worth, adj. *valēre*, 2 c.

Worth, (it is) *valet*
——— adj. *valens*
Worthily, adv. *dignè*
Worthy, adj. *dignus, a, um*
Would you be? *esses ne?*
——— have, (he) *haberet ne?*
——— not have, (you) *tu non haberes*
——— you not have consented, *an tu non assentires?*
Wound, s. *vulnus*, 3 d. n.
——— v. *vulnerāre, sauciāre*
Wounded, part. *vulneratus*
Wrath, s. *ira*, 1 d. f.
Wreck, s. *naufrăgium*, 2 d. n.
Wretch, s. *miser, perditus*
Wretched, adj. *miserabilis, miser*
Wrinkles, s. pl. *rūgæ*, 1 d. f.
Wrist, s. *carpus*, 2 d. m.
Wristband, s. *brăchiāle*, 3 d. n.
Write, v. *scribĕre*, 3 c.
Writer, s. *auctor, scriptor*, 3 d.
Writing, s. *scriptum*, 2 d. n.
——— master, *magister vel institutor*
——— desk, *scriptorium*, 2 d. n.
Written, p. p. *scriptus, a, um*
Wrong, adj. *malus*
——— (to be in the) *fallĕre, errāre*
——— (you have done) *malè fecisti*
Wrong side, *pars contraria, contrario*
Wrongfully, *injuriosè*
Wrote, pret. *scripsi, isti, it*
Yatch, s. *navicula*, 1 d. f. *cĕlox, ōcis*, 3 d. f.
Yard measure, *virga*, 1 d. f. *ulna*, 1 d. f.
Year, (new) *novus annus*
Yearly, adj. *quotannis*
Yellow. adj. *flavus, fulvus*
Yes, *imò, certè*
——— I am, *imo ego sum*
Yesterday, (the day before) *nudiustertius*
Yet, *at, tamen*
Yew-tree, *taxus*, 2 d. f.
Yield, v. *cedĕre*, 3 c. *submittĕre*, 3 c.
Yoke, s. *jugum*, 2 d. n.
Yonder, *illic*
You, pers. pron. *tu*
——— (I love) *amo te*
——— (he speaks to) *tecum loquitur*
Young, adj. *juvenis*
——— people, *juvenes*
Younger, *junior, minor*
Young lady, *virgo nobilis*
Youngest brother, *frater minimus natu*
You, yours, pron. *tuus, a, um*
Yourself, pron. *tu ipse*, nom. *te ipsum*, acc.
Youth, s. *juvenis, adolescens*, 3 d.
Youthful, adj. *juvenilis*
Zealous, adj. *studiosus*
Zephyr, s. *zĕphўrus*, 2 d. m.

FINIS.

LONDON:
G. SCHULZE, 13, POLAND STREET.

CPSIA information can be obtained at www.ICGtesting.com
Printed in the USA
BVOW011839221012

303644BV00006B/4/P

9 781165 676200